DANCING CHIEF

DANCING CHIEF

THE TRAGIC LIFE OF LIEUTENANT FREDERICK F. KISLINGBURY

Douglas W. Wamsley

American History Press
Staunton Virginia

Copyright © 2025 Douglas W. Wamsley

All rights reserved. No part of this book may be transmitted in any form by any means electronic, mechanical or otherwise using devices now existing or yet to be invented without prior written permission from the publisher and copyright holder.

American History Press

Staunton, Virginia

Visit us on the Internet at:

www.Americanhistorypress.com

First Hardback Printing – December 2025

To schedule an event with the author or to inquire about bulk discount sales please contact American History Press.

Note: Full Library of Congress Cataloging-in-Publication Data is in process.

Names: Wamsley, Douglas W., 1958- author.

Title: Dancing Chief -

/ Douglas W. Wamsley.

Description: First edition. | Staunton, Virginia : American History Press, [2025]

Identifiers: ISBN 9781939995476 (paperback)

Subjects: Kislingbury, Frederick F., 1846-1884.

Cover design by Rick Burkart; interior design by David Kane

Printed in the United States of America on acid-free paper.
This book exceeds all ANSO standards for archival quality.

CONTENTS

Acknowledgments	ix
Introduction	xii

CHAPTER ONE
A Respectable Young Gentleman ... 1

CHAPTER TWO
With the Pawnee Scouts ... 7

CHAPTER THREE
"The Most God-Forsaken Part of Uncle Sam's Dominions" ... 18

CHAPTER FOUR
The Great Sioux War ... 32

CHAPTER FIVE
Indian Scout Leader ... 41

CHAPTER SIX
Fort Yates ... 49

CHAPTER SEVEN
Dancing Chief ... 61

CHAPTER EIGHT
Trying Times ... 72

CHAPTER NINE
The Lady Franklin Bay Expedition　　　　79

CHAPTER TEN
Seeds of Discontent　　　　96

CHAPTER ELEVEN
Fort Conger　　　　112

CHAPTER TWELVE
The Farthest North　　　　127

CHAPTER THIRTEEN
Season of Despair　　　　142

CHAPTER FOURTEEN
"Here We Are Dying Like Men"　　　　156

CHAPTER FIFTEEN
Home Again　　　　171

CHAPTER SIXTEEN
Aftermath　　　　184

Appendix　　　　198
Chapter Notes　　　　205
Bibliography　　　　225
Illustration Credits　　　　232
Index　　　　234
About the Author　　　　243

Acknowledgments

While completing a biography of Lieutenant Frederick Schwatka, a military man turned arctic explorer, I was intrigued by the thought of other arctic explorers whose frontier experience was considerable, but completely untold. These were markedly talented soldiers whose military service, coupled with an adventurous nature, served as a springboard for their polar endeavors. Frederick Kislingbury was just one of those men who emerged from the plains to seek his destiny in the Far North. Familiar with him as a participant on the ill-fated Greely Expedition (1881-84), I was surprised to chance upon a field report of his 1880 engagement at the Musselshell River, Montana Territory, while stationed at Fort Custer. That unexpected find led to the more dedicated search that culminated in this work.

Kislingbury's path to the Montana Territory was a protracted one and indicative of his persistence and singleness of mind and spirit. Marty Miller, archivist at the Nebraska State Historical Society, helped locate documents as to Kislingbury's volunteer service with Major Frank North and the Pawnee Scouts. This little-known aspect of Frederick Kislingbury's early military career served a critical role in obtaining his long-sought commission in the Regular Army. Archivist Eunice Tibay at the Fort Concho Research Library and Museum was particularly helpful in locating documentation regarding Kislingbury's first duty station as an officer in the U.S. Army in remote West Texas. Standing in the officers' quarters and walking the grounds of the now restored Fort Concho National Landmark gives a sense of daily life at the post for military families like those of Kislingbury. The Abraham Lincoln Presidential Library in Springfield, Illinois, holds correspondence of Colonel Benjamin Grierson while stationed at Fort Concho. Archivist Christopher

Acknowledgments

Schnell filled my multiple requests for the Grierson manuscripts relevant to the Kislingburys' stay at the post.

The U.S. National Archives hold a multitude of records that detail Frederick's military service, including his Appointment, Commission, Personal (ACP) file, as well as post returns, agency correspondence, reports and orders from various stations. Those papers opened a door to his relationship with his Indian allies and as an Indian scout leader. The archives also hold the many unpublished diaries of the members of the Lady Franklin Bay Expedition. As always, Andrew Brethauer and research assistants in the manuscripts division were particularly helpful in locating hard-to-find records. The staff of the Library of Congress helped with the many requests for the voluminous Greely papers, which tell a great deal of the budding, but later soured, relationship between Kislingbury and his commander.

Kislingbury's closest friend and executor, Charles Clark, deserves much credit for the painstaking attention he paid to Frederick Kislingbury's instructions and to the wellbeing and upbringing of his sons. The heavy burden under which Clark labored to fulfill those obligations over many years is reflected in the myriad personal records at the William L. Clements Library at the University of Michigan. During visits and in response to remote requests, Meg Bossio aided in retrieving those documents.

Other institutions that merit thanks for their assistance include the following: The Explorers Club, New York, NY; Leddy Library, University of Windsor, Windsor, Ontario; Library of the University of Wisconsin-Madison, Madison, WI; Montana State Library, Helena, MT; Rauner Special Collections Library, Dartmouth College, Hanover, NH; Raclin Murphy Museum of Art, University of Notre Dame, Notre Dame, IN; Department of Rare Books, Special Collections, and Preservation, River Campus Libraries, University of Rochester, Rochester, NY; Shelburne Museum, Shelburne, VT; State Historical Society of North Dakota Archives, Bismarck, ND; The Ulysses S. Grant Presidential Library, University of Mississippi, Starkville, MS. The printed records carried through many newspapers and periodicals were located in digital form and helped fill out many aspects of Kislingbury's life.

Acknowledgments

David Kane at American History Press was supportive with the project from the start. He provided his usual pointed editorial focus to help deliver a far better presentation. Robert Cronan of Lucidity Design, called upon to deliver maps from the southern border to the far north, provided precise and visually appealing depictions of the varied locales of Frederick Kislingbury's travels.

A number of individuals stand out for their assistance. Most importantly, I am greatly indebted to Linda Kislingbury Cain, the great-granddaughter of Frederick Kislingbury and devoted historian of the Kislingbury family. By virtue of a single telephone call, she opened her trove of unpublished letters, photographs and diary of her great-grandfather and supplied background details that would otherwise have been impossible to obtain. Without her assistance, this project would not have been possible. Linda was also an unceasing source of encouragement throughout the entire process. No doubt, Fred would be proud. Paul Hedren, ever knowledgeable historian of the Great Sioux War and all matters related thereto, provided helpful advice on Kislingbury's various duty stations in the northern plains and a number of aspects relevant to his time served there. Historian Glenn Stein lent his knowledge of the Greely Expedition, its trials and tribulations, and its various personalities. Glenn was especially helpful understanding the varied writings of Sergeant David Legge Brainard.

Of course, this project could not have been completed without the support of my wife, Leslie, who deserves special mention. To her, my love and grateful thanks.

Introduction

On August 26, 1881, the crew of the sturdy-built steamship *Proteus*, under the command of whaleman Captain Richard Pike, bid farewell to the members of the U.S. International Polar Expedition. At Lady Franklin Bay, within five hundred miles of the North Pole, twenty-five men prepared themselves for at least one year of isolation. With mixed emotions, they watched their last connection to the outside world fade below the horizon. Freeing the vessel from the packed floes which hemmed her in the harbor, Captain Pike forced the ship through the heavy, treacherous ice of Kennedy Channel. As the transport nudged southward following the coast, Lieutenant Frederick F. Kislingbury, the young and adventurous second-in-command, abruptly elected to resign his position and take leave of the expedition. Despite an overwhelming desire to make a name for himself in the High Arctic, with a heavy heart, all his thoughts had turned to returning home aboard *Proteus*. After penning a formal resignation letter and parting with his commander, he hastily packed a handful of personal belongings, shouted a few goodbyes to his companions, and hurriedly chased the fast-departing ship, keenly following its billowing trail of smoke.

Sliding and tumbling about slippery hillocks and slogging through slushy ice along the shoreline, his diminishing profile, a mere speck within the prodigious landscape, passed unobserved by the crew of the retreating ship. Lieutenant Kislingbury could only watch in disappointment as the *Proteus* steamed away leaving him behind. Ironically, as one historian noted, had Frederick Kislingbury hastened his departure by a matter of minutes, he might have met the retreating *Proteus*. In retrospect, that unsuccessful last-minute withdrawal by Kislingbury sealed his fate. With the benefit of

Introduction

hindsight, the episode would prove to be one of the most poignant events of the expedition, an expedition that would suffer many fateful consequences.

The disaster that occurred during the Lady Franklin Bay Expedition of 1881–1884 has captured the attention of a mainstream audience through modern retellings and compelling documentary films. Under the command of Lieutenant Adolphus W. Greely, it was one of the twelve expeditions from eleven nations forming the so-called International Polar Year (IPY). The objective of the IPY was to unify scientific work across the Far North through a spirit of cooperation and simultaneous observations, in contrast to what had formerly been a hodge-podge of individualistic competitions for geographic firsts.

For two years, members of the Lady Franklin Bay Expedition dutifully fulfilled their scientific obligations and found time to complete record-breaking sledge journeys. When relief ships failed to arrive, its members undertook a desperate retreat through ice-riddled Kennedy Channel, hundreds of miles south. Despite their efforts, many of them eventually faced a tragic and ghastly end on a desolate, forlorn location at Cape Sabine, off the Ellesmere Island coast. Gradual starvation, food thefts, and allegations of cannibalism made for a harrowing storyline that highlighted the best and worst of character. The ultimate toll of its dead, nineteen of twenty-five men, including Kislingbury, speaks to its grim outcome.

For one man, the expedition was to be an outlet for his own personal misfortune. Frederick Foster Kislingbury, a thirty-six-year-old lieutenant in the U.S. Eleventh Infantry, eagerly joined the expedition on the heels of the sudden and tragic death of his second wife. For Kislingbury, the grief was even more unimaginable as he had laid to rest his first wife less than three years before. For Frederick Kislingbury, what started as an exodus from personal despair, quickly led to a rude falling out with his commander Lieutenant Greely. Even as the expedition's transport ship, *Proteus,* touched high in the Canadian Arctic at Lady Franklin Bay to onload its cargo and expeditioners at their northern station, the two became awkwardly estranged. Kislingbury's sudden resignation from the expedition and failed attempt to withdraw onboard the departing *Proteus* left him

Introduction

stranded at the arctic post. No longer an expedition member, he became an outcast trapped within a closed community and a thorn in the side of its commander.

As the official chronicler of the expedition, Greely cast his own view as to their relationship and Kislingbury's professional fitness, views that Kislingbury's siblings believed had distorted the truth and maligned the deceased lieutenant. Even modern commentators have diplomatically brushed Kislingbury off as "a poor choice for the disciplined teamwork required in the Arctic," or even more bluntly concluded that "Greely made an error" in his selection of Kislingbury. Another assessed his mental state and determined that "Kislingbury may have been suffering from a nervous breakdown when he signed on the expedition." At best, Kislingbury has remained a fringe player in the accounts of the Lady Franklin Bay Expedition, but even as an outcast he managed to contribute to the well-being of the expedition.

Frederick Kislingbury was more than a disgruntled malcontent, and the complete story of his brief but venturesome life has never been fully revealed. For Kislingbury, the Lady Franklin Bay Expedition was the culmination of a lengthy and commendable career as an officer in the U.S. military. Indeed, public service occupied his entire adult life.

Youthful fervor had given Kislingbury his first measure of military life when he joined a volunteer regiment during the American Civil War. The experience kindled a desire for a professional career in arms, with its attendant hardships and dangers. In the late 1860s, with limited opportunities and skills, many enlisted men had simply joined the service by default, a matter of last resort to escape hard times. By way of but one example, Kislingbury's companion on the Lady Franklin Bay Expedition, Sergeant David L. Brainard, joined on a lark. After leaving the Centennial Exposition in Philadelphia, he changed trains in New York City, but found himself dead broke, without fare for even a ticket home. With no better options, he enlisted after spying a recruiting station.

Frederick Kislingbury took to the field under far different circumstances. Already a married man with two young children, he surrendered a comfortable homelife and a secure financial position

Introduction

in metropolitan Detroit for active duty, petitioning long and hard for an officer's commission in the Regular Army. His adventurous nature would place him in some of the most remote and inhospitable locations in the American frontier.

As the nation turned its eyes to the West, Kislingbury came of age on the Great Plains. Far from the label of "malcontent," as a junior officer he worked exceedingly well within the rigid confines of a tightly knit military command. He was a determined, highly regarded soldier who dutifully executed orders, displayed sound judgment both in leadership and under the stress of combat. In contrast to his frayed relationship with commander Adolphus Greely, Kislingbury was uniformly well-liked and respected by both his superiors and his comrades in the field. The surviving records, official reports, regimental and post returns, letters, and newspaper accounts tell a story of commendable accomplishments.

Unfortunately, it would not be stretching the truth to state that his successes as a promising young officer in the unsettled West are virtually unknown today. In his time, those accomplishments reached beyond his immediate superiors to the senior military brass. Hard-driving Lieutenant General Philip Sheridan, later commander-in-chief of the Army, as well as Brigadier General Alfred Terry, commander of the Department of Dakota, expressly complimented Kislingbury's conduct and judgment. Even Lieutenant Greely begrudgingly and belatedly acknowledged his service and hard work during the polar expedition.

But Kislingbury was not simply a frontier fighter. In an understaffed military that by necessity served multifaceted roles, like other talented and ambitious officers, Frederick Kislingbury fashioned a distinct position for himself. As a successful leader of Indian scouts, he worked side-by-side with Indigenous peoples, including the Pawnee and Crow, building relationships based on mutual respect. He succeeded in the field by virtue of an open mind that was prepared to learn from and utilize his companions' tactics and techniques.

By way of but one example, his Indian language skills were considered equal to the West Point graduate Captain William Philo Clark, a self-directed Indian linguistic expert who had made a

Introduction

special study of their sign language. The ties between Kislingbury and his scouts were strong. In the face of life-and-death encounters, his Indian allies risked their own lives in his defense. Kislingbury also worked hard to advance the welfare of the Indians and their families. His companions even adopted a name for him, Dancing Chief, a compliment to Kislingbury's willingness to participate in their ritual dance.

Frederick Kislingbury's military career attends some of the most significant conflicts of the Indian wars and the country's "Manifest Destiny" westward from 1869 through 1880. His path followed the final tragic events from the central plains of Nebraska, Kansas and Colorado to the far southern Texas/Mexican border, and ultimately to the northern plains in the aftermath of Custer's defeat.

Kislingbury's service would not place him in the pantheon of arctic explorers or field servicemen. But he represents the quintessential frontier officer, committed to duty and willing to endure extended hardships. In many respects, his story reflects the lives of a multitude of frontier soldiers who made valuable contributions but who have since passed without recognition. A look at his career sheds light on his personal merits and accomplishments, as well as the history of the U.S. Army in the Arctic and on the Plains. This work attempts to provide a more complete record of Frederick Kislingbury, and with it further recognition of his brief and tragic but eventful life.

Chapter One

A Respectable Young Gentleman

FREDERICK FOSTER KISLINGBURY WAS BORN on December 16, 1845 in the quaint parish of East Ilsley, Berkshire, England, some sixty miles west of London. At the time, East Ilsley was a pastoral sheep-farming community and the site of one of the largest sheep markets in England. On a clear day, atop one of its lush, rolling hills, the Round Tower at Windsor Castle, then the royal residence of Queen Victoria and Prince Albert, could be viewed in the distance. The grassy downs that characterize the region were the playground of the wellborn, where their thoroughbreds trained and raced, and pedigree hounds pursued their quarry.[1]

By contrast, the laboring class of the community could spare little time for such leisure pursuits. So it was with the Kislingburys, an old established family that could trace their ancestry back to the 1086 Doomsday Book. Frederick's father, John Kislingbury (1814-1893), was a versatile tradesman, working several skilled jobs as a glazier, painter and plumber. In 1840, John Kislingbury had married Maria Chenery (1820-1868), originally from Malton, a small market town in North Yorkshire. Frederick Foster was the second son and fifth of their seven children. By religion, the Kislingburys were Anglican, Church of England.[2]

In 1855, in search of improved economic fortunes following a bankruptcy, and with their young children in tow, John and Maria Kislingbury boarded the packet ship *Daniel Webster* in Liverpool. After their transatlantic crossing, they eventually settled in the city of Rochester, New York. Their assimilation into the new country was eased somewhat by the fact that John Kislingbury's sister, the children's aunt, accompanied them on the voyage. Rochester was chosen because Margaret Kislingbury, a sister-in-law of John

Kislingbury and a widow, had relocated to that city with her daughter a year or two before.[3]

Rochester looked to be an attractive choice for a skilled tradesman like John Kislingbury. The 1825 opening of the Erie Canal, which ran through the heart of the city, had been an economic boom for the city, dubbed "The Young Lion of the West." By the time the Kislingburys arrived, the city's grist mills were grinding out bushels of flour by the thousands, establishing it as the "leading Flour City of the world." Twenty years later, in an economic transition, its horticultural fruit and seed business would establish it as the "Flower City of the world." With such a vibrant economy, the city became a haven for thousands of immigrants from Europe. By 1850, it boasted 36,000 citizens, and was the twenty-first largest city in the country.

In Antebellum America, the city was also at the forefront of the reform and abolitionist movements, sheltering fugitive slaves and serving as an important stop on the Underground Railroad, and free blacks had formed a vibrant community within the city. Rochester became the long-time home of Frederick Douglass in 1847, and the center for publication of his influential anti-slavery newspaper, *The North Star*. Although the Kislingburys were not necessarily spirited activists, the family had relocated to a city whose residents were more open-minded and tolerant toward the anti-slavery and other reform movements than many other northern cities.[4]

John and Maria Kislingbury settled comfortably into their new home. Between 1857 and 1859, they welcomed three more children into their household, for a total of ten. Few details regarding the youthful Frederick Kislingbury or his family are recorded, but young Kislingbury was remembered by one Rochester resident as an active church member and always "upright, honorable and honest." He attended the public schools and later received some private schooling. As a teenager, he worked in the wholesale grocery business of Smith, Perkins & Company with thoughts of a possible mercantile career. By all accounts, he was considered a respectable young gentleman within the community.[5]

Momentous events outside Rochester would soon stir an interest in the young man toward more adventurous pursuits, altering that

A Respectable Young Gentleman

Frederick F. Kislingbury near the time of his military enlistment.

comfortable homelife and reshaping his future. Three months after reaching the age of eighteen, the minimum enlistment age, Frederick Kislingbury volunteered for service in the local militia during the American Civil War. A patriotic spirit had gripped the city after the fall of Fort Sumter in 1861, and an enlistment frenzy had quickly caught hold, with both immigrants and citizens answering the call. The city raised volunteer militias and regulars throughout the war, from the opening Union disaster at the First Battle of Bull Run. On July 24, 1864, Company E, of the Fifty-Fourth Regiment, New York National Guard, was organized in Kislingbury's hometown of Rochester, and Frederick Kislingbury enlisted for service with the company on the same day. Whether Frederick was overcome by patriotic fervor on behalf of his adopted land, as one acquaintance suggested, or had simply been compelled by peer pressure is unclear. He remained on duty for one hundred days, mustering out on November 10, 1864. During this entire period, young Frederick remained out of harm's way, stationed in Elmira, New York, serving as a prison guard for captured Confederate soldiers and civilians.[6]

The Elmira prison was the largest detention center in the Union but only operated as such for a one-year period. Designed for a maximum of 5,000, its 12,000 prisoners stretched the facility well beyond its capacity. Dubbed "Hellmira" by its inmates, a combination of insufficient rations, unsanitary conditions, harsh winter weather and lack of adequate medical care led to a dreadful number of deaths (nearly 3,000). As a volunteer enlisted man, Kislingbury had no say in the executive management that contributed to the appalling conditions within the prison. The devising of methods to break the sheer monotony of standing sentry occupied much of his time. In contrast to the plight of its inmates, for some guards prison duty sounded almost jocular. According to one veteran, Elmira's various regiments "had indeed acquired a great reputation during our life in camp for being possessed of an inexhaustible store of fun.... There was not an hour in the day but that one might enjoy a hearty laugh over the pranks of one or more of the boys." During Kislingbury's entire military service, his most dangerous scrape was not suffered on the field of battle, but rather on a parade ground when a clumsy horse trod on his foot. There was concern that his big toe might need to suffer amputation, but it was ultimately saved. The incident, though considered minor at the time, took on major significance in his identification after his death. Kislingbury was well regarded by his commanding officer though, performing well enough to have been promoted to corporal.[7]

For several months after mustering out, Kislingbury returned to work at Smith, Perkins & Company, but evidently military service held more appeal for him than storekeeping. His stint as a volunteer had set off a spark that would become all-consuming. On June 3, 1865, less than two months after the end of the Civil War, Kislingbury enlisted as a regular in the U.S. Army as a private in the U.S. Fourth Infantry for a term of service of three years. At nineteen years of age, the tall, blonde, blue-eyed soldier cut a handsome figure in his military uniform. Those who knew him personally were taken by his engaging personality and softspoken demeanor that could quickly become excitable when championing a cause. Underlying all those attributes was a fierce, gritty determination to prove himself capable of the demands in the field. With little active experience, Kislingbury was relegated to clerical positions at various army headquarters, first stationed at the Department of the East in Troy, New York. With the aid of Lieutenant Colonel Orson H. Hart, Kislingbury managed to a transfer to offices at the headquarters of the Department of the Ohio in Detroit, Michigan.[8]

During that time, on March 1, 1866 in Christ Church, Detroit,

Agnes ("Aggie") Bullock, first wife of Frederick Kislingbury.

Frederick married twenty-two-year-old Agnes "Aggie" Struther Bullock (1843-1878). Aggie was the daughter of George Bullock and Agnes (Findley) Bullock of Amherstburg, Ontario, Canada. George Bullock was a retired sergeant major in the British army, a bar owner and a local politician. The scant few references to his life and character cast him in a decidedly unfavorable light. After allegations of embezzlement as county treasurer, George fled for nearby Detroit (his wife had died in 1860). It was while Aggie and the Bullock family were rooming in a Detroit boarding house that they made the acquaintance of Fred, then a fellow lodger.[9]

Of those children, the most recognizable is Aggie's younger brother, the legendary westerner Seth Bullock, who would make a name for himself as a prominent politician, businessman and lawman in several territories in the West. Seth Bullock's reputation as a steadfast lawman grew while sheriff of rough-and-tumble Deadwood, Dakota Territory, during its heady gold rush days of the 1870s. Legend has it he arrived in Deadwood shortly after James Butler (aka "Wild Bill") Hickok was shot in the back of the head by Jack McCall in a saloon. A powerfully built man, his imposing demeanor could maintain law and order without the violence of gunplay. Enamored with the natural beauty of Yellowstone, he was also instrumental in its designation as a national park. In an oft-repeated statement, his friend President Theodore Roosevelt later characterized Bullock as a "true westerner, the finest type of frontiersman." With Roosevelt as vice president, Bullock was appointed the first supervisor of the Black Hills Reserve (now the Black Hills National Forest). Bullock's legendary character featured prominently in the HBO series *Deadwood* (2004-06) and *Deadwood: The Movie* (2019). In real life, Seth Bullock would also play an outsized role in the family of Frederick Kislingbury.[10]

Chapter 2

With the Pawnee Scouts

AFTER THEIR MARRIAGE, FREDERICK AND AGGIE KISLINGBURY settled into a comfortable metropolitan lifestyle. On Frederick's military pay they were able to live in a modest home in the city center of Detroit at a time when the city was on the cusp of its rise as an industrial powerhouse in the Midwest. The first commercially feasible steel production process in operation at mills in nearby Wyandotte had spurred manufacturing industries. The city's population was approaching 70,000 citizens, more than half of whom were immigrants. The Kislingburys were within walking distance of the city's center, Campus Martius, where both the Old Detroit Opera House (destined to become the premier theatre in Detroit) and the magnificent city hall were nearing completion. Recreational boat houses dotted the riverfront along the Detroit River separating the United States and Canada from which they could view Aggie's former hometown in Ontario.

The blissful couple welcomed a first son, Howard "Harry" Grant Kislingbury, on June 18, 1867. Despite his growing family, an adventuresome spirit within Frederick Kislingbury would find less and less favor with an urban office-bound role. Perhaps his family connection to the westward-leaning Bullocks had aroused an interest in the western frontier. Coincidentally, Aggie's brother Seth Bullock had left his home in Michigan for the Montana Territory not long after the marriage of Aggie and Frederick Kislingbury. In any case, throughout his brief life, a basic thirst for adventure, more than anything else, seemed to drive him from one venturesome undertaking to the next.[1]

After his company was transferred to the Department of the Platte in Omaha, Nebraska, Kislingbury continued to serve as a clerk in the department's headquarters. Aggie willingly uprooted from her snug Detroit home and transferred with her husband to the small but growing city on the Missouri River. Frederick beamed with great pride about Aggie, writing to his mother in October 1867 that "I have already got the name of having the prettiest lady in Omaha for a wife."

Kislingbury had other reasons to be upbeat. A cholera epidemic had raged through the Great Plains, striking Omaha in 1867, sickening dozens of citizens and stoking panic and fear in far more. Lieutenant Kislingbury had fallen gravely ill to the scourge in September and his life had hung in the balance for more than a week. Once the doctors declared him out of danger, he still remained physically weak. In a more relieved state of mind, he admitted to his mother that "poor old Fred came near going."[2]

He wasted no time in re-enlisting in July 1868. Kislingbury's assignment to the military headquarters in Omaha would prove fortuitous to his future. With several years of experience at command posts, Kislingbury was convinced that the military was his proper career choice. However, from behind his desk, he dreamed longingly for a vastly different role in the service, one of a position in the field rather than at a mundane clerical job.

With the conclusion of the struggle between the northern and southern states, the nation had turned with even greater focus to the west. The unceasing and expanding intrusion into longtime Indian tribal lands exacerbated an already growing discontent and led to numerous conflicts. At the time, the Department of the Platte, Kislingbury's duty station, administered a vast region that included the state of Nebraska and the territories of Wyoming, Utah and a corner of Idaho. Forging a pathway to the west, troops were engaged in safeguarding workers on the Union Pacific Railroad from Indian threats as the line pushed westward, as well as protecting settlers and Indians. This was the military service that attracted young Kislingbury.

Fellow officers strongly urged him to seek a higher position. He confided to his mother that he "was a little ambitious myself," and that at their next meeting she might see him in an officer's uniform. Though coveting a commissioned role in the U.S. Army, he realized that his prospects were slim. The army was undergoing massive demobilization, from over one million soldiers in 1865 to approximately fifty-five thousand by 1866. With hardnosed veterans of the Civil War unable to maintain rank, Kislingbury stood no chance of advancement. To his credit however, Kislingbury did manage to raise his profile within the downsized army. Impressed with Kislingbury's abilities and his spiritedness, Brigadier General Christopher C. Augur, commanding the Department of the Platte, found an active service role for the eager young man. In June 1869, Augur secured an appointment for Kislingbury in the Nebraska volunteer battalion, the so-called "Pawnee Battalion," of Major Frank J. North (1840-1885).[3]

At the time, North was already a respected leader of the Pawnee Scouts. While employed at the Pawnee Agency in central Nebraska during the early 1860s, North had become conversant in the Pawnee language and familiar with their customs. His ability to communicate in their language, as well as his own ample fortitude and battlefield courage, made North a greatly respected leader of the Pawnee Scouts. North permitted the Pawnee to maintain many of their methods and practices in the field, recognizing that attempting to force the Pawnees to conform to standard military practice would be unworkable. Having won their confidence and respect, North made a name for himself and his scouts in active fighting in the plains against the Cheyenne and Sioux, traditional archenemies of the Pawnee. Frederick Kislingbury would learn much about leadership and frontier fighting from both Major North and the Pawnee Scouts.[4]

The Pawnees were once a prosperous and dominant people who had settled along the fertile river courses of the central Great Plains of Nebraska and northern Kansas. Less nomadic than their northern counterparts, the Sioux, Cheyenne and Arapaho, the Pawnees lived in earth-lodge communities, tending crops for much of the year with a break for several months while hunting buffalo. By the 1860s, the traditional way of life of the Pawnees was under pressure. Through the early part of the 19th century, a series of virulent epidemics had dramatically reduced their population. The Pawnees also contended with the intrusion of the more numerous nomadic Northern Indians into their traditional homeland and game country, sparking armed conflict. They also faced an unremitting influx of settlers sparking further competition for limited resources. In the face of these mounting difficulties, the Pawnees took a pragmatic approach, aligning themselves with the U.S. government and its military. Though ceding much of their ancestral homeland through treaties, the move vastly improved their security. In return, the Pawnee proved good partners.[5]

Kislingbury's enlistment as a first lieutenant in the Pawnee Scouts coincided with the U.S. Army's "Republican River Expedition," organized in the spring of 1869. Like many regions of the west, the rapid infiltration by homesteaders into the rich buffalo hunting grounds of the Republican River and South Platte River valleys had initiated conflict with the Northern Indians in pursuit of game. In May 1869, Major Eugene Asa Carr and several cavalry companies had led two spirited engagements against Chief Tall Bull and his Cheyenne "Dog Soldiers" (together with a small number of Sioux and Arapaho), in which more than twenty-five Indians were killed. Following those encounters, the Dog Soldiers had attacked several settlements in the western frontiers of Kansas and Nebraska, destroying property, killing settlers, and taking captives. In response, in June 1869, eight companies of the 5th U.S. Cavalry under Major Carr were ordered to remove the hostile Indians from the region. Attached to the command was a battalion of three companies of Pawnee Scouts (ultimately comprising some 150 Indians, and five or six officers) mustered by Major Frank North.

The larger-than-life plainsman, William "Buffalo Bill" Cody, also accompanied the party as chief scout. He did in fact manage to acquire his legendary horse, and long-time companion, "Buckskin Joe" by trade from the Pawnees prior to the campaign. Cody also boasted with some pride that he acquired the name "Big Chief" from the Pawnees, after claiming to have improved their methods of hunting buffalo. If the story is true, atop Buckskin Joe, Cody dashed headlong into a buffalo herd and killed thirty-six within a half-mile run, much to the astonishment of the Pawnees.[6]

Kislingbury was assigned to Company A of the Pawnee battalion. He would quickly learn that marching with the scouts, and frontier campaigning in general, was a far more demanding

Major Frank North, leader of the Pawnee Scouts, in 1867.

lifestyle than shuffling paperwork in a comfortable office chair. He also garnered his first taste of Indian warfare, with its privations and brutal consequences. Kislingbury's appetite for the service was markedly single-minded. At the time of his acceptance of his appointment in June 1869, Aggie was well on her way to delivering a second child, Walter Frederick Kislingbury, who was born on August 13, 1869 while Kislingbury was in the field.

From Fort McPherson in central Nebraska, the ponderous expeditionary force, with its troopers, Indian scouts, teamsters, and some fifty wagons, plodded through rough terrain along the meandering course of the Republican River, some 150 miles through Nebraska and Kansas. The first few days were a slow slog as the command adjusted to life on the rough trail under sweltering hot temperatures, mixed with heavy thunderstorms. Compounding the delays, Carr had to attend to personnel matters, since his civilian teamsters were fond of drink and disruptive to the march. One of his officers, Captain Jeremiah C. Denney, suffered a nervous breakdown after having recently lost his wife (ordered back to the fort, he died of a self-inflicted gunshot wound).[7]

A brief encounter with an Indian hunting party on June 12 broke the monotony, though the Indians did manage to elude the pursuing Pawnees. Several days later, within the Republican River Valley near Prairie Dog Creek, an Indian marauding party attempted to stampede the mules, killing two teamsters. But they were held off, with the Dog Soldiers suffering two casualties at the hands of the fast-responding Pawnees.

Dancing Chief

On alert, the scouts continued to lead the command, following a nearly-concealed Indian trail through short buffalo grass that even Cody, an inveterate tracker, failed to discern. Once visible horse tracks were spotted, by forced marches the command followed telltale campsites in pursuit of the band, slowly closing the distance. According to Cody, observing a white woman's shoe print at each stop increased their desire to find and free female captives (though the truth of that tale has been disputed). To minimize detection of their trail, the Indians employed diversionary tactics that hindered pursuit. They scattered upon breaking camp and reassembled on the hard-packed ground of the high prairie. Their horses and mules were also driven in different directions until rejoining at the next encampment.

An advance patrol led by Major William B. Royall, 5th Cavalry, and one Pawnee company, tracking some thirty miles in advance of Carr's main party, caught the trail of the Indians, surprising a war party of some ten Dog Soldiers. Without awaiting an order from Royall, the Pawnees immediately charged the Dog Soldiers. In a brief, but spirited encounter, several Dog Soldiers were killed, two by the sergeant of the Pawnee Scouts, Mad Bear.

On the evening of July 8, along the North Fork of the Platte, three soldiers lagging several miles behind the main column were attacked, and that evening the Dog Soldiers attempted unsuccessfully to stampede the command's horses. During the latter engagement, on his own initiative Mad Bear dashed out alone on horseback ahead of the regular soldiers and Pawnees in pursuit of one mounted Indian. From a distance, in a friendly fire incident, he was shot and wounded by one of his fellow soldiers. At the recommendation of Carr, on August 29, 1869, Congress awarded Mad Bear the Medal of Honor for his actions, the first Indian recipient of the award.

The major engagement occurred in the mid-afternoon of July 11. Patrolling ten miles ahead of Carr's main force, scouts led by Cody and six Pawnees spotted the main village, some nine hundred persons, encamped near Summit Springs in the northeast corner of Colorado. Cody galloped back to Carr with the information. Taking advantage of depressions among the sand hills through which his force trudged, Carr managed to conceal his forces within a mile of the Indian camp when the order to charge was given. Some reports state that the Indians had burned the grass to erase their trail, leaving a smoky haze obscuring visibility. Outpacing the troopers, the spirited Pawnees seized the moment, leading the attack on the village and catching Tall Bull and his followers by surprise. Many were finishing their noonday meal, performing chores or simply relaxing under the warm midday sun. Finally spotting their attackers, a group of Dog Soldiers quickly dashed to meet the oncoming force. Greatly outnumbered, they quickly retreated.

Regular soldiers and officers joining the Pawnees, stormed the village. With no time to saddle or bridle their horses, the startled and confused defenders gathered what weapons they could manage. In the midst of the clamor of shouts and war whoops of the attackers and stampeding horses, they hustled the screaming women and children to safety. Small groups fled on foot and fought valiantly. Their leader Tall Bull led two wives and several others into a steep ravine for protection. In a heated fight there, Cody boasted of killing Tall Bull, a claim similarly made by Major North, and later attributed to at least three others, including a Pawnee.[8]

The engagement was a harsh, one-sided affair. Tall Bull and his people suffered fifty-two killed, many at the hands of the Pawnees. Seventeen Indian women and children were captured. In addition, a large number of horses and mules, which had scattered across the prairie, were rounded up. So many lodges, buffalo robes, provisions, arms and equipment were captured that Cody overheard one grieving Sioux remark that they "had lost everything and were ruined." Carr's attackers suffered only one soldier "scratched by an arrow" and the loss of a few played out horses. Luther North, Major North's brother, claimed that he had been hit by a spent ball, but that it struck his belt buckle, leaving him only with a black-and-blue mark.[9]

The two white captives suffered different fates. Maria Weichell, a homesteader originally from Bavaria, was rescued after suffering a dreadful pistol shot to her back by her captors. The other captive, Susanna Alderdice, a mother of four children and pregnant with another, was killed by the Indians as the troopers arrived, her skull crushed by a tomahawk.

That evening, a particularly violent hail and thunderstorm raked the plains, marking an end to the terrible affair that day. A lightning strike killed one horse with its trooper astride it, leading some soldiers to speculate that the wrath of God was punishing a sinful humanity. Some sixty miles distant at Fort Sedgwick, Major E. F. Townsend, 9th Infantry, recorded in the post returns, not normally a forum for daily weather events, that the storm "surpassed anything of the kind for severity known by persons in the country." Six buildings at the post were unroofed.[10]

Luther North had learned from the Dog Soldiers that the Indians made a fatal delay at Summit Springs. With the military close on its heels, Tall Bull had urged the break-up and scattering of the party. However, there were claims that their medicine man objected and had pushed to postpone the separation until July 12, which as it turned out, was the day after the encounter.[11]

The Pawnees took a decisive role in the engagement. Kislingbury may have been officially in command of a Pawnee company, but in battle, his Pawnee allies often pursued their own methods and tactics consistent with their culture. Kislingbury gained first-hand knowledge of Pawnee martial practice. The military's eye-catching blue uniforms were discarded, and a minimum of distinctive apparel was worn to distinguish them from the enemy. Pawnee Scouts sported warrior face paint, ditched saddles or bridles to ride bareback and fit ropes in the mouths of their mounts. The Pawnees were fearless fighters and individual displays of courage and bravery in battle were honored and held in great respect.

Kislingbury's assignment with the Pawnee scouts, although a means of gaining a commission in the Regular Army, would prove fortuitous to his future military career. Though officially serving under the overall command of Regular Army officers with their attendant military protocol (certainly helpful for that commission), Kislingbury's practical experience differed markedly from that of the traditional cavalry officer. As the neophyte to frontier fighting, Kislingbury was a student of the Pawnees, observing and absorbing their methods of scouting, travelling, and fighting, practices that differed from the rigidly disciplined conduct instilled by the Regular Army. Kislingbury understood that the Pawnees would never fully surrender their cultural identity and practices while serving the U.S. Army. However, through Major North and his interaction with the Pawnees, Kislingbury gained an understanding of how to bridge the two disparate cultures such that they could work together productively in the field. Though unaware at the time, lessons learned from the Pawnees would distinguish him from the rank-and-file cavalryman and fit him for a distinctive role in the Regular Army.[12]

Despite the victory at Summit Springs, the campaign was not yet completed. Through August and September, the 5th Cavalry and Pawnees marched northward across the South and North Platte Rivers to northern Nebraska in an exhausting pursuit of scattered refugees (the little-heralded campaign was known as the "Niobrara Pursuit"). Major Royall led the command as Major Carr had been granted leave to attend to the tragic death of an infant son.

With his Pawnee allies, Lieutenant Kislingbury experienced some of the worst of frontier campaigning. One of his ten-day dashes during the pursuit with Royall's troopers, hot on the trail of the Cheyenne and Sioux, was through a region characterized by Royall as "the most desolate I have ever travelled, a succession of sand hills, destitute of timber, unpassable for loaded teams, and terribly wearing upon horses." The command endured long forced marches under a scorching sun, with only scant few waterholes (dug at fifteen feet) that were low or unfit for drinking. Exhausted mounts simply dropped dead by the wayside. Despite the strain on his forces, Royall continued to close the gap; a trail of scattered lodge poles and skins, together with an absence of overnight camps, confirmed that the harried Indians were pushed to the limit. Without time to hunt, there was even evidence they were eating their own animals.[13]

On August 11, Royall abandoned the accompanying wagon train to make a fast move in a last-ditch effort to reach the Indians. With five companies of the 5th Cavalry and Kislingbury leading one hundred Pawnees, sixty-five miles of hard travel took the command to the banks of the Niobrara River. But with his horses failing and rations low, Royall was reluctantly forced to abandon the chase and make for nearby Fort McPherson. The hostiles, with extra riding mounts, had saved themselves. Royall's return march, completed on August 21, was physically exacting. Seventeen horses gave out and were mercifully shot. One Pawnee, a nineteen-year-old scout in Kislingbury's company, had died, possibly of a heart ailment. Some forty weak animals abandoned by the fleeing Indians were captured.[14]

At the post, Royall turned over command to Lieutenant Colonel Thomas Duncan, 5th Cavalry, as the expedition entered its unheralded final phase. Kislingbury and the Pawnees received a brief reprieve from field service, as the troops and mounts slowly recovered over the course of three weeks. Kislingbury briefly returned home to visit Aggie and his newborn son, delivered during the midst of the Niobrara Pursuit.

On September 15, a newly energized command under Duncan, five companies of cavalry, and two Pawnee companies (including Kislingbury and his Company A), scouted the region southwest of the Republican River. After an uneventful ten days, on September 26, Cody and North were off hunting buffalo about one-half mile ahead of Lieutenants William J. Volkmar and George F. Price, who were leading a group of some twenty civilian volunteers who were two miles behind, engaged in trail-breaking for the main force. Cody and North had dismounted when a party of six Indians, concealed in a ravine, quickly emerged and attempted to cut them off, charging full speed and firing at the exposed and outnumbered pair. According to Duncan, "just as the Sioux were almost certain of their success," Volkmar and Price sighted the attackers, and joined by the fast-approaching civilian party, routed the Indians. Duncan was certain that the charge by the two lieutenants and civilians "undoubtedly" saved the lives of Cody and North. A determined pursuit of the Indians was made until horses gave out and darkness fell. Though the main party escaped to the northwest with their animals and guns, their hastily abandoned village of fifty-six lodges was secured. An enormous stock of buffalo robes, food stocks and supplies were captured. A scouting party the following day, comprised of two regular companies and Kislingbury with his Pawnee companions, failed to locate the fleeing Indians.[15]

After several further scouting missions confirmed the flight of the Indians, the Republican River Expedition was completed.

Pawnee Scouts, including Lieutenant Kislingbury, mustered out on November 10, 1869. Writing in his official report of the expedition, Major Carr, a previous skeptic of the utility of the Pawnee Scouts, now remarked that the Pawnees "were of the greatest service to us throughout the campaign." Lieutenant Colonel Duncan echoed similar comments, but also added that Major North's several officers, including Frederick Kislingbury, "always acted promptly and cheerfully in the performance of every duty assigned to them." The Nebraska legislature also passed a resolution expressly recognizing the service of the Pawnees.

Even Buffalo Bill benefitted from the campaign. The campaign became a popular feature in his "Wild West show," carrying the history of the affair long beyond its occurrence and, in some sense, preserving its significance. Summit Springs was a cornerstone frontier event, marking the end of major Indian conflicts within the Republican River region.[16]

Chapter Three

"The Most God-Forsaken Part of Uncle Sam's Dominions"

FOLLOWING THE REPUBLICAN RIVER EXPEDITION, Kislingbury returned to a familiar position in the Regular Army, serving as chief clerk at the Department of the Lakes in Detroit. He and Aggie celebrated a joyous Christmas as they welcomed a third son, Louis Pelouze Kislingbury on December 25, 1870. The joy was only short-lived, however, as the infant died shortly after birth. In what was a tragic and devastating coincidence, another child was born on October 2, 1872 and given the same name, but also died shortly after birth. (The dates and circumstances surrounding their deaths are unknown).

These personal tragedies failed to dim Kislingbury's venturesome nature. Though outwardly settled in his home life and his professional station, he again was deeply unsatisfied with what he viewed as a mundane clerical post. Steadfast in his conviction for active field service, he set about to make it a reality. On September 10, 1872, he submitted a written request directly to President Ulysses S. Grant seeking an appointment as a second lieutenant in the Regular Army. His appeal was straightforward, remarking to the commander-in-chief that "having a taste of military life, I desire to enter the service with a view of making it my profession."[1]

He approached the potential appointment in earnest. Under the guidance of a well-qualified tutor, he knuckled down to his studies for the better part of a year. Armed with multiple character references, a modicum of frontier fighting experience and the backing of U.S. Senator Zachariah Chandler (MI), Michigan governor Henry P. Baldwin and heavyweights in the military brass (Brigadier General Philip St. George Cooke and Adjutant General of the Department of the Lakes Louis H. Pelouze, among others),

Frederick F. Kislingbury in 1872.

Kislingbury stood as a more qualified candidate. His portfolio now contained a bevy of favorable recommendations.

Kislingbury successfully passed his examination at the offices of the Department of the Lakes on October 11, 1873, and obtained his coveted appointment as second lieutenant. Overjoyed at his accomplishment, he was promptly assigned to the 11th Infantry, Company H, a long-storied regiment that had seen action in the War of 1812, the American Civil War and the Mexican-American War.

His first duty station was Fort Concho, a far-flung outpost in the Concho Valley of West Texas, at the confluence of the North Concho River and the combined South and Middle Concho Rivers. Remote and isolated, the post stood some ninety miles southwest of the railroad cow town of Abilene. Austin, the largest nearby city, was a full 225 miles to the east. The post was established in 1867 to protect settlers and cattle ranchers migrating to the region and homesteaders steering farther west.

By the 1860s, Texas Longhorns were being driven to New Mexico and Colorado along dusty trails adjacent to the fort. At times, Fort Concho served as a staging point for large cattle herds, and the army provided escorts to prevent attacks by marauding gangs and cattle thieves. Remorseless buffalo hunters, whose pursuit of hides denuded the plains of the remaining animals, also frequented

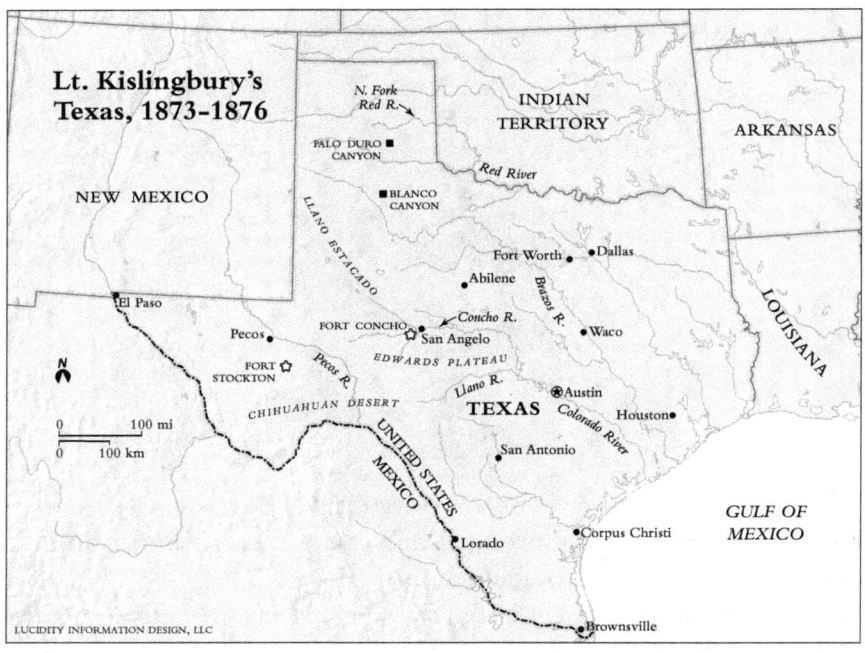

the area. From Fort Concho, the result of their efforts could be seen in the relentless procession of overloaded wagons that rolled beyond the station towards markets in the east.[2]

Fort Concho was situated on the western shoulder of a wide plateau (the Edwards Plateau), from which a visitor could view the far-reaching horizon across a vast prairie grassland dotted by scrubby mesquite trees and shrubs. The rugged banks and shorelines of streams, creeks and watercourses supported stands of pecan, oak and junipers. By 1870, an abundance of buffalo and pronghorn antelope still grazed in the grassy highland beyond the confines of the post.

The ramshackle fort was an eye-opener in contrast to Kislingbury's comfortable duty station in the metropolitan city of Detroit. At the time of his arrival in 1873, the fort was comprised of barracks for eight companies, eight sets of officers' quarters, a hospital, and work and storehouses. Contemporary reports paint a picture of a neglected and tumble-down assemblage of buildings with the grounds littered with trash and weeds, and scores of unleashed dogs roaming at will. Unsanitary conditions in the outhouses posed health hazards. Today, the restored post (encompassing some twenty

"The Most God-Forsaken Part of Uncle Sam's Dominions"

View of Fort Concho from above the Concho River.

well-maintained buildings) stands as a National Historic Landmark, library, archives and museum, preserving a fine example of military life on the frontier of West Texas in the mid-to-late 1800s.

The station's location on the plateau left it plagued by drastic extremes in weather—sleet and ice in winter and blistering heat and severe storms in summer. Heavy rains could swell barren rivers, creeks and fords almost instantly, while droughts could turn lush prairie grass to dust almost as quickly. Despite its variable weather, the Concho Valley offered a natural pathway for movement farther west in a region where both terrain and environment were extreme. To the north and west of the post, the Llano Estacado (or Staked Plains), a southern extension of the North American High Plains, rises in dramatic fashion above the Edwards Plateau. From the time of the Spanish conquistador Francisco Vázquez de Coronado, observers have labelled the rising tableland an unbroken landscape without a bluff, outcropping, protruding rock, or even a tree or shrub by which to orient. During an 1852 expedition its scarcity of water led Captain Randolph B. Marcy, 5th Infantry, to remark that the Llano Estacado region was "the Sahara of the Americas," though its lush buffalo grass supported large herds of buffalo in winter. Its edges are marked by sheer-walled canyons and arroyos. South and west of Fort Concho lies the Chihuahuan Desert, a dry and parched region broken by intermittent ranges of small mountains.[3]

There was little relief in the nearby town of San Angela (San

Angelo after 1880), located within a stone's throw of the fort. At the time an unkempt "hovel" of brothels, saloons, and gambling dens, the town was well known as a haven for outlaws, bandits, cattle and horse thieves. As the military could technically exercise no enforcement powers outside their fort, lawlessness was rampant, and shootings and robberies were common occurrences. Alice Grierson, wife of Colonel Benjamin Henry Grierson, 10th Cavalry (transferred to Fort Concho in April 1875), matter-of-factly wrote to her son that the town recorded five killings in one week during the month of December 1875. With no civil law enforcement within several hundred miles, military commanders at the post felt compelled to bend the rules and step in and restrain civilian lawbreakers when matters got too far out of hand.[4]

John Grierson, brother of Colonel Grierson, characterized the post as "the most God-Forsaken part of Uncle Sam's dominions." Contributing to the family's contempt of the post may have been the tragic death of Colonel Grierson's thirteen-year-old daughter Edith, who succumbed to typhoid fever at the station. Her ghostly apparition, mysteriously appearing while playing jacks, was said to have plagued overnight guests in the officers' quarters. Colonel Grierson spoke for those unlucky enough to be stationed there when he wrote to his wife that many officers would simply resign if they had any other employment opportunities. Overflowing with enthusiasm and naive to the hardships of extended frontier service, the army would have found little hesitation in assigning the tenderfoot Kislingbury to the woeful post.[5]

At the time of his arrival, some two hundred enlisted men were on duty. In April 1875, when Colonel Grierson arrived at the station, the regimental headquarters for the 10th Cavalry was also transferred to Fort Concho. In 1867, Grierson had organized the 10th Cavalry, a regiment of black troopers, the "Buffalo Soldiers," so-called due to the belief among the Indians that their hair resembled that of the buffalo. After serving in the central plains, companies of the 10th Cavalry served in posts along the West Texas frontier, including Fort Concho. Many of the men of the regiment were freed slaves from southern border states. They excelled in their service, performing the same duties as the other cavalry units at Fort Concho.[6]

Frederick and his dutiful army wife Aggie made the best of the situation. She faithfully accepted her role as a soldier's wife, caring for their small young family and fostering a home life under the shadow of an omnipresent military command. That shadow could prove rather oppressive at times, since assignments to quarters were based on rank rather than family size. This made for shifting accommodations for the Kislingbury family as Colonel Grierson and more senior officers had arrived. Upon the colonel's arrival, he selected the quarters that were occupied by the Kislingburys, ultimately necessitating the family's relocation to more cramped and uncomfortably warm quarters, even in the springtime of the year. At the time, Frederick was away on escort duty, so Grierson's introduction to the Kislingbury family was by virtue of Aggie. Grierson's first impression of Aggie was favorable, writing to his wife Alice that she was very "ladylike," but her children were very "noisy." Under the circumstances, the courteous colonel declined to move the Kislingbury family until Frederick returned, thus easing the burden on Aggie.[7]

Children too young to board away from the fort, including young Harry and Walter Kislingbury, received rudimentary schooling from the sole teacher on post. To break the dreadful monotony of isolated frontier life, harmless diversions were devised to cope with the boredom. When freed from domestic chores, the women were occupied with teas, carriage rides and croquet matches. The arrival of the weekly mail run was a cause for excitement. With fish and game abundant outside the fort, officers were often on sporting excursions. It was here that Frederick Kislingbury honed his skill with firearms.

In the evening, families competed in games such as chess, checkers, whist and backgammon. After a parade of lackluster commanders through the fort, the arrival of the jovial and well-liked Colonel Grierson (acclaimed for his Union cavalry raid during the 1863 Vicksburg campaign) brought a notable rise in spirits and a welcome upgrade to the shabby post. In the absence of any cultured society in San Angela, Grierson made a point of holding festive banquets, dinners and "hops" at Fort Concho. The regimental band, often led by Grierson, an accomplished violinist, provided lively music and entertainment.

One photographic image of the celebrations at the post has survived—a sepia-toned stereoview of the Valentine's Day masquerade ball held on February 14, 1876. Military uniforms, commonplace wardrobes and work clothing were replaced by bright, colorful costumes, among them familiar "Little Red Riding Hood," and the "Queen of Hearts." Posing in Grierson's backyard with the officers and ladies, Aggie Kislingbury is dressed as a "Gypsy," perhaps a thinly veiled statement hinting of her peripatetic military lifestyle (the fact of her sixth month of pregnancy is indiscernible from the photo). She stands to the right of Lieutenant John T. Morrison, dressed as "Old Nick," with his hand on his knee. Frederick Kislingbury was not present for the photo, likely on duty in the field.

The Kislingbury's welcomed two more children while at the station—Douglass Ebstian Kislingbury, born March 2, 1874, and Wheeler Schofield Kislingbury, born June 21, 1876. Both children carried the names of senior officers at the post, a reflection of the comradery and mutual respect that developed among the officers and the closeknit family groups. The youngest Kislingbury, Wheeler Schofield, took his name from career officer Major George Wheeler Schofield (1833-1882), 10th Cavalry. The Kislingbury's son Douglass was named after another senior officer, Major Henry Douglass (1827-1892), 11th Infantry, commander of the post prior to Grierson's arrival.

There were other family matters to contend with at the post. Eyebrows were raised and tongues were wagging among the officers' wives when forty-three-year-old Major Schofield married Aggie Kislingbury's sister, twenty-one-year-old Alma ("Allie") Bullock (1855-1879). The festive ceremony at the post came on the heels of a mere seventeen-day acquaintance between Major Schofield and the young Allie.

Whirlwind courtships on the frontier were not unusual in light of the isolation and fleeting opportunities for meeting members of the opposite sex. Moreover, the country's population mix had changed dramatically by virtue of the catastrophic loss of men during the American Civil War. Marriage opportunities for single women fared far better at frontier posts where men largely outnumbered

"The Most God-Forsaken Part of Uncle Sam's Dominions"

Masquerade party at Major Grierson's lodging, Aggie Kislingbury is fifth from left.

women. This was especially true at Fort Concho. Grierson noted that when he had arrived, there was but one unmarried lady at the post, who had "many devoted admirers among the young scouts." Aware of Allie Bullock's impending arrival at the outpost, he had presciently joked to his wife that when Allie arrives, "the same spirit will no doubt gather about her, like ants to a sweet biscuit."[8]

Major George Schofield and his wife Alma would remain close with the Kislingbury family. With no children of their own, Major Schofield would be asked by Frederick to serve as guardian of several of the Kislingbury children and as executor of Frederick's estate. As an experienced veteran of the Civil War, Schofield had been breveted brigadier general by war's end. Of an inventive mind, the major had tinkered with modifications to the standard .45 Smith & Wesson revolver, developing the so-called "Model Schofield." The weapon received rave reviews from soldiers in the field and Schofield pocketed a handsome royalty from the manufacturer for non-governmental sales. Ironically and tragically, reportedly with the same make of weapon, at isolated Fort Apache, Schofield would commit suicide on December 17, 1882. Perhaps he never overcame the grief of losing his wife Allie three years before. Curiously, George Schofield's brother Frank had also committed suicide, in 1879. Another brother, John McAllister Schofield, was a high-ranking military leader with a long and distinguished record during the Civil War, and later served as Secretary of War under President Andrew Johnson (1868-69). In 1876, he was serving as Superintendent of West Point Military Academy (through 1881), and in 1888, he would be appointed commanding general of the Army, a position he held until 1895.

Both cavalry and infantry were well-utilized at Fort Concho. Cavalry units were constantly in the field on scouting duty. Heavily fatigued troopers did their best to forestall, or to respond to, isolated attacks, as well as to horse and cattle thievery by Indians and marauding bandits. Infantry detachments guarded and escorted settlers, buffalo hunters, Indians and railway construction workers. Those soldiers also manned several sub-posts, protecting stage and mail routes and settlements, ranging from twenty-five miles up to eighty miles from the post. Soldiers also had to contend with other enemies. Medical reports disclose that about fifteen percent of the post's command was regularly out sick, largely due to stomach ailments which originated from contaminated water supplies.

Kislingbury arrived at Fort Concho at an unsettled time in Indian relations. Historically, the Concho Valley was the domain of the Indians who had relied on its natural resources for generations. With the westward movement of an increasingly larger number of emigrants, settlers and buffalo hunters, competition for land and resources inevitably led to confrontations. A similar pattern played out in West Texas as it had in other parts of the American frontier. Threatened by the onslaught, some Indians surrendered to reservations, while some remained steadfastly determined to maintain their way of life. By the 1870s, poor conditions and management at the reservations had led large numbers of dissatisfied Comanche, Kiowa, and Cheyenne to take to the plains and become openly hostile. They were joined by free roamers in the Staked Plains of northwestern Texas.

Following continued unrest, in the fall of 1874 several posts, including Fort Concho, prepared to strike a punishing blow to remove the hostiles from West Texas and move them back to reservations in the Indian Territory, today's Oklahoma. Five columns were organized from different posts, comprising more than 3,000 soldiers. At Fort Concho, the largest column, as many as eight companies of cavalry and five of infantry, including Kislingbury's Company H, were consolidated under the command of career officer Colonel Ranald Slidell Mackenzie (1840-1889).

Mackenzie was a highly competent officer during the Civil War and, at the time, praised by U.S. General Grant as one of the Union's "most promising young officers." He was known as a hard-driving officer and strict disciplinarian, traits for which he was not particularly well liked by those who served under him. Wounded on several occasions, consequently having lost several fingers, he was known as "Bad Hand" by his men. After the conclusion of the war, he remained in active service on the plains through his retirement in 1884.

Mackenzie had already introduced aggressive tactics and extended campaigns against the Indians in West Texas. His objective was to take the fight to the home grounds of the Comanches while making life off the reservation untenable. In 1871, marshalling a large force and marching some two hundred miles, Mackenzie faced the Comanches from within the Blanco Canyon of the Llano Estacado. The following year, scouting new routes across the Llano Estacado, he led an engagement against the Comaches along the North Fork of the Red River. To the south, in 1873, to quell cattle depredations along the Rio Grande, he made a rapid incursion into Mexico to surprise the Kickapoos and Lipans.

Starting from Fort Concho on August 22, 1874, a fiercely determined Mackenzie pushed his sizable column hard for miles through drenching rain, sleet and mud. The Indians were harried and kept constantly on the move. With the element of surprise, spotting the main Indian encampment in the bottomland of the Palo Duro Canyon within the Llano Estacado (Staked Plains), Mackenzie's force made a difficult traverse, single-file down through the sheer canòn. Reassembling the column and attacking, the Indians briefly held the ground as their women and children retreated. The fleeing Indians were pursued for some twenty-five miles until sunset. Returning to the abandoned camp, Mackenzie's force succeeded in confiscating their entire winter supplies of food, arms and equipment. In another devastating blow, more than 1,000 captured Indian horses were shot by the cavalry to prevent them from falling back into the hands of the Indians (the location, known as "The Bone Pile," became a gruesome and distinctive landmark for years). Lacking transportation, food and supplies, through the winter of 1874-75, the Indians were also harried by a column led by Colonel Nelson A. Miles (known as "Bearcoat" for his overcoat of bearskin). The campaign broke the resistance of the Indians, and ultimately brought an end to any further significant Indian hostilities in West Texas.

Frederick Kislingbury had a busy time of it during the grueling four-month campaign. His infantry company supported the main body of Mackenzie's force in the field by escorting supply trains and scouting missions. Supply wagons were vital to the extended operation, and were in constant motion to and from temporary camps and permanent posts carrying food stocks, munitions and necessary equipment. At times, the escorts lent a hand with picks and shovels in road building. Stubborn pack animals were urged by whip and blade, and soldiers helped push and pull wagons up steep and slippery slopes, over broken ground and frequently through deep mud and driving rain and sleet. In the busy month of September, with Kislingbury in charge, his Company H covered over 429 miles ferrying supplies between those supply camps and posts.

Even as a support unit, field reports noted that Kislingbury's escorts faced the occasional hostile Indian encounter. One soldier and messmate of Kislingbury who later penned an account of the campaign in the *United Service Magazine* had nothing but praise for the young lieutenant. Impressed with Kislingbury's soldierly qualities and character, he wrote that "Kislingbury was one of the best-hearted fellows that ever wore shoulder-straps, and a true man."[9]

In the aftermath of what later became known as the "Red River War," Kislingbury returned to Fort Concho, serving as commander of his company in the continued absence of Captain Erasmus C. Gilbreath. A welcome break in routine escort and guard duties presented itself during the fall of 1875. Kislingbury chanced

"The Most God-Forsaken Part of Uncle Sam's Dominions"

Lieutenant Adolphus W. Greely, U.S. Signal Corps.

to work with a fellow visiting officer, one who would change the course his life—Lieutenant Adolphus W. Greely (1844-1935). From a proud working-class background in the bustling port city of Newburyport, Massachusetts, a youthful Greely had been ingrained with an almost absolute "obedience to authority and love of country and faith in God," as he later noted in his autobiography. Now, at age thirty-one, he was tall and lean, sporting a wooly beard while wearing fashionable pince-nez glasses, looking more the professor than soldier.[10]

Nonetheless, "Dolph" was a battle-hardened veteran of the American Civil War. Stirred by pro-Union fervor and what he characterized as an almost religious belief in "duty for my country," at the onset of the war he enlisted as a private in the 19th Massachusetts Volunteers. Only seventeen years old, he lied about his age to meet the minimum requirement (eighteen). According to his own whimsical storyline, Greely claimed that he chalked the number "18" on the sole of his shoes so he could truthfully answer that he was "over eighteen."

Humor aside, his fortitude and battlefield courage were unmistakable. He survived a fusillade of musket and cannon fire at Second Manassas, endured weeks of misery in the swamps of Chickahominy, was badly wounded in his regiment's decisive defense at Antietam, and recovered to fight house-to-house and hand-to-hand at Fredericksburg. At Antietam, the bloodiest day of the war, his 19th Volunteers lost 136 men out of 384, with his particular unit suffering losses of more than fifty percent. Greely was rightly proud of his claim that he was the first of three million Union volunteers to reach the rank of general officer in the Regular Army.

After the war, he remained in the army as an officer in the newly formed Signal Corps, an army branch tasked with improving military communications and advancing the nascent science of meteorology. With an innovative mindset, Greely was adept at devising and implementing practical solutions within the multifaceted Signal Corps. After introducing new means for forecasting weather conditions along the flood-prone Mississippi River basin, his organizational skills were quickly put to use in completion of a telegraphic system of communication across the unsettled West to collect weather data, as part of the fledgling U.S. Weather Bureau.

At Fort Concho, Kislingbury and Greely struck up a friendship. The two shared a common background that may have facilitated their cordial relationship. Greely was less than two years older than Kislingbury, though with vastly more battle experience. Both hailed from modest hard-working families. As Greely stated in his autobiography, "the gaining of one's living by labor was the rule," a maxim that applied equally to the Kislingburys. As New Englanders (including for that matter upstate New York), they were possessed of a strong Republicanism, and both had volunteered to serve the Union cause. The two were possibly already acquainted. Greely had served as an aide to Major Eugene Carr during the Republican River Expedition of 1869, while Kislingbury served with the Pawnees. In fact, in his own account, Greely claimed to have discovered the first traces of the Indian trails that led to the Summit Springs victory. In any event, Greely may have been impressed by young Lieutenant Kislingbury, a non-West Pointer like himself, who had matured in the four years since his Pawnee days and had persevered to earn his commission in the Regular Army.[11]

For the Signal Corps, West Texas had proved a daunting field for telegraph installations. The boundless prairie, devoid of serviceable trees and sweltering in the summer heat, made for enormous logistical problems and trying conditions for physical work. After

"The Most God-Forsaken Part of Uncle Sam's Dominions"

earlier failures and undefined "embarrassments," a frustrated Colonel Albert Myer, commanding the Signal Corps, directed Greely to take charge in April 1875.[12]

Greely excelled at organizational tasks, and the telegraph communication across Texas required every bit of problem-solving skills, coupled with back-breaking labor. The desolate plains from Fort Concho to El Paso were considered some of the most difficult stretches in the United States. A dearth of suitable trees in the region forestalled progress until Greely ingeniously arranged to import poles by boat and wagon from Tidewater Virginia, a journey of over 1,000 miles. At the fort, telegraph wire was cut in half-mile lengths and carted by wagon to the hitching point. Enlisted men toiled in the unrelenting heat to cut poles and dig post holes three to four feet deep, and string the wire.

Kislingbury evidently grew to know Greely well. From October 1875 through mid-March 1876, Kislingbury commanded construction parties, and his Company H supplied manpower and protection for more than 100 miles of military telegraph construction toward Fort Stockton. The telegraph system supported not only vital communications from remote outposts for the protection of settlers and Indians, but trained soldiers also transmitted daily meteorological information which could assist the Signal Corps in the budding field of weather forecasting. Kislingbury was one of several officers commended for "zeal and efficiency" in rendering assistance to the construction parties.[13]

Chapter Four

The Great Sioux War

FOR FREDERICK KISLINGBURY, HIS NEXT ASSIGNMENT would serve to prove his mettle and gain him recognition within military circles. From Fort Concho, in the fall of 1876, companies of the 11th Infantry received orders to proceed some 1,000 miles north to the Dakota Territory, home of the Sioux. The wheels had been set in motion for the transformation of the Sioux Country well before Kislingbury's arrival on the scene. For years, the inexorable westward expansion of white settlement into Sioux lands had forced tribes to migrate further west to the Dakota and Montana Territories. A series of treaties in the 1850s and 1860s with tribes that had little choice but to accept their terms led to tensions, and in some cases bloodshed, when treaty obligations went unfulfilled or were set aside to further land grabs.

There followed Red Cloud's War, a series of conflicts initiated by settlers moving along the Bozeman Trail through favored Indian hunting grounds in the Powder River region of northeast Wyoming and southeast Montana. It had ended with the signing of the Fort Laramie Treaty of 1868, an agreement which would have great consequences for the Northern Indians. The treaty had established the "Great Sioux Reservation," an exclusive tribal area encompassing that portion of South Dakota west of the Missouri River, which included the Black Hills region. In the "unceded Indian Territory" within the adjacent disputed Powder River region, an area rich with herds of buffalo, the Indians were granted travel and hunting rights. The treaty also stipulated that annuities would be furnished to the Indians. Moreover, their traditional nomadic life, following game and the seasons, was to be transformed to an agrarian and stock-raising one with the goal of self-sufficiency and future land allotments.

With the discovery of gold in the Black Hills within the lands covered by the agreement, it was inevitable that the frenzy to extract valuable minerals would lead to government renegotiation or even outright disavowal of its stipulations. For a time, the Army had served to maintain treaty obligations and had removed prospectors and settlers from the area. The growing friction exacerbated between white men infiltrating the region and the Northern Indians intent on preserving their traditional way of life. In an unprecedented attempt at reconciliation, Indian representatives, including Chiefs Red Cloud and Spotted Tail, had travelled to the nation's capital to meet with President Grant and administration officials. Efforts on the part of the government to purchase the treaty lands outright were rejected by the tribesmen. In response, the government changed course, concluding that the desire for precious metals and settlement outweighed the interests of the Indians. Without resolution of the matter, President Grant opened the region to prospectors and instructed the military to condone unrestricted access. Frustrated by the inability to coerce the Indians into surrendering treaty lands, the government lost patience and issued an ultimatum.

The Indians were ordered to return to the Great Sioux Reservation by January 31, 1876, and any who failed to comply by that date would be considered hostile. It was a futile order that was largely a pretext for action. Some tribes discussed the one-sided terms but decided that the need to procure game in advance of winter made compliance impossible, even had they elected to do so. Others simply wanted no part of agency life and a surrender of the deep-rooted traditional lifestyle they knew well. The Indians felt betrayed, and they found it difficult to reconcile the government's action.

The failure of the majority of the Northern Indians to comply led Brigadier General George Crook, commander of the Department of the Platte, to commence his first action, a winter campaign. A thoughtful fighter, Crook had applied novel tactics in his campaigning: the extensive use of Indian scouts, winter campaigning, and increased mobility through the use of mule packs instead of unwieldy wagon-trains that slowed troop movements.

Dancing Chief

The campaign opened on a disagreeable note. A large but unknown number of well-armed warriors roamed the vast territory of the unceded region. They remained resolute in their belief that they could successfully oppose or avoid the small frontier armies that had been assembled to confront them. Crook believed that a decisive blow in mid-winter would leave the Indians physically weakened, at the mercy of the elements, and broken in spirit. Such a bold strike might facilitate a quick change of heart on their part. On March 1, 1876, Crook advanced troops from Fort Fetterman to Fort Reno (a Bozeman Trail relic) in the Wyoming Territory, establishing a base there. The weather was unbearably cold, and the troops trudged through deep snow in heavy wool and furs, subsisting on meals of frozen bacon and beans served with lukewarm coffee. Proceeding along the Tongue River, they located a large Indian village near the Powder River in southeastern Montana Territory. Colonel Joseph Reynolds was dispatched with three hundred men to attack and destroy the village.

At sunrise on March 17, Reynolds stormed the Indian village, comprised largely of Cheyenne and a smaller number of Oglala Sioux all on their way to the Red Could Agency in response to the government's directive. On that ironic circumstance, the Great Sioux War had begun. Despite the element of surprise, the Indians managed to escape to safety outside the village. Reynolds destroyed the camp, its food and stores, but he quickly retreated from the smoldering settlement, enabling several hundred horses to fall back into the hands of the Indians.

The incomplete action by Reynolds marked the end of any further winter campaigning, so General Crook turned his attention to the upcoming summer operation. Soon dubbed the Big Horn and Yellowstone Expedition, the Army now adopted a three-pronged approach, using a total strength of some 2,400 men converging on the Northern Indians in the Tongue and Powder River regions to either push them back to the reservations or to destroy them. Colonel John Gibbon from Fort Ellis, near Bozeman, would move east; Brigadier General Alfred H. Terry (with Custer's 7th Cavalry) at Fort Abraham Lincoln, near

The Great Sioux War

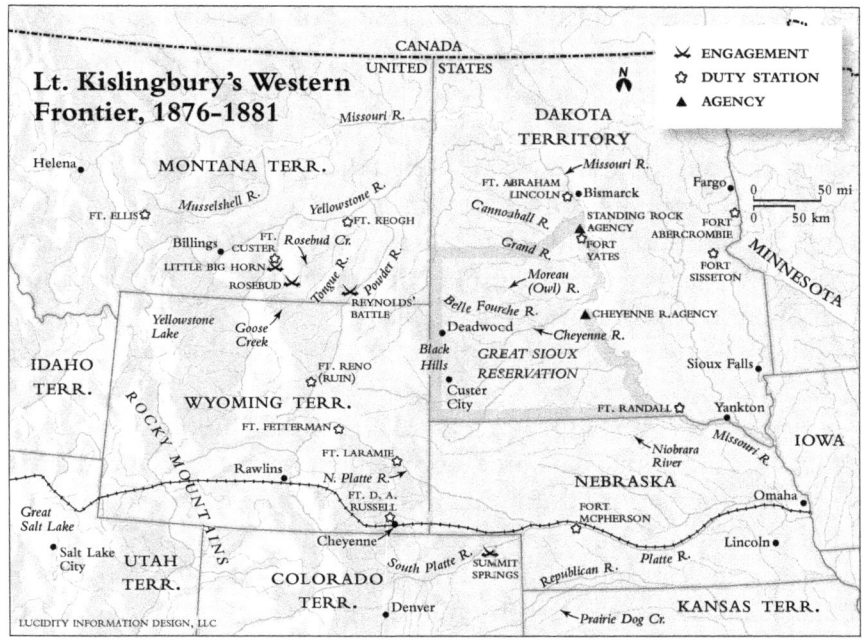

Bismarck, would move west, and Brigadier General Crook would start north from Fort Fetterman near Douglas, Wyoming.

The disappointing engagement by Reynolds had more profound consequences; it galvanized the Northern Indians. Fearing a threat to their traditional way of life, they were forced into action in an unprecedented manner. After a wearying march along the still frozen Powder River, the beleaguered stragglers from the Reynolds' engagement had arrived in the camp of Crazy Horse instead of returning to the Red Cloud Agency. After hearing their pitiable story, Crazy Horse looked for assistance from others, including Sitting Bull's Hunkpapas, who had always been opposed to treaties and reservation life. For Sitting Bull there was no hesitation, he would respond to the threat. The legendary leader summoned a call to action. During the following weeks, Sitting Bull, Crazy Horse and the others undertook a slow, inexorable spring march, with their horses grazing lazily along the way as the weather warmed. As they crossed paths with additional newcomers, many so-called "traditionals" who shunned reservation life, their ranks swelled. Disgruntled agency Indians also received word from Sitting Bull.

Already smarting from the frustrating loss of the unceded region, a scarcity of game and scrimping by agents on rations and arms at the agencies, they needed little incentive to join the ranks.[1]

In late May, General Crook left Fort Fetterman again, leading two battalions of cavalry and a battalion of five companies of infantry, comprising some 50 officers and 1,000 enlisted men. Some 250 Shoshone and Crow allies, considered a vital component to the overall force, also joined the movement. Crook's scouts had obtained information that a large Indian village sat along Rosebud Creek, a sluggish tributary of the Yellowstone River, inside Montana Territory.

On June 17, a large force of Sioux and Cheyenne attacked Crook's command. The fierce engagement at the Rosebud lasted more than six hours until the Indians retreated. Crook suffered some nine or ten killed and some fifty wounded; his Indian scouts suffered one dead and about seven or eight wounded. The Northern Indian casualties were largely unknown but easily counted in the dozens. Though by definition Crook was the victor by holding the field at the day's close, he was well aware that he had been stymied. He withdrew his force to Goose Creek. Doing so prevented Crook from joining Terry's command.

In the meantime, Brigadier General Terry and his soldiers, including some 600 cavalry and 400 infantry, had departed Fort Abraham Lincoln and headed west, as planned. Following the Yellowstone to the mouth of the Rosebud, Terry communicated with Colonel Gibbon, whose force was stationed at the mouth of the Big Horn River, a tributary of the Yellowstone. The 7th Cavalry proceeded up Rosebud Creek. Encountering an Indian trail, they followed it to the Little Big Horn River, where a large Indian camp was spotted. The ensuing engagement led by Custer ended with his immediate command killed to a man. The outcome would have profound consequences for the Sioux.

Prior to the Great Sioux War, the military maintained a limited and widely scattered presence along the confines of the Sioux Country for purposes unrelated to defeat of the Sioux. These included the oversight of a handful of reservations established under the Fort Laramie Treaty of 1868, and the protection of Indian Bureau agents and employees, as well as westward moving settlers and commerce. In the aftermath of the Custer defeat, the region quickly became the focus of attention of Lieutenant General Philip H. Sheridan, commanding the Division of the Missouri which encompassed the Sioux Country. There was a massive influx of soldiers, an assemblage of forts, and the transport of equipment and supplies with Sheridan's goal of once and for all breaking the Indian resolve and ultimately readying the region for settlement. Troops from within and without the departments of the Dakota and the Platte were redeployed to the theatre to assist in the construction and guarding of sizable posts in support of troops in the field. At Fort Concho, companies of the 11th Infantry received orders to proceed some 1,000 miles north to Sioux Country.

༺❦༻❦༺❦༻

Lieutenant Kislingbury and multiple companies of the 11th Infantry were transferred to the military post at Fort Yates, Dakota Territory, arriving via steamer from Yankton in September 1876 (the post had originally been named the Post at Standing Rock until renamed Fort Yates in 1878 after Captain George W. Yates, 7th Cavalry, who was killed at the Little Big Horn). Located on the west bank of the Missouri River in Dakota Territory, the post stood adjacent to the Standing Rock Agency and within two hundred yards of its buildings. Kislingbury would play an integral role at Fort Yates and Standing Rock for more than three years, gaining the respect of both his military commanders and his Indian agency companions.

The agency was initially established in 1869 (as the Grand River Agency) and formed part of the Great Sioux Reservation to oversee the Yanktonai, Cut Heads, Hunkpapa and Blackfeet. In 1874, it was moved some fifty miles north of the Grand River and renamed Standing Rock Agency. The agency buildings were situated on level ground above the steep banks of the west side of the Missouri River, offering a striking view of the surrounding area, and convenient access by steamer. The agency was sizable, both in terms of territory and population, the largest on the Missouri River. Spanning more than several million acres, its grounds still stretch across vast prairie grasslands, interspersed by rolling hills, wooded streambanks and bottomlands, dotted by the occasional crumbling butte or outcrop (today, the reservation straddles the South Dakota and North Dakota border). At the time, populous Indian camps dotted the riverbank for miles above and below the agency.

During its first few years, the lightly manned post (two infantry companies, about 200 men) served to maintain order and peaceful relations at the agency. Relations with the Indians may have been peaceful, but the military command at Fort Yates and the civilian Indian agents of Standing Rock were habitually at odds, a microcosm of the broader raging tug-of-war between the military and civilian control over the agencies. Though authority for Indian Affairs had been transferred from the War Department to the Interior Department as early as 1849, the agency remained dependent upon the military for protection of its employees and agents, and as an enforcement arm. With differing viewpoints on the handling of Indian matters, interdepartmental disputes were commonplace. Such was the case at Standing Rock, where cantankerous relations between the two departments escalated into scathing personal attacks.

When Kislingbury arrived, a reliable census of the number of Indians present at the agency, upon which ration distributions were calculated, had become one of several nasty flash points. In his 1875 report to the Interior Department, Agent John Burke identified some 7,000 Indians at the agency. Unconvinced as to its accuracy, the then-commander of the military post, Captain John S. Poland, 6th Infantry, who undertook his own count, found closer to 4,000. The fluid nature of Indian movements on and off the agency and estimates based on lodge numbers rather than actual headcounts, made anyone's calculation uncertain. In any event, Poland was incensed by what he viewed as an outright lie by the agent as to the headcount. He believed that the overstatement led to added rations being served to hostiles outside the agencies. In Poland's opinion, the agent should be relieved. For his part, Burke was incensed that Poland had retained the services of a man named Allison as an Indian interpreter, after Burke had recommended his dismissal for theft of property.[2]

At the time, Poland was actually the one who was relieved. From mid-August 1876, the companies were under the command of Lieutenant Colonel William Passmore Carlin, 17th Infantry. Forty-seven-year-old Carlin was a no-nonsense career soldier who had fought the Indians on the plains before the Civil War and was involved in active fighting throughout the war. As successor to Poland, Lieutenant Colonel Carlin was no less critical of Agent Burke, and was perhaps even more fault-finding, declaring him "treacherous to the interests of the Government and the Indians." Carlin similarly concluded that the ration numbers of Burke bore no relation to the true number of Indians. As a result, Carlin claimed that Burke had fraudulently issued more than $200,000 a year in rations. In addition, Carlin claimed that Burke had defied Carlin's orders by issuing rations to Kill Eagle, who had been in the hostile camp at the Little Big Horn battle.[3]

Standing Rock, with its large Huckpapa Sioux population, had close bonds of both friendship and blood to Sitting Bull and his followers outside the agency. Agent Burke had recognized that influence had been "brought to bear upon [the agency Hunkpapa] by the hostile camp" after the events of the Little Big Horn. Burke maintained that despite the pressure, the local residents "have uniformly and constantly resisted all the influence" of the hostile camp. However, Burke mischaracterized the situation at Standing Rock. In his annual report, Burke claimed that no more than one hundred had departed and only for "visits" to the hostile camps, "for the sake of trade, novelty, and curiosity, without any hostile intentions." Carlin had a very different take on the matter. In his annual report to the assistant adjutant general, Carlin noted that upon his arrival in August 1876, he found the residents "insolent and defiant." Carlin reported that "the agent at that time [Burke] had apparently instilled into their minds a bitter feeling against the military. They were in constant communications with the hostiles and were sending supplies of all kinds to them." In any event, Burke's days as agent were numbered. With the military assuming control of the agency, on August 16, 1876, Lieutenant Colonel Carlin wasted no time in selecting Captain Robert E. Johnston, 1st Infantry, to replace the agent.[4]

By the fall of 1876, the previously small, sleepy military post was quickly cramped with nine infantry companies, establishing it as a sizable military garrison with a distinct mission. Lieutenant Kislingbury superintended the work parties to house the swelled ranks, a hurried construction project that raised roughhewn officers' quarters and barracks for the enlisted men. Log structures chinked with mud, dirt roofing, and wooden plank floors offered little relief from the elements. Poor ventilation, particularly during the shut-in winter months, added to the discomforts. With their completion though, Lieutenant Kislingbury would soon have scant time to experience the discomforts of the post quarters.[5]

Chapter Five

Indian Scout Leader

BELIEVING THAT THE INDIANS, particularly those at the Standing Rock Agency and the Cheyenne Agency, were actively supporting the hostiles through supplies and shelter, Lieutenant General Sheridan set about to neutralize them. Though many were peaceful, all were painted as hostiles, and Sitting Bull's Hunkpapa tribe was declared an enemy of the government.

The matter of Indian horses continued to be of particular concern to Sheridan. The thought that mounted and well-armed hostiles could again mass in large numbers in Sioux Country bedeviled the military man. To the nomadic tribes, horses were the lifeblood of mobility, instrumental in hunting, traveling and warfare. The horse had been integrated into Indian culture, so much so that the Indians held a spiritual connection to their animals. Removing them would have profound consequences to their traditional way of life and belief system.

Integral to Sheridan's plans to wrest control of Sioux Country was the necessity of appropriating those means of transport and confiscating arms. Colonel William H. Wood, 11th Infantry, writing from the Cheyenne Agency, stated the matter more bluntly, writing in his 1876 annual report that "a Sioux without his horse is, comparatively, a very harmless being." In advance of a spring offensive, Sheridan commanded officers at the agencies of the Upper Missouri to take active steps to dismount and disarm the agency Indians.[1]

At Standing Rock, Carlin immediately issued orders that bands outside Standing Rock would be attacked if they did not return and surrender their arms and ponies. Fearful of Carlin's threat, on September 15, 1876, one large band of 124 Indians surrendered, bringing with them 100 ponies and 29 firearms. Those who did return and had been present at the Little Big Horn or had spoken to participants, offered their own accounts of that fateful day. One of those who surrendered on September 15 was Kill Eagle, who offered one of the most lengthy reports as to the events, and his interview was published in newspapers across the country.[2]

In accordance with Sheridan's orders, on October 22 Brigadier General Terry, with companies of the 7th Cavalry, also arrived at Standing Rock Agency for the purpose of disarming the agency Indians and collecting their mounts. Similar actions proceeded against other Upper Missouri agencies. Threatened with suspension of food rations, and bewildered by a prodigious show of force, agency Indians at Standing Rock encamped on both sides of the Missouri River were left with little choice but to surrender as requested. Some Indians outside the camps who learned of the action avoided returning from fear of confiscation. All nine infantry companies at the post under Carlin, together with four companies of the 7th Cavalry under Major Marcus A. Reno, eight more companies of the 7th Cavalry, and three infantry companies under Colonel Samuel D. Sturgis, fully surrounded the camps. The search was conducted lodge by lodge. Though some 700 ponies were collected, and small numbers of firearms, Crook believed advance notice provided time to seclude both ponies and arms outside the agency. Crook advised the agency Indians that the horses rounded up would be transported to St. Paul for sale and the money used to purchase cows and cattle, a step on the road to "civilization" and assimilization.[3]

In Washington, Congress was taking action to attempt to resolve the crisis in Sioux Country. A commission was appointed to negotiate the purchase of the Black Hills country and other lands outside the reservation and to relocate the Red Cloud and Spotted Tail Agencies to the Missouri River. Shortly thereafter, representatives of the U.S. government arrived at Standing Rock to negotiate for the approval of a treaty for the surrender of the Black Hills and the unceded hunting territory. On October 11, Indian signatories at Standing Rock, who were promised assistance by the government to become self-sufficient farmers and ranchers, signed the treaty though constituting less than the three-quarters of the adult males, as required by the 1868 Fort Laramie Treaty. A similar practice was followed at other agencies. In February 1877, following Senate approval and the signature of President Rutherford B. Hayes, under the context of the treaty, the U.S. government formally confiscated the Black Hills.

At the same time, Carlin diligently continued to follow orders to arrest and return Indians captured roaming outside the agency and to confiscate their horses and arms. Lieutenant Kislingbury's experience with the Pawnees enabled him to implement that directive through a specialized role, one that he came to fully embrace. At the time, no cavalry units were assigned to Fort Yates. In order to provide the means of accomplishing those orders, Lieutenant Colonel Carlin formed a mounted detachment of Indian scouts and enlisted men. Kislingbury was extremely pleased to be given the command of the detachment, an assignment far more appealing than supervising construction parties.[4]

Though Indian scouts had long been of service to the military, in 1866 legislation formally approved their enlistment in the U.S. Army. Terms of enlistment generally ran for short-term stretches. At Fort Yates, enlistments ran for six-months, and re-enlistments were common. Scouts were generally paid the same rate as cavalry soldiers and received horses, rations, clothing, and weaponry. Most lived near the post with their families, and family members benefitted from the privilege of drawing rations. The Indian scouts of Standing Rock were drawn largely from the Yanktonai, considered a more peaceful band.[5]

On November 21, 1876, Kislingbury was pleased to lead his first operation with mounted soldiers and Indian scouts. Through year-end, operating under less-than-ideal weather conditions, Lieutenant Kislingbury had a particularly busy time with a series of four mounted patrols, each from five to fourteen days in length. His travelling parties were typically small, comprised of some five or six mounted soldiers and several mounted Indian scouts. In the midst of falling temperatures and shortening daylight hours, his detachment could still manage to cover between thirty and forty miles per day.[6]

The Grand River basin and its tributaries, which ran through unsettled areas of the agency some thirty miles south of the post, offered excellent grazing; thus it was a prime search area for secluded ponies. From the convergence of the South Fork and the North Fork branches of the Grand River in northwestern South Dakota, the Grand River flows some two hundred miles in a southeasterly direction through the Standing Rock Agency until its confluence with the Missouri River. Fanning out for two-to-three miles on each side of their line of march, Kislingbury's scouts searched through valleys and ravines, and from the highest hilltops, for scattered Indians and herds. The party was constantly on the march except when bedding down in rough field encampments. Though scouting occupied a significant portion of their time and effort, the detachment was kept busy with caring for their own mounts, herding and driving captured animals, as well as maintaining a watchful eye on those animals at all times of the day and night.

His final march of the year reflected the varied nature of the command and the severity of the elements. Leaving the post on December 13 with one sergeant, six enlisted men and four Indian scouts, five days travel took the party to the Cheyenne Agency. There additional provisions were obtained to supply them as far as Owl Creek in search of ponies thought to be kept there by Chief Thunder Hawk. During the eighty-mile march to Owl Creek over the next three days, the party crossed paths with a group of two Indian families with seven ponies, two of which were branded "U.S." Though the group was absent from Standing Rock Agency without permission, Kislingbury exercised good sense, wisely permitting the party to continue to Cheyenne Agency, confiscating four ponies and one firearm. Kislingbury reported that "they had nothing upon which to subsist, expecting to get food at the Cheyenne Agency Indians, and with only rations for my command, I could not have provided for them; and if I had taken all their ponies it would have left them on the open prairie without shelter, and their women and children would have suffered extremely as the weather was bitterly cold."[7]

Kislingbury fulfilled his primary mission. At Owl Creek, the scouts recovered fifty ponies of Chief Thunder Hawk, a number of which were branded. Battling the elements on a frigid Christmas Day while shepherding sixty-seven captured ponies to the post, he returned on December 26. Kislingbury reported that despite the cold weather, "the men have been uncomplaining, and the ponies are in almost as good condition as they were when I started although they have travelled, at a low estimate, at least 280 miles in eleven marching days without forage and the ground covered with snow." Post commander Carlin praised Kislingbury's action, forwarding Kislingbury's report to Brigadier General Terry with the comment that "Lieut. Kislingbury and his detachment deserve credit for their service."[8]

All told, in those four separate patrols, Kislingbury and his mounted infantry detachment and Indian scouts rounded up more than 200 horses through the six-week period ending December 31, 1876. Kislingbury was relentless in his pursuit and evidently had made a name for himself among the Indians. A letter written by a correspondent visiting Standing Rock and published in the *Chicago Tribune* singled out Kislingbury's efforts, remarking that "this young officer [Kislingbury] has made himself a terror of the Indians. They say; 'It is no use to lie to the white man any longer; he is too smart for us; we cannot hide our ponies-he [Kislingbury] finds them in some way.'"[9]

Kislingbury's effectiveness in the field was a product of an open mind willing to place his reliance on the knowledge of his Indian companions. In his first report to the post adjutant, he praised those skills, noting that "the Indians had proved themselves invaluable in their superior knowledge of the country and the most likely places to find ponies." His early reports also served as a scouting primer, passing along helpful details for the benefit of future patrols. At the outset of his first excursion, in what he characterized as a "trial," he adopted Indian methods of travel, making for a more mobile party capable of lengthy marches. In lieu of military horses, Kislingbury adopted smaller Indian ponies, which he found showed "peculiar" endurance and were more self-sustaining on the dry winter grass (a point he would also have learned from the Pawnees). In contrast, military horses relied on forage, such as oats, which necessitated transport by wagon. Rather than burdening their horses with heavy packsaddles, Kislingbury found that two or three travois (a type of sledge) could transport more supplies in a manner less burdensome to the animals. However, greater mobility came with a cost. Supplied

Dancing Chief

Eagle Man in 1872. Photograph by Alexander Gardner.

with only government-issue blankets for sleeping, below-freezing nights in the open air were particularly trying. A welcome campfire and hot coffee at the day's end marked one of the few comforts on the winter trail.[10]

But life off the post offered some additional advantages. On the trail, the young lieutenant exercised the final authority and reveled in the freedom from the officialdom that marked life on the post. In contrast to his soldiers, Kislingbury rode an Indian pony and shunned the military accoutrements of his rank for the more practical buckskin attire and moccasins.

The cornerstone to his detachment's success rested with the Indian scouts. Several were already long-serving veterans with distinguished records. The intrepid Indian scout "Cold Hand" had been honored by Terry in 1873 for holding off an armed band of thirty Indians with only three other scouts while on route with a mail delivery between Standing Rock Agency (then Grand River Agency) and Fort Rice. The same year, the same fearless scout was credited with leading a party that brought back ten horse thieves. Another scout, the highly regarded "Eagle Man," was part of the delegation that travelled to Washington, D.C., to negotiate ownership of the Black Hills region.[11]

With the success of the roundup, Lieutenant Colonel Carlin now had to deal with the large numbers of confiscated ponies. In October and November 1876, some 1,300 ponies, largely those collected during Terry's show of force at the agency, were sent to Fort Lincoln by Major Reno. From there, the massive and unwieldy herd was marched to St. Paul. The tragic fact was that of the 1,300 ponies that left for St. Paul, only some 700 ever reached that final destination in Minnesota. A large number died of disease or succumbed to exposure, while others simply wandered away due to inattentiveness and even the drunkeness of soldiers on the trail. In some instances, civilian herders were complacent in thievery and rustling. Proceeds from auction sales were intended to benefit the Indians by the purchase of cows and cattle, but after expenses, little remained to be spent on animal purchases.[12]

In February 1877, Kislingbury had his own opportunity to drive ponies to St. Paul. Taking up the role of "trail boss," he was tasked by Carlin with leading another 250 ponies overland some 400 miles to market in St. Paul, via Fort Sisseton and Fort Abercrombie. At any time of year, the trip would be formidable, but during a stiff Dakota winter, it could be deadly. One newsman from the *Chicago Tribune* reporting from Fort Yates found Kislingbury's approaching task so daunting that he remarked:

> One thing is certain: if silent Kislingbury should succeed in getting his herd to St. Paul, without great loss, he will deserve much credit. It is a dreadful trip to contemplate – 430 miles, over snow and ice, in January and February, in Dakota and Minnesota, without a house or even a tree, to shelter one for hundreds of miles! It is not pleasant to dwell upon.[13]

Forage for the ponies was scraped and pawed from under snow cover. Water was hard to come by in frozen streams. With just an Indian lodge and basic camp equipment transported by travois, Kislingbury drove the ponies by day, and huddled around a campfire at the evening bivouac. Simply managing and keeping the herd fed was a challenging undertaking, but Kislingbury needed all his diplomatic skills to retain his scouts. The enlistments of several scouts, whose services were vital to the drive, had expired while on the trail. Without enlistment papers (or even a writing tool) to confirm their reenlistment, Kislingbury was forced to "imperatively demand" their retention and convince them to accept his verbal assurance of reenlistment. With five soldiers and eight scouts, he proved equally up to the task, arriving at St. Paul with only "a trifling loss," noted Carlin in his annual report. Kislingbury's efforts caught the attention of military's senior brass. Terry added an endorsement to Kislingbury's report, expressing "his appreciation of the very excellent manner" in which Kislingbury and party brought the herd to St. Paul. In the overall context of the pony drives in the fall and winter of 1876-77, Kislingbury proved far more competent at his task, and under far more adverse conditions, than the earlier dismal drive in October 1876.[14]

Chapter Six

Fort Yates

IN A REMARKABLE CAREER CHANGE, Kislingbury had left behind an office-bound administrative position and fashioned a far more challenging role for himself. Approaching his third year as a veteran commissioned officer, in the spring of 1877 Kislingbury and his scouts were back on the hunt, demonstrating an untiring persistence in accomplishing their task. Their efforts paid off. Three marches during May and early June secured another eighty-seven ponies and several weapons.

Encounters with armed Indians outside the agencies could be exceedingly dangerous affairs. During one such encounter near Grand River, Kislingbury, along with two mounted soldiers and five scouts, attempted to secure arms from two mounted Indians, both of whom were absent from the agency without passes. Outnumbered and outgunned, the two surrendered peacefully. However, a third Indian, spotted by Kislingbury several miles away, attempted to flee on horseback. In hot pursuit by the scouts, he was doggedly chased over some ten miles of rolling hills, steep ravines and high grass, all the while dodging and hiding. The scout Good-Toned Metal, riding a fitter horse than the others, closed the gap on the fleeing Indian, reaching near enough to order him to halt. Ignoring the command, the pursued rider turned in the saddle, fired and missed, but a well-placed return shot by Good-Toned Metal, riding at full speed, clipped his pony's hip at 500 yards. Leaving the now-wounded animal, the dismounted Indian fled on foot another two to three hundred yards before being apprehended. A Colt pistol, with holster and belt that he had tossed away, was traced back to being a 7th Cavalry weapon from the Little Big Horn.[1]

Kislingbury's resourcefulness with his Indian companions

evidently added to his already heavy workload. In May, his detachment marched 109 ponies to Bismarck for sale, netting them $1946. In order to avoid notorious "rings" that sought to take advantage of hasty military dispositions at bargain prices, Kislingbury engaged in private sales at fixed prices, and organized auctions of small numbers of ponies several days apart outside of the city center. By spreading auction sales in this manner, transient buyers could not afford to remain for all the sales, and Kislingbury achieved more favorable prices for the government.[2]

In a rather epic two-month journey, during August and September, in accordance with orders from headquarters, his detachment of two enlisted men and eight scouts herded some 200 cows and bulls from Fort Abercrombie to the Standing Rock Agency. Despite travelling in the warm season of late summer, through Kislingbury's careful management only one animal was lost over their 200-mile cattle drive (the hapless animal jumped off the boat while crossing the Missouri River and drowned). Upon arrival, the animals were distributed proportionally to each tribe based on the number of families in each.[3]

Raising livestock at the agency figured in large part with Terry's plans for the Indians. Like many other officials, Terry was a firm believer in "civilizing" the Indians, the notion that they could abandon their nomadic way of life for one of farming and ranching. Terry was of the mindset that raising cattle and cows at the agencies was a far more practical pursuit than farming. According to him, transition to "the pastoral state" (i.e., making Indians into shepherds and herdsmen) was an easier "first step" to civilization than the backbreaking work of farming. In addition, on a more practical level, according to Terry, agency lands were ill-adapted to agriculture, but ideal for pastorage and grazing.[4]

Kislingbury likewise embraced Terry's notion. In addition, he had built personal bonds with the agency Indians beyond their service as scouts. Having lived and travelled in close quarters with them on the trail, he had gained the trust of his companions. His relationship with them led Carlin to place Kislingbury in charge of working with the Indians to advance Terry's plans. (Carlin was also a strong advocate of such plans). Kislingbury wrote optimistically to his captain at length in regard to his efforts:

> You will be pleased, I think, to know that the Indians are getting along nicely with their cows. They have entered heartily into the business of cattle raising, and I believe that this time it is going to be a success. [Lt. Colonel Carlin] still retains control of the cows, and has placed me in charge of them. I inspected them about a week ago; found each chief with the number issued him, and the cows in the very best condition. Each band's cows are kept separate, and herded by herders detailed by the chiefs. They have put up hay to carry the cows through storms, and I expect to see the cows in fine condition in the Spring. The promptness of the military in giving the cows first (before the Agent) has pleased them decidedly. . . Quite a number have expressed their appreciation of General Terry in his keeping his promise to them. They are very much pleased to know they are to get another herd of cows in the spring. Many of them have told me how proudly they look forward to the time when the cattle shall have increased, and that the herds can be seen covering the hills.[5]

Kislingbury's report made its way to Terry, who took great satisfaction in forwarding it to the U.S. Secretary of War, George W. McCrary. With some satisfaction, Terry noted for McCrary's benefit that "you expressed so much interest in my proposition regarding the civilization of the Indians that I am prompted to send you an extract of a letter received by one of my staff officers from an officer at Standing Rock. Two hundred and fifty cows were sent to that place in August and September last and I expect to send one hundred more there in the spring. This letter seems to dispose of one objection to my plan which has been urged; that is, that 'the Indians cannot be made to put up the hay necessary in winter.'"[6]

Kislingbury's glowing optimism overlooked the reality of the situation at Standing Rock Agency. Even when highly motivated, Indians found that the agency lands were often ill-suited for farming or even husbandry. Severe weather, droughts and insect infestations were a constant plague. Moreover, a shortage of plows and mowing machines for crops and hay feed often severely hindered their best efforts. Over the next few years, though agents claimed sporadic progress in both increasing the herds and in crop production, the results were far below the initial heady expectations, and never proved viable on a larger scale.

Coincident with Kislingbury's service, there were other important matters for the Great Sioux War. Numerous bands surrendered to the Red Cloud and Spotted Tail Agencies that spring, and with them the legendary Crazy Horse, a significant step in the close of the war. Crazy Horse spent a few tense months at Red Cloud Agency during the summer of 1877. Ahead of Crook's order to arrest him, he fled to the Spotted Tail Agency. On September 5, 1877, following his return to Red Cloud Agency, he was tragically killed in a jailhouse struggle.

Sitting Bull and his followers continued to resist surrender, and in May of 1877, they crossed into Saskatchewan, Canada. Separately, in October, after a running fight, Colonel Nelson Miles engaged and captured Chief Joseph and some four hundred followers at Bear Paw Mountain in northern Montana, just shy of the Canadian border. This brought the Nez Perce War to a close.

By the fall of 1877, Kislingbury was back to handling his principal responsibility, a long-distance pursuit of another band absent from the post. In October, Kislingbury marched more than 250 miles from Fort Yates to the outskirts of the Black Hills. His sizable party included an assistant surgeon, five soldiers, seven Indian scouts and two "volunteer" Indians from the post. While marching along the Belle Fourche River, his scouts spotted a group of three Indians approaching from the opposite direction. Kislingbury quickly gathered his party and concealed them and their mounts behind a tall bluff. With the element of surprise, Kislingbury's party suddenly emerged from their hiding place and managed to surround and disarm the Indians "before they could recover from their surprise at seeing us" noted Kislingbury in his report.[7]

Continuing along the river, another Indian party was soon observed approaching, unaware of the earlier encounter. Employing a tactic used successfully in the past, Kislingbury sent the Indian scouts with pony travois ahead while the soldiers remained concealed. The approaching Indians, believing the scouts were defectors from the agency, let their guard down, and were captured before they could flee. All were armed with .45 and .50 caliber carbines and pistols, and carried "belts well filled with ammunition." According to Kislingbury they "acted very surly." One attempted to draw a pistol on one of the scouts and would have shot him, but one of the volunteer Indians, "Fair Heart," grabbed the pistol before it could be fired.[8]

Kislingbury managed to learn from the captives (now twelve in number) that their sizable and heavily armed camp was within several miles, adjacent the Belle Fourche River near its confluence with the Cheyenne River. Its exact size was unclear, but large numbers were communicated to Kislingbury, leaving him in a quandary as to how to proceed. Several Indians had been seen perched on a high precipice nearby. They had observed the recent encounter and had moved speedily toward the direction of the main camp, likely raising the alarm.

As the numbers ahead and behind his party swelled, he found himself in a precarious situation, but his decision making was decisive and bold. He considered taking flight, but rather than attempting a desperate retreat, Kislingbury decided to "go on toward their camp, gather in and disarm as many as I could on the way, and then if I found them too many for me, I would get out of the scrape the best way I could either by talking or fighting." Nonetheless, he still sought to gain advantage in some way. Believing that talk was better than a fight, he released one "prisoner," with instructions to return to his camp with a request to meet their leader.[9]

Ominously, within the hour, a line of some twenty-five armed Indians approached, dotting the escarpment high above the bluffs. Steadying himself, Kislingbury halted the now-approaching Indians within one hundred yards and requested their chief to come forward. Out stepped their leader Blue Cloud, who demanded to know why his men were captured and their arms taken. Kislingbury replied that he feared that the lives of his group were in danger. Tensions started to rise as Indians started pressing closer on all sides, only reluctantly halting as Kislingbury repeatedly demanded they stop.

Blue Cloud told Kislingbury that he was from Spotted Tail Agency, and that he had left that agency because some of his people had moved or were planning to relocate. He added that his group was intent on a successful deer and antelope hunting mission and would return to Cheyenne or Standing Rock Agency. He claimed that he was unfamiliar with those in his group from other agencies and why they had left their agencies, but they too were hunting and would return to their assigned agencies.

At this point Kislingbury and his men found themselves in the midst of at least fifty well-armed Indians, whose demeanor appeared threatening. Some had their faces blackened in preparation for fighting and several had slipped cartridges into their gun chambers. According to Kislingbury, their chief was quite defiant and warned that his young Indians "were growing impatient and they might forget themselves in their excitement and do us mischief if I did not give them (the prisoners) back their guns and let them go." Nonetheless, Kislingbury bluntly told the chief that if they dared to shoot, his men "would do the same thing," and though fewer in numbers, each of his men "would lay out a good many of them before they got us." Much credit is due to Kislingbury's scouts, who stood shoulder-to-shoulder with Kislingbury and added much needed backing to his threat. The scouts spoke up fully in support of Kislingbury, stating that they had sworn to stand by him as soldiers and Indians, and that any injury would bring a large military force upon Blue Cloud and his followers. With tempers rising, Kislingbury realized that he needed to defuse the situation with as much diplomacy as possible. With much regret and humiliation, he released the twelve Indian prisoners and handed back their arms. Then Kislingbury's party cautiously withdrew without further incident. (His scouts later estimated that there were a total of 80-90 men in Blue Cloud's camp, with 200-300 ponies, and that he was expecting additional lodges to join him).[10]

Lieutenant Colonel Carlin quickly forwarded Kislingbury's report of the affair to the adjutant general, with a sense of alarm, noting that the large, heavily armed band was "in a position where they can do much harm if so disposed, as they can receive aid from all the agencies and can raid the people of the Black Hills." Carlin fully backed Kislingbury's peaceful settlement of the confrontation, remarking that "I fully approve the decision arrived at by Lieut. Kislingbury." Carlin was so impressed with the "energy and zeal of Kislingbury and the fidelity of his men" that he invited senior staff to read the report. Kislingbury's tactful conduct caught the attention of hard-driving Lieutenant General Sheridan, who concurred with Carlin's assessment, remarking on his endorsement that "I approve the conduct of this young officer on the occasion referred to in his report." Deemed a matter of importance, the report was forwarded to both the secretary of the interior and the secretary of war.[11]

Slanted coverage by the press recounted the affair differently. According to a special dispatch to the *Deadwood Pioneer-Press,* under the disparaging title "Scared by Savages," Kislingbury's scouting party "was taken in by a band of Brule Indians on the north bank of the Cheyenne River and only escaped by surrendering their arms and a few captive Indians they were bringing in to Standing Rock. The party has just arrived safely at their post, but badly scared." In an unusual public retort, Carlin penned a letter to the paper, looking to set the record straight and defend Kislingbury's action. Carlin wrote that "your issue of the 16th, headed 'Scared by Savages' does great injustice to Lieutenant Kislingbury and his party." According to Carlin:

> Lieut. Kislingbury did not surrender the arms of his party. He had captured twelve Indians with arms, and in trying to find their camp was surrounded by about fifty more, who were within less than one hundred yards of him and numerous enough to have killed his party at the first volley. Observing hostile demonstrations on the part of the Indians... and posted and prepared to attack him, he voluntarily released his prisoners and restored them their arms.... A different course would have been foolhardiness. When he found that a fight would result so disastrously, he displayed high moral courage and good sense in avoiding it. None of his friends would have escaped alive if a fight had taken place.[12]

Dancing Chief

☙☙☙☙☙

As fate would have it, Kislingbury's detachment, scouting east of the Black Hills in the fall of 1877, also happened to cross paths with one of the finest western photographers of the era, Frank J. Haynes. Born in 1853 in Saline, Michigan, by 1876, with an apprenticeship under his belt, Haynes had opened his first photographic studio in Minnesota. A roving spirit, in 1877 he accepted an offer from the Northern Pacific Railroad that led him westward to Bismarck, taking photographic views that did much to publicize the railroad and its scenic locales. By 1883, Haynes would become the official photographer for the Northern Pacific Railroad and of Yellowstone National Park. His views of the park and its environs did much to attract interest in the national treasure.

In the fall of 1877, the nascent western photographer was continuing his tour along the recently completed 250-mile Bismarck to Deadwood stage trail, where he chanced to meet Kislingbury's outfit on the Belle Fourche River. The meeting proved fortuitous, as Haynes evidently found Kislingbury's detachment a fit subject for his camera. At least six on-the-spot photographs of the detachment have survived. Those images provide a fine visual record of the party and offer a sample of the conditions under which they operated. In several images Kislingbury's party poses expressionless in their makeshift encampment, set in the midst of a clearing of thick scrub brush and barren trees under threatening grey skies. In the center stand his well-armed Indian scouts wrapped in blankets, looking uncomfortably cold but appearing staunchly resolute. Reflecting the irregular nature of his party, an unassuming Kislingbury wears a tired, well-worn uniform that has endured miles of arduous conditions, but he stands in a relaxed pose, hands in pockets. Seven armed Indian scouts are present in two of the photographs, as are the two Indian "volunteers," noted by Kislingbury in his official report. A separate staged image by Haynes demonstrates Indian surprise tactics.

Not all Kislingbury's exploits involved Indian encounters. In another sign of his now accomplished wilderness prowess, the

Fort Yates

Lieutenant Kislingbury and Indian Scouts on the Belle Fourche. Photograph by F. J. Haynes.

newspaper man Charles Hackett, owner and publisher of the *Parker New Era* (Parker, SD), recalled how "mild-eyed, blonde" Kislingbury spearheaded the capture of a marauding group of horse thief bandits and marauders, the so-called "Davis band," named after George Davis. After receiving word that a group of men were travelling with wagons and horses under cover of darkness along the wooded banks of the east side of the Missouri River opposite Fort Yates, Lieutenant Colonel Carlin dispatched Lieutenant Kislingbury to ascertain their identity. Travelling in the darkness with twelve scouts, Kislingbury managed to cross the frozen river, follow their tracks below the post, and in absolute silence approach the gang. By this time, Kislingbury had proved himself a master in the art of covert wilderness pursuit, a skill of which he was immensely proud. In recounting the capture to Hackett, Kislingbury boasted that Kislingbury and his men were so quiet on their approach that "not even a twig or dead limb crackled under their moccasined, silent feet, and the surprise was complete.... So close did the scouts approach before the gang observed them, as the bandits sat eating their lunch, that the scouts' rifle barrels pressed their breasts before the quarry knew the scouts were near." A number of 7th Cavalry horses, saddles and bridles, stolen from Forts Lincoln and Rice, were recovered. The prisoners later received harsh sentences in the federal penitentiary. Hackett went on to add his own fond personal recollections of Kislingbury, observations

Surprise tactics demonstrated by the Indian Scouts. Photograph by F. J. Haynes.

that echoed those of others who were impressed with his genial disposition and underlying personal courage. Hackett remembered Kislingbury as "mild mannered as a woman, as tender as a sister and brave as a knight."[13]

As for Kislingbury, that he was successfully performing an important and difficult service was attested to by Brigadier General Terry from the headquarters of the department in St. Paul, Minnesota. After reviewing one of Kislingbury's 1877 scouting reports, Terry advised Carlin (by letter from Assistant Adjutant General George Ruggles), that Terry "highly appreciates the excellent service performed by Lieutenant Kislingbury, who he requests be advised of the compliment."[14]

In August 1877, that service was poised to change. Kislingbury was suddenly ordered to join his company at Tongue River, Montana, several hundred miles to the west. Strongly opposed to the order and fearful of losing Kislingbury, Carlin appealed to Ruggles to permit Kislingbury to remain in command of the scouts at Fort Yates. No higher compliment to Kislingbury's services exists than Carlin's plea to the assistant adjutant general:

> While another officer might be selected to discharge the duties heretofore by Lieutenant Kislingbury, I know of none so peculiarly fitted for it. The Indians all know him

and fear his little detachment. When this detachment is present they fear to run away from the Agency. The only Indians known to have left for other agencies or unknown parts, did so in his absence on other duties in June and when the weather was so rainy that their departure was not discovered until it was too late to overtake them all. Some of them however were overtaken on the trail towards Fort Totten and Manitoba and brought back by the scouts under Lt. Kislingbury's command.[15]

Carlin's plea was persuasive and successful. Lieutenant Kislingbury would continue to remain in charge of his mounted detachment at Fort Yates through May 1879. Tellingly, the post records at Fort Yates record only one mention of a scout detachment under the command of an officer other than Kislingbury. In that instance, while Kislingbury was dispatched to St. Paul, Lieutenant George L. Rousseau led a party from Fort Yates.

The Indian scouts at Fort Yates had also proven their worth to Carlin. Writing to the assistant adjutant general, Carlin added that the Indian scouts "are the cheapest and best soldiers for hunting in rough country and better travelers than white men." For that reason, he requested more scouts, while at the same time pushing the requisition to retain Kislingbury.[16]

But the hard life of frontier service had its downsides. The stress of extended journeys away from family and the post took a physical and emotional toll on Kislingbury. One incident that flared from a matter of minor consequence perhaps reflected the strain of that duty. On the morning of July 10, 1877, private William Brown, 14th Infantry, charged with filling water buckets, had refused the request of Aggie Kislingbury's aide to empty her water bucket before filling it with clean water. The soldier gruffly advised the aide that he had no orders to do so and therefore would not oblige. Informed of the rebuff, Frederick Kislingbury, not known for a hotheaded temper, nonetheless hurled a string of profanity at the soldier. According to the soldier, Kislingbury exclaimed "G-d d-mn you if you speak to my servant again I'll put you in the jug." Kislingbury was then alleged to have drawn back his fist as if he was going to strike the soldier. An irate Kislingbury ordered the soldier to empty and clean the bucket, which he did. Kislingbury was said to have replied: "G-d d-mn you, if you don't empty these barrels every morning, I'll put you in the jug and G-d d-mn you, don't ever let me hear of your saying another word here."[17]

The affair led to the soldier's official claim for redress. In his formal response to the soldier's charge, far from apologizing for the act, Kislingbury justified his conduct on the basis that "my duties have kept me away from my family most of the time for a long period; and my wife at times has greatly missed my assistance in securing her the necessary and proper attentions allowed others at the post in the way of duties performed by fatigue parties...." Kislingbury did add that Brown had on several occasions refused to empty the dirty water for Kislingbury's wife and her aide, at one point "declaring an oath" to the aide. Kislingbury concluded his remarks with the statement that "I judge he is a stubborn insubordinate soldier." No discipline followed from Kislingbury's outburst.[18]

Fortunately for Kislingbury, protracted scouting missions were winding down as Carlin soon ceased the confiscation of ponies and weapons. In retrospect, as a military strategy Sheridan's so-called "Pony Campaign of 1876-77" had limited long-term value. Sitting Bull and other Northern Indians remained mounted, armed and at large for several more years. Moreover, the action was indiscriminate as peaceful, agency Indians were caught up in the aggressive operation and subject to deprivation of their property. At the time, they failed to receive adequate compensation in cash or cattle for the number of ponies confiscated. Restitution for the shortfall became a protracted process extending over many years, so long that some original owners never lived to receive their payments. Beginning in 1891, sums of up to $200,000 were finally authorized to deprived Indians at Standing Rock and Cheyenne Agencies as compensation for up to 5,000 ponies. Over the next forty years, after continual back-and-forth, additional claims were settled with relatives and descendants of the former owners with the government ultimately paying a total of $320,000 for more than 8,000 claims.[19]

Chapter Seven

Dancing Chief

THOUGH MONOTONOUS AND EVEN DREARY at times, life was made as tolerable as possible by the soldiers stationed at Fort Yates. During the holiday season, Christmas was celebrated in festive style. Captain Thomas M. McDougall's Company B, 7th Cavalry, prepared a sumptuous spread of turkeys, mince pies, cakes and even canned oysters from Baltimore, somehow still deemed "deliciously fresh" by the soldiers. The quarters were appropriately decorated with flags and bunting and lit by candlelight chandeliers. Despite cold, even blizzard conditions, Lieutenant Colonel Carlin hosted a lively dancing party for the officers and their spouses, including Lieutenant and Mrs. Kislingbury.[1]

In the spring of 1878, Lieutenant Kislingbury's service was interrupted under tragic circumstances of a wholly personal nature. At the post at Standing Rock Agency, Aggie Kislingbury died suddenly on April 2 at the young age of thirty-five. A fever epidemic which raged through the post claimed her life and those of several other military family members. It is possible that Frederick Kislingbury blamed himself for the fateful circumstances that befell his wife, based on his own single-minded desire to pursue a career in active duty. Whatever the case, he may never have fully recovered from the blow. Years later, distraught on his own death bed, it was claimed that he was heard to cry "Aggie, Aggie." With a heavy heart, he was granted leave to proceed with her remains to her hometown. In a sorrowful procession she was escorted to her burial in the churchyard of St. John's Anglican Church, Sandwich (today part of Windsor), Ontario alongside other family members. Trying his best to put his grief behind him, Kislingbury quickly returned to Fort Yates by April 25,

Jessica ("Jessie") Lillian Bullock, second wife of Frederick Kislingbury.

perhaps too quickly in retrospect (cutting his 30-day leave short by a week).

Shortly thereafter he managed a rough one-month-long cow drive from Fort Sisseton to Standing Rock Agency, but all may not have been settled with Kislingbury. On May 17, prior to starting the cattle drive, Frederick requested a four-month leave of absence, which was deferred until September. During that break, while still grieving, Kislingbury had his hands full settling estate matters and arranging safe keeping for his four young children: Harry Howard, age ten, Walter Frederick, age eight, Douglass Ebstain, age four, and little Wheeler Schofield, age twenty-three months. Fortunately, Major George Schofield and Alma Schofield generously offered to care for little Wheeler Schofield (the major later had thoughts of adopting the child after his wife Alma died in 1879). In another act of generosity, Jessica ("Jessie") Lillian Bullock, the younger unmarried sister of Kislingbury's deceased wife Aggie, left the comfort of her home in Detroit to accompany Kislingbury to his post to oversee the other three children. It was relationship that would blossom quickly on the northern plains. On May 22, 1879 Frederick Kislingbury married Jessie Bullock in a small ceremony in Bismarck. Seth Bullock and all three Bullock sisters (Aggie, Jessie and Alma) had come to play vital roles in the life of Frederick Kislingbury.

While in Bismarck, Joseph Culbertson, post interpreter at Poplar River Agency, caught Kislingbury's ear. The two had previously met when Kislingbury visited the agency to assist in a headcount. From Cuthbertson, Kislingbury received news of Sitting Bull's whereabouts during the winter of 1878-79, and the alleged misconduct on the part of the Indian agent at Poplar River. Believing the information valuable, Kislingbury bypassed department protocol and sent his report directly to Brigadier General Terry. The information was already largely known to Terry, who nonetheless felt obliged to forward it to Sherman, with the added comment that "Kislingbury is a very intelligent young officer."

Leaving Bismarck with his new bride and the three children, Kislingbury was now in far brighter spirits as he made his way to his next station at Fort Custer. His departure from Fort Yates was not without the appreciation of his former post commander, hard-driving Lieutenant Colonel William Passmore Carlin. On his departure, Carlin offered a highly praiseworthy testimonial: "the Lt. Colonel commanding feels it due to him to express his high appreciation of [Kislingbury's] meritorious services while commanding the Indian Scouts of this command for two years past;...on many occasions while in command of the Indian Scouts, Lieutenant Kislingbury has displayed unsurpassed energy and fortitude especially in scouting the Indian country during the very severe weather in the winter of 1876-77."[2]

On June 11, 1879, after a brief honeymoon (five days leave), he and his family reached the new post. Fort Custer, originally known as Post Number Two, was built in July 1877, and was renamed after the legendary cavalryman on November 7, 1877. In accordance with Sheridan's vision of a permanent military presence within the heart of Sioux Country, Fort Custer, on the Bighorn River, and Fort Keogh (formerly Post Number One), at the mouth of the Tongue River, had been approved by Congress. The military forces brought to bear on the Sioux Country through these and several other posts were instrumental in the quelling of Indian resistance. Important to that control, though less recognized, was the rapid deployment of telegraph lines to improve communication in the unsettled region. Urgent requests from anxious settlers and ranchers seeking protection, and the need for rapid military communication, led to the establishment of a lengthy system of these lines.[3]

Dancing Chief

Lieutenant Greely was already acquainted with Kislingbury from their time together in West Texas and from his success in deploying telegraph wires in that desolate region. Greely had been given orders to extend telegraphs over the lengthy stretch from Bismarck, Dakota Territory, to Fort Ellis, in southwest Montana Territory. With the assistance of enlisted men at adjacent posts, Greely supervised the installation of this system between August 29, 1878 and January 30, 1879. It passed through Forts Buford, Custer, and Keogh, with a branch line from Fort Keogh to Deadwood, Dakota Territory. At great effort, wooden posts were brought in by steamboat along the Yellowstone River. Greely succeeded in installing some 600 miles of communication lines in the time span of only five months. The chief signal officer commended the work, remarking that it was "performed in unusual rapidity in the presence of great difficulties." While Greely was so engaged, it is possible that he rekindled his earlier friendship with Kislingbury, as soldiers from Fort Yates were deployed on the project at the time Kislingbury was stationed at the post.[4]

Unlike his service at Fort Yates, Kislingbury initially had a different, but no less active role at Fort Custer than commanding Indian scout detachments in search of ponies. More time was spent ferrying supplies to Terry's Landing, a depot established on the Yellowstone River a few miles upstream from the mouth of the Big Horn River, as well as visiting St. Paul for his testimony at a court-martial and, upon his return in January 1880, serving as company commander. He was also plagued by an undisclosed ailment that sidelined him for several weeks that spring and summer.

At the time, the frontier army continued to be understaffed. Small detachments were obliged to cover vast swaths of territory, often at risk of engagement. Lieutenant General Sheridan, always arguing for greater strength, carped that the overworked troopers led lengthy scouting missions, and when not on the trail were manfully engaged in erecting forts, protecting settlers, Indians and exploring and railroad parties, all while guarding the borders and responding to hostile Indian raids and bandits.

Kislingbury embodied the overworked frontier officer. In late March, he was verbally ordered back in the field to support of

Dancing Chief

Fort Custer in 1880.

Captain Eli L. Huggins and Lieutenant John H. Coale, 2nd Cavalry, who were leading some fifty enlisted men, ten Crow scouts and a long lumbering mule train. The detachment had set out in pursuit of more than one hundred ponies belonging to post scouts that were stolen by a daring Sioux raiding party. According to Huggins, several days of wearying travel took them from Fort Custer, along and across Rosebud Creek, and through "innumerable windings, up and down, often as if through sheer wantonness, through the worst 'Bad Lands.'"[5]

Maintaining a vigorous chase, the command made daily marches of extraordinary length (one as long as sixty miles, another fifty) on short, meatless rations and weak mounts, all in frigid weather and occasional white-outs. Fording the Powder River, and leaving the feeblest of horses and pack mules, the command approached O'Fallon Creek, a meandering twenty-five-mile tributary of the Yellowstone. At the head of the creek, Huggins' scouts spotted the main Sioux camp resting in a fringe of cottonwood trees, the stolen ponies huddled in a ravine to their left. Fearful of detection, Huggins quickly concocted a plan. Kislingbury, with ten men, was ordered to pass undetected between the Indians and ponies, cutting off a possible retreat and recovery of the animals. Huggins and Coale proceeded with their men straight through and to the right of the camp. The plan proceeded and the alarmed Indians, forestalled by Kislingbury's party from recovering the ponies, scrambled for cover in a deep gully with near vertical walls that were lined with thick brush. Ill-fated Sergeant Joseph Johnson, 2nd Cavalry, was killed almost immediately, shot through the head as he dismounted, falling at Coale's side. Realizing that to dislodge the Indians would lead to bloodshed on both sides, Huggins attempted to negotiate a surrender. He only partially succeeded, as a handful capitulated, while the balance slipped away under cover of darkness.

The scouting mission was one of the more successful however as the entire stolen herd was recaptured, as were a number of the perpetrators. Terry highly commended the action, writing in a letter that was published in district orders: "The gallantry displayed by Captain Huggins, Lieutenants Coale and Brett, 2nd Cavalry, Lieutenant Kislingbury, 11th Infantry, A. A. Surgeon Terry, J. A. Campbell Chief of Scouts, from Fort Custer, merits and receives from the Department Commander the expression of his highest commendation."[6]

The affair at O'Fallon Creek was quickly put aside by Kislingbury. After that pursuit, he was on detached service, hot on the tail of military deserters in the Big Horn Mountains. Then followed a two-month trek to deliver the convicts to Fort Snelling, Minnesota. Finally, in September, Kislingbury returned to his more comfortable position as commander of Indian scouts.

Despite the hardships and discomforts of frontier duty, Kislingbury fully relished his military service on behalf of his adopted country. One of his foremost desires was to see his own young sons enter one of the service academies, either West Point or Annapolis. A fellow-soldier with Kislingbury in Montana Territory characterized Kislingbury's commitment to the service as follows:

> No one knew Lieutenant Kislingbury in life better or more thoroughly than his brother comrades. He was one of us, living here on the isolated frontier in daily companionship with us for many years. He came here when this part of the country was full of perils. A man without fear, when assigned to duty wherein the chances

of life and death were about even, he never hesitated nor failed to do the right thing. He was one of the best men in the service to handle Indians....[7]

In preparation for an anticipated winter campaign against Sitting Bull and hostile Sioux encamped north of the upper reaches of the Missouri River, during the fall of 1880 Brigadier General Alfred Terry requisitioned some eighty tons of rations, forage and ammunition. The material was to arrive by the steamboat, *F. Y. Batchelor*, at a depot to be established on the Missouri River at the mouth of the Musselshell River.

By 1879, steamboat traffic was on the wane along the Missouri and Yellowstone Rivers, a victim of the ever-expanding railroads. After the Northern Pacific Railroad reached Bismarck, the *Batchelor* was the only boat still making the run from Yankton to Bismarck. In the upper stretches of the Missouri, from Bismarck to the Yellowstone and Fort Keogh, where the railroad had yet to make inroads, the *Batchelor* maintained its schedule, making several trips during the boating season (generally from April 15 to November 15).

The *Batchelor* was at Fort Buford, near the confluence of the Missouri and Yellowstone, making what Captain Grant Marsh believed was a final delivery of the season when Terry's request came through. With the river low and temperatures threatening a freeze, Marsh, an experienced river pilot, questioned whether even reaching the Musselshell, some 200 miles further west along the Missouri River, was even possible. He only took on the task after his inflated fee was accepted by Terry.[8]

From headwaters in central Montana, the Musselshell flows in an easterly direction some 150 miles, at which point it turns sharply to the northeast, some thirty miles above Fort Custer. For some 200 miles from the big bend, the river runs through progressively more rugged and broken terrain until it enters the Missouri at today's Fort Peck Reservoir. By 1880, by virtue of its relative isolation and rough country, the northern Musselshell watershed offered one of the few remaining safe havens for large herds of buffalo.

Dancing Chief

White Swan. Photograph by Frank Rinehart.

On October 30, Lieutenant Kislingbury, leading an impressive contingent to meet the steamer and retrieve those supplies, took to the trail from Fort Custer to the mouth of the Musselshell. Kislingbury's command included three non-commissioned officers from Company C, 2nd Calvary, ten enlisted men of Company C, some ten Crow Indian scouts, and an interpreter, known as "Le Forgey" (Thomas Leforge). In contrast to his lightly-burdened mounted detachments, their cumbersome pack train of fifty-four animals was handled by eleven packers, their riding mules, and a lead bell horse.[9]

One of the detachment's Crow scouts was White Swan (1850-1904), a highly-regarded veteran of the Indian wars with a lengthy career. Enlisted as one of six Crow scouts in Custer's 7th Cavalry, White Swan was attached to Major Marcus Reno's command. A fearless warrior, at the Little Big Horn he aggressively engaged with the Sioux and Cheyenne who had mounted a threatening charge from their village. Fending off multiple attackers, he suffered several debilitating gunshot wounds, a badly mangled right hand and wrist, and an injured leg that left him with a pronounced limp. At some point, a blow to the head left him partially deaf. Despite his severe injuries, he recovered and continued to serve as an effective scout for an additional five years. Lieutenant Kislingbury would soon be an eyewitness to his battlefield courage.

Winding their way due north from the fort, the first few

days of travel along the wide valley of the Bighorn River were tolerable as the caravan settled into a daily routine. At the mouth of the Yellowstone River, they were ferried across the still unfrozen waterway. On November 4, striking across country and crossing the east spur of Bull Mountain, they reached the Musselshell River, having averaged a creditable twenty-three miles a day. Some concern was expressed for the absence of the packer, "Tex," who had planned on joining the party at that location. Kislingbury blamed his absence on whiskey, but unknown to Kislingbury other circumstances had delayed his arrival. Two scouts sent to locate him returned unsuccessfully.

The detachment's fortunes changed for the worse on the fifth day, due to a combination of a whipping and blinding snowstorm and a trail virtually impracticable for the pack train. Ordeal was none too strong a word as they worked through a series of backbreaking ravines, gulches and deep coulees carved by numerous creeks and streams, all of which were equally hard on the men and animals. Kislingbury aptly noted that the broken ground of the region was a "frightful country" for wagons, which kept on the backbone of the ridges or along watercourses whenever possible. Adding to their travails, the ground appeared burned out, leaving little edible forage for the animals.

As they moved through the bottomlands of the Musselshell, Kislingbury's anxiety mounted for a different reason. Indians were spotted both on the hilltops and crests cautiously eyeing the movement of the pack, but keeping well back. These ominous signs compelled Kislingbury to attempt to dispatch couriers to Fort Keogh. However, the sharp-eyed Indians were "too thick and watching too closely for them to get through," noted Kislingbury. The Indians made attempts to divert a detachment to pursue them into the hills. Kislingbury kept his head and maintained his position, keeping the pack train close.[10]

At the mouth of the Musselshell on November 6, the eighth travel day, Kislingbury finally reached the depot. Tents were hastily pitched along the riverbank in front of several ramshackle log huts used by the hunter, Paddy Rohls. A battalion of the 7th Cavalry had been stationed at the location during the summer of 1879.

Dancing Chief

The timeworn remnants of their sizable camp—rifle pits, brush shelters, bowers and adobe chimneys—were ordered destroyed by Kislingbury to prevent their use as hiding places for any attackers. In retrospect, though time consuming and burdensome to the footsore command, the decision turned out to be a prudent one. A smaller barricaded perimeter with rifle pits was constructed from the remains.

Feeling more secure, Kislingbury noted that "am now in good position and can stand them off any number they want to send along." On the morning of the November 7, lookouts observed Indians approaching at some distance from the camp. White Swan and four other Crow scouts set off to meet the approachers. At about 400 yards from the site, the scouts were ambushed by ten or so attackers hidden in the underbrush. In the immediate heated skirmish, one scout's horse was killed and three other horses were wounded. Though briefly at a disadvantage and heavily outnumbered, the experienced and coolheaded Crow scouts displayed great courage and composure under fire. Without hesitation, they responded vigorously, killing two of the attackers and wounding several others without suffering any casualties. Afterwards, they finally retired to Kislingbury's camp.[11]

One little known pictorial account of the encounter by a participant, the indomitable White Swan, has been preserved. White Swan was an accomplished Crow artist, with a legacy of warrior art, comprising some thirty paintings on hide, muslin and paper. Though most of White Swan's works document the events of the Little Big Horn and his own prowess in that engagement, White Swan thought enough of the affair at the Musselshell and his own valor to memorialize it. Using graphite, ink and watercolor on muslin, White Swan graphically highlighted his individual bravery in detail. Heavily outnumbered, sporting his carbine in one hand and a U.S. guidon in the other, White Swan leads a mounted bareback charge into the heated fire of the group of ten partially secreted attackers. One attacker has been dispatched and lies prone under White Swan's mount.[12]

As White Swan and the scouts returned to the camp, a local ranchman, whose knowledge of the territory lent credibility to his

Dancing Chief

White Swan (Apsáalooke, 1851/52-1904), Pictographic War Record, ca. 1887.

opinion, informed Kislingbury that they were "Sitting Bull" Indians, and more would be on the way in force. Not doubting his word and fearful that a more substantial contingent under Sitting Bull would take up the call, Kislingbury looked to dispatch a courier to carry a message by fast horseback to Fort Assinniboine with the details of their predicament. However, no volunteers in his immediate command stepped forward. According to Kislingbury, "none of the men of his command knew the country and none desired to take their chances." Kislingbury forked over $100 to Paddy Rohl, who knew the country well, to make the hazardous run. Despite his fear that he was outnumbered, Kislingbury was still fully prepared to fight to the end. In his dispatch he noted "I shall do the best I can and they shall not get in our shack until they get us all."[13]

Rohl's fearlessness was quickly put to the test; his departure was full of peril and personal risk. As he left the confines of the makeshift fort at daybreak the next morning, watchful attackers quickly caught sight of the messenger. A concentrated fire immediately fell upon Rohl from as many as fifteen Indians. With a fit horse, he managed to stay out of range of his attackers, who finally broke off the chase. The anxious Kislingbury could do nothing but wait.

Chapter Eight

Trying Times

FOR SEVERAL DAYS AFTER ROHL'S GETAWAY, the Indians made a conspicuous showing on nearby hills and highlands. Their smoke signals added to the growing uneasiness that hostile reinforcements would soon be on their way. Desperate for information, on November 11, four days after the initial attack, Kislingbury sent two enlisted men downriver disguised as ranchmen to try to find any information about the *F. Y. Batchelor*.

Lieutenant Frederick Monroe Kendrick, 7th Infantry, had assumed command of the steamboat from Fort Buford onward. On the morning of November 13, after picking up the two soldiers sent by Kislingbury, the *Batchelor* arrived at the Musselshell in the midst of floating ice. Wasting no time, Kendrick and his crew hurriedly unloaded a hefty measure of supplies: 1,000 sacks of oats and 4,000 rations. To avoid the *Batchelor* becoming locked in the ice and with the knowledge that Kislingbury had sent to Fort Keogh for relief, Kendrick and the *Batchelor* beat a hasty departure the same afternoon.

The welcome relief finally managed to arrive under the command of Major Guido Ilges on November 19. Major Ilges was a well-liked and competent Bavarian-bred officer, with commendable service in both the Civil War and the Indians wars. On the evening of November 11, after attending a dance at Miles's residence at Fort Keogh, Ilges had retired, only to be awakened at midnight by an orderly. Summoned by Miles, Ilges was informed that Paddy Rohls had managed a difficult night trip travelling across snow and ice to Fort Assinniboine with the desperate request for Kislingbury's relief in hand. His request was telegraphed to Miles at Fort Keogh.

With one company of the 2nd Cavalry and two companies of the 5th Infantry, supported by mule teams for faster travel, Ilges marched 150 miles through snow and freezing temperatures to the mouth of the Musselshell in four days. Goaded on by three ambitious young lieutenants, the fourth day was a forced march of some sixty-five miles in one day, rather than the usual two.

Ilges arrived in time to see the attackers scattered but Kislingbury still on high alert. With the improved circumstances, after a hot meal of venison and potatoes, Kislingbury entreated Ilges to mount a counterattack on Sitting Bull's forces north of the Missouri River. Ilges remarked that "Kislingbury was full of fight, . . . and his plans were feasible and sanguine of success." Nonetheless, absent explicit orders, Ilges would not risk the venture. However, in his report on the affair, Ilges advocated a strike on the Indian camps between the Missouri and the American-Canadian border.[1]

In fact, after his relief of Kislingbury, Major Ilges left Fort Keogh on December 23 in pursuit of Sitting Bull, in what became known as the "Poplar River Campaign." Ilges now took command of five companies of the 5th Infantry and one company of the 7th Cavalry, along with an artillery detachment. In early January 1881, near Poplar Creek north of the Missouri River, his forces secured several Indian villages and hundreds of hostiles. Another engagement on January 29, 1881 resulted in the surrender of another 60 Indians.

In his own report on Kislingbury's engagement, Ilges reported that the Indians that had attacked Kislingbury's Crow scouts at the Musselshell were not Sitting Bull's warriors, but rather a group of some thieving Yanktonai on a horse-stealing mission from the Poplar Creek Agency. Ilges commented that "they [the Yanktonai] would not have attacked but for the presence of the Crow scouts, their hereditary enemies."[2]

Ilges was taken with Kislingbury. He had met him briefly on two occasions, but quickly "learned to love and admire him for his genial and soldiery qualities." To a reporter after Kislingbury's death, Ilges offered one of the finest descriptions of Kislingbury's bearing and character:

Lieutenant Kislingbury was at that time about forty years of age, of middle stature, but of powerful frame. He was very fond of wearing moccasins and other trinkets, such as belt and tobacco pouch. His gait was that of a natural born sailor. His features were remarkably impressive-a strong, massive forehead, dark blue or grey eyes, a large aquiline nose, a handsome firm-set mouth and ruddy complexion. He was of unusual intellect, of vivid imagination and of a mercurial as well as highly sanguine temperament. He was a good talker, and loved to sit for hours and relate incidents of the late war and camp life since. But, above all, warmheartedness and kindly acts to everyone-brother officer, soldier and Indians alike-will never be forgotten by those who had the good fortune of his personal acquaintance. The Crow Indians fairly worshipped him and called him the Dancing Chief, because he had, I believe, upon one occasion, participated in a few steps with them at a war dance. He was one of the most accomplished and graceful sign-talkers I have ever observed, and of him it was said that he could make an Indian ashamed of himself in that language. He almost equaled Captain Clark, of the Second U.S. Cavalry therein.[3]

Ilges's reference to Captain William Philo Clark reflected an impressive compliment on the part of Ilges. Clark was also an Indian scout leader and had made an extensive study of Indian culture and the sign language used by the Indians. Over many years, his work led to the publication of his comprehensive work, *The Indian Sign Language*.

But Ilges touched on other significant aspects of Kislingbury's personality, traits that helped to form loyal bonds with his Indian companions. As with Frank North and the Pawnee Scouts, Frederick Kislingbury came to be respected by the scouts because he treated them as individuals and equals. No doubt, Kislingbury's success was influenced by his own experiences under North, as well as Kislingbury's own grasp of Crow culture. Kislingbury was possessed of an open-minded disposition that avoided the rigid imposition of regular military practice, particularly when Indian methods were more effective. Given the freedom to act consistent with their culture, the scouts excelled under his leadership. Kislingbury's ability to communicate with the Crow helped facilitate his acceptance by them and also set him apart from the regular army soldier, many of whom held the Indian in disdain, even when considered allies. Crow culture also respected individual bravery, and Kislingbury's courage under fire served as an example the scouts were prepared to follow.

For Frederick Kislingbury, however, military matters fell to more pressing personal matters at the Musselshell, with the arrival of reinforcements and the surrender of command. When Kislingbury left Fort Custer, his wife Jessie had been suffering from "swamp fever" (likely scarlet fever). Ilges, arriving from Fort Keogh, had carried no information as to her status. The next ten days were an unceasing mental agony for Kislingbury while awaiting news about his beloved, as well as the equally delayed orders to return to his station. Despairing over his wife, and still with no news, Kislingbury finally received orders to return to Fort Custer with the pack train on December 2. That courier also brought more alarming news. Kislingbury's wife had taken a turn for the worse. "Poor darling has been sick ever since I left and still very weak," he despondently noted. "I ought to be with her but must grin and bear it." Those orders included a message from a nurse caring for Kislingbury's wife which he scribbled in his diary:

> My wife is still (November 25) very dangerously ill with swamp fever and yet I have been left all this time in total ignorance. Her life at one time despaired of per letter of Miss Whelan. They would not tell me and sent no officer to relieve me. Pack train just got in. Worn out and used up by trip to Carroll and Fort Maginnis. Four or five lame mules and sprained by bruises from falling. I have asked to be allowed to start ahead alone and let the train follow under sergeant or officer but here is my order to go with the worn out pack mules. God forgive them at [Fort] Custer for not relieving me before and God help me if anything happens to my poor Jess. Why can't I fly there?[4]

According to Ilges, Kislingbury, with tears in his eyes, broke the sorrowful news of his wife to the amiable major. "The poor fellow wanted to go so much, yet his high sense of duty forbid me to ask my indulgence," remarked Ilges. Only the district commander could grant the request. Moved by Kislingbury's pitiable situation and the zealousness of junior lieutenants who volunteered to undertake Kislingbury's duties, a sympathetic Ilges claimed to have dispensed with protocol and freed Kislingbury to leave the pack train with a scout and a packer. "My poor Jess. I will be with her soon–as soon as the horse flesh can get me to [Fort] Custer," Kislingbury recorded. By a long ride of 180 miles covered in four days, at breakneck speed day and night, over ground almost impossible during the season, Kislingbury returned to Fort Custer.[5]

At the post, he found Jessie at death's door, two hours from her demise. As the story goes, with only a faint glimmer of recognition of her beloved husband, and without uttering a word, she died in his arms on December 8, 1880. Evidently, it had always been her wish to be buried beside her family in the churchyard in Sandwich, Ontario. But her funeral ceremony would not occur anytime soon in the midst of a Montana winter. Heavy snow blanketed the northern plains, bringing stage and railroad transit to a halt. Not until April 4, 1881, with a four-month leave, could Kislingbury start on another mournful journey to Canada.

In the meantime, Kislingbury had to cope with yet another potential family tragedy. An outbreak of scarlet fever had raged through the post, threatening both Douglass and Wheeler. Just three days after Kislingbury had "placed my poor darling in her temporary resting place [at the post], my youngest child [Douglass] was taken down with the disease in all its worst features," he told a friend. In addition, six days later Douglass's older brother [Wheeler] "who had been sent out of the house at first, returned with the disease fully developed." Both boys recovered, but there had been deep concern that Douglass would not survive the struggle.[6]

After the long convalescence of his children, through Herculean efforts, the faithful Kislingbury made good on Jessie's final wish. In the absence of a rail line to Bismarck, with a small escort he made his way with a rough army wagon to Bismarck on what would become a desperate, month-long trudge. Winter was still firmly settled on the northern plains, and temperatures had fallen well below zero. Besides exposure to the bitter cold day after day, heavy snow still blanketed the party's trail. A brief warm spell brought on by a passing chinook caused a momentous change, but also brought torrential rains and sudden flooding to the valleys through which they travelled. While attempting to ford one swollen stream, the wagon holding his beloved's coffin overturned and the casket was swept downstream. Only by sheer force of will did Kislingbury manage to save himself and secure the coffin. A full month was spent on the march to Bismarck.[7]

Now traveling by train, Kislingbury finally reached Detroit, a broken man in spirit and health. Friends in the city helped the weary and forlorn soldier to travel to the churchyard in Sandwich, Ontario, on the south side of the Detroit River opposite the city of Detroit. On May 11, 1881, in Jessie's hometown, as the solemn procession commenced, the second one Kislingbury had borne in thirty-six months, the distraught husband and father remained fixed in his hotel room with his departed. He could only be removed by the physical force of his friends while caretakers carried the coffin to the burial ground. An observer present at the ceremony sadly noted that:

> I never saw, nor may I never see again, a sadder sight, than met my gaze that cold bleak day when "poor Jess" was laid away in the narrow portals of her last resting place, with husband-father and four young motherless boys kneeling with joined hands reverently by her side. In the deep snow their loving thought in silent prayers following her departed spirit and the tears flowing in streams from their eyes.[8]

The emotional burden on the young boys was equally as heavy. While they joined hands in grief with their father, it would be the last time they would be together as a family for some time. Each was destined to be raised by different foster parents, and little contact was maintained over the next few years. As late as 1884, after receiving a letter from Douglass and Wheeler, Walter poignantly wrote back to them, thankful that his two brothers could even remember him. As for Frederick Kislingbury, he returned to his post at Fort Custer to perform routine garrison duties, though the sad circumstances of the preceding several months weighed heavily on him.

Kislingbury was pulled from his lethargy rather quickly, when a request came from Lieutenant Greely soliciting Kislingbury's interest in an arctic expedition then being organized under Greely's command. Perhaps seeking to remove himself from a place of such disheartening memories, or from a spirit of adventure which always seemed to motivate him, Kislingbury did not hesitate to offer his services.

Chapter Nine

The Lady Franklin Bay Expedition

BY 1881 INTERNATIONAL INTERST in the polar regions had culminated in the scientific program known as the First International Polar Year. The concept of multinational cooperation to investigate polar phenomena had originated with the scientist Karl Weyprecht. The forward-thinking Austrian believed that simultaneous scientific observations from multiple northern locations would produce more meaningful results than what had been a long history of disparate expeditions motivated by personal ambitions and agendas. Weyprecht also sought to foster a spirit of cooperation among nations, rather than what had been a free-wheeling competition for geographic discoveries.

As a result of Weyprecht's prolonged efforts over a period of several years, eleven nations finally established research stations in the Arctic as part of the First International Polar Year. The U.S. Government, principally by virtue of the Army Signal Corps, was persuaded to support the program with two expeditions. The U.S. International Polar Year Expedition 1881-84, more commonly known as the Lady Franklin Bay Expedition (or Greely Expedition, after Adolphus Greely, its leader), was one of the two expeditions supported by the United States to further Weyprecht's objective. The second U.S. contribution to the program was the expedition stationed at Point Barrow, Alaska from 1881-83, under the command of Lieutenant Patrick Henry Ray, 8th Infantry.

The U.S. Army Signal Corps, a logical name for the army branch tasked with communications and weather forecasting, had been led by the aging administrator, Brigadier General Albert J. Myer. Officers of the Signal Corps were well aware that Arctic weather systems of Alaska, Greenland and Northern Canada had

Dancing Chief

Lieutenant Henry W. Howgate, U.S. Army Signal Corps.

some effect on local weather patterns within the continental United States. Although they were unsure of the extent of such systems, they were considering methods to analyze just how they affected area weather conditions. As Weyprecht pushed for his own plan of scientific observations, Lieutenant Henry Williamson Howgate, an ambitious Signal Corps officer who had served with distinction in the American Civil War, had concluded that the best way to analyze those weather patterns and engage in exploring activities in the Arctic was by establishing a long-term station or "colony" in the Far North. Unfortunately, Howgate's position as disbursing officer for that department would lead to his embezzlement of thousands of dollars.

In August 1877, Howgate managed to privately outfit a modest preliminary expedition in advance of a long-term "colony," at a cost of approximately $10,000. This advance party wintered on the coast of Cumberland Sound, off the southern end of Baffin Island, a relatively well-known area frequented by whalers and home to an Inuit community. During the course of the winter of 1877-78, the party made some scientific observations, tried its hand at whaling, and assembled equipment and manpower necessary for a potential future colony.[1]

Delays beset Howgate's follow-up plans, and it was not until 1880 that he could marshal the funds and governmental support for his proposal to establish a colony at Lady Franklin Bay on the northeast coast of Ellesmere Island. Unfortunately, the fate of the expedition was sealed before it had even left Washington, D.C. Howgate had hastily purchased a decrepit 200-ton sealing steamer, *Gulnare*, to transport the party to its intended destination. Though most of the money for this acquisition technically came out of his own pocket, it was likely stolen by Howgate from the U.S. government.

Overly anxious to proceed with his plan, Howgate neglected to perform a thorough examination of the vessel before committing to its purchase. Since military personnel were attached to the project, the U.S. government demanded an inspection by a board of naval officers, who immediately condemned the vessel. As a consequence, the government withdrew its support for the expedition. Howgate was undeterred, and the expedition became his personal quest as he set about to remedy the *Gulnare*'s deficiencies.

The expedition's command was initially offered to Lieutenant Greely but Greely prudently declined after the ship had been condemned. Evidently, before Greely had bowed out, he had discussed the proposed expedition with Frederick Kislingbury, who expressed a desire to go after having lost his dear first wife Aggie. With Greely's absence from the expedition, Kislingbury's desire to join went unfulfilled.[2]

Two other military men, Lieutenant Gustavus C. Doane, 2nd Cavalry, and Lieutenant William H. Low, Jr., 20th Infantry, requested leaves of absence to serve on the expedition. Inspired by the explorer-soldier Major General John C. Fremont, Doane had led several noteworthy excursions in the Yellowstone region. An equally ambitious and adventurous pathfinder, Doane saw Howgate's budding arctic venture as a means to achieve his own fame. For the *Gulnare* expedition, Doane obtained leave to join over the objection of General William T. Sherman who declared Doane "a Cavalry officer of too great value to be banished to the polar regions." Low, a highly regarded West Pointer with experience in the Indian wars, was likewise approved.[3]

From within the Department of the Missouri, the 2nd Cavalry made a sizable contribution to the expedition. At a time when the military was hard-pressed for mounted manpower on the plains, ten enlisted men from four posts of the 2nd Calvary volunteered and were accepted. They included several who would later volunteer to serve on the Lady Franklin Bay Expedition: Sergeant David L. Brainard, Corporal Daniel C. Starr, and Privates Nicholas Salor, James Ryan and Julius R. Frederick, the last was known as "shorty," for his five-foot two-inch height.[4]

One addition to the expedition, Dr. Octave Pierre Pavy, would display some negative personality traits during the brief venture, which would presage worse conduct in the future. Born in New Orleans in 1844, the son of a cotton merchant in the Antebellum South, Pavy had enjoyed the advantages of a privileged lifestyle and European education. Enrolled at the medical school at the University of Paris, through his father's influence, he had the benefit of working alongside Alfred-Armand-Louis-Marie Velpeau, clinical chair at the medical school and one of the leading surgeons of the time. Pavy's upscale background and acceptance among Europeans elite at an early age may have contributed to a sense of self-importance and superiority that would affect his subsequent personal dealings. While in France, Pavy's interest turned exclusively to one subject, the exploration of the North Polar regions. In 1867, his friendship with Gustave Lambert, a hydrographer for the French government, fueled his obsession for an arctic voyage. The two planned a trip to the North Pole, a venture that came to nothing after the untimely death of Lambert during the Franco-Prussian War. But Pavy persisted with his polar passion, and "monomaniac" was the term most frequently used to define his headstrong personality. This persistence paid off when Lieutenant Howgate accepted him as naturalist and physician for the *Gulnare* expedition in 1880, a decision that would have profound consequences for the subsequent Lady Franklin Bay Expedition.

Pavy's addition to the *Gulnare* expedition would lead to considerable confusion regarding its command structure. Howgate had placated the ambitious Pavy with an informal promise that he would be granted command after landing. In truth, Howgate had no intention at all of awarding Pavy the leadership position because the military men, Doane and Low, could not serve under civilian authority, and Howgate believed that placing the military men in command would serve his purpose of maintaining the favorable support of the U.S. Army for the next season.

With the navy board refusal to clear the *Gulnare*, the government pulled the enlisted men from the expedition. Undeterred, Doane and Low were willing to risk their lives and take their chances in the unseaworthy vessel. After minor repairs, *Gulnare* finally departed Fort Monroe on June 21, 1880 with both Doane and Low still in Washington, D.C. and planning to join the expedition at Halifax. Matters began to take an ominous turn as Pavy began to exercise his control over the expedition. To Doane's alarm, Pavy directed *Gulnare* to bypass its intended stop in Halifax and sail directly to St. John's. Without approval, Pavy also contracted for $5,000 for repairs to the malfunctioning boiler.

With the arrival of Doane and Low at St. John's, Pavy learned that Lieutenant Low would be placed in charge of the expedition after disembarking. Outraged, Pavy telegraphed his dissatisfaction to Howgate and threatened to leave the expedition. A flustered Howgate quickly recruited a replacement surgeon, Dr. Leonard Rohe. But for the intervention of Lilla May Pavy, Octave Pavy's more sensible wife, matters for both the *Gulnare* and Lady Franklin Bay Expeditions would have been far different. Writing to Octave Pavy in St. John's, Lilla May dissuaded the headstrong Pavy from quitting. Even though she believed that Howgate had been "slippery" and "underhanded," Lilla May advised Octave that he would ruin any future opportunity by walking away.[5]

Pavy accepted Lilla May's advice to remain with the expedition, but Pavy leveled some stinging personal comments at Rohe, who had graciously offered to permit Pavy to remain as surgeon, with Rohe simply staying on as a subordinate volunteer. Thoroughly insulted by Pavy's criticism, Rohe left the expedition at St. John's. The affair highlighted some of Pavy's most negative traits—a tendency to overstep his authority and a personality that was easily provoked when matters were not to his liking.

Upon reaching Greenland for supplies, it soon became obvious that the ship's failings would risk disaster if it attempted to sail for Lady Franklin Bay. Doane was advised by whalers that ice in Davis

Strait had been particularly heavy that year. Disgusted with the situation, Doane was prepared to simply abandon the project and return to the United States. Pavy, however, was not about to concede. After what he characterized as "a long bitter battle," Pavy persuaded Doane to leave Pavy and another member, Henry "Harry" Clay (a Louisville prosecutor and the grandson of the famous Kentucky statesman) at the tiny settlement of Rittenbenk, on the far end of Disko Island, Greenland, with all the provisions Doane could supply.

While in Greenland, Pavy accompanied Mr. Krarup Smith, Royal Inspector of North Greenland, on his regular tour of settlements along the coast. Pavy gained the basics of Inuit language and worked hard at learning how to use dog teams for effective arctic journeying, how to erect snow huts and how to successfully hunt arctic game. His longest sledge excursion was a 750-mile round trip from Godhavn (Qeqertarsuaq) to Upernavik with eighteen dogs and one Inuk, a grueling trip during which Pavy fell through the ice and was badly frostbitten. He prided himself on having adopted an Inuit lifestyle and his skills far exceeded any other member of the expedition from the United States, including Lieutenant Adolphus Greely.

In the spring of 1881, Pavy was anxiously awaiting the arrival of the Lady Franklin Bay Expedition at Rittenbenk, with thoughts of his own northern glory. Meanwhile, as Pavy was polishing his survival skills in Greenland in the aftermath of the *Gulnare* fiasco, the government was moving toward approval of the U.S. commitment to the First International Polar Year. Chief Signal Officer William Hazen (successor to Myer) had forwarded his plan for the Lady Franklin Bay Expedition to Secretary of War Robert Todd Lincoln for approval. That plan did not sit well at the headquarters of the Army. Overlooked in the numerous tellings and retellings of the Greely Expedition is the intradepartmental friction caused by the expedition's recruitment efforts and its impact on understaffed field units. William T. Sherman, commander-in-chief of the Army, continued to believe the Regular Army was already stretched far too thin, and that his military men had no reason to be staffing exploratory or scientific jaunts. In response to the plan, Sherman remarked that:

> This application contemplates the detail of an officer and 21 men of the Army to establish some sort of a base of operations for the exploration of the Polar Regions. The Signal Corps has now 500 men and I have not a partial objection to their being used for this purpose or any other. But I do most seriously object to using the officers and enlisted men of the Army proper for that purpose. Every Division and Department commander reports his active size of men too small for the present duties and Gen. Sheridan especially reports his men overworked. The Army is too small to admit of this detachment and therefore I disapprove.[6]

Notwithstanding Sherman's objection, the plan (including the use of Regular Army personnel) was approved by both President Rutherford B. Hayes and Secretary of War Lincoln. Hazen selected Adolphus Greely for command of the Lady Franklin Bay Expedition, and Greely hastily set about selecting the manpower for the expedition. Brigadier Generals Alfred Terry and George Crook were ordered to "call to service men of sound health, discipline and good character and acclimated to cold climate" as volunteers from within their commands.[7]

Greely's first choice was Lieutenant Frederick Kislingbury. In contrast to every other man selected for the expedition, Kislingbury was the only one with whom Greely had made a personal acquaintance. In fact, Greely knew Kislingbury well, an ironic circumstance in light of later events. Day in and day out, over several months, while building out a communication system across the hardscrabble West Texas prairie, the two had lived and labored together in the field in an environment of harsh extremes. What better surroundings within which to assess the young man's mental and physical qualities for a polar expedition. Later, while the two were stationed on the northern plains, Greely had discussed his potential future polar plans, and Kislingbury affirmed an overwhelming desire to join the expedition if it ever came to pass. Now, with the formal approval of the expedition in hand, Greely thought highly enough of Kislingbury's character, ability and work ethic to offer him the important role of second-in-command. According to Frederick's brother John Kislingbury, Greely not only recruited Frederick Kislingbury, but "urged" him to join the expedition. Wasting no time after receiving Greely's communication, Kislingbury swiftly telegraphed him that he was "grateful and hasten to say yes; write me full particulars, plans and details and what will be expected of me."[8]

In response to Greely's offer, in a lengthy letter filled with emotion, Kislingbury explained his reasons for accepting the position:

> My friend, you will not wonder if I speak of grief and sorrow. This was my reason for wanting to go before. I had just lost my first wife. Now my second, the last of three sisters. First, my wife Agnes, then Mrs. Schofield [Major Schofield's wife and Seth Bullock's third sister], and now my wife Jessie. All taken within three years. With you, up there in the cold north, I can find relief. It will be like leaving a world that has been so cruel to me. I can find up there hard work and plenty of it. Overland trips through snow and ice, and the kind of exposure that will do me good. Ah! My friend, the future looked very dark to me and your good letter comes as a boon. It awakens me from a fit almost of despondency. It seemed as though all sources of joy and even sorrow were dying up in me. But now the future looks brighter. The separation from my children will be nothing compared to the prospect there will always be of having been with those who may accomplish some great and lasting good to mankind. I look upon it as a great and useful work; and even if nothing should be accomplished my children will love me better when I return and will be proud of their father who dared to brave the dangers, the depressing influence, in fact, everything we imagine and have read about of a

The Lady Franklin Bay Expedition

sojourn in the Arctic regions.... I am with you heart and soul in the enterprise and you will find me a devoted friend and more devoted servant. My aim shall be to do everything in my power to earn your approbation and make the expedition a success.... If you want a man to control men, to lead them through hardships, to go through exposure, to make dangerous and important expeditions or anything wherein resolve, patience and endurance is concerned, then I am your man! I can say no more, I think, to convince you of my eagerness to go.[9]

Should Greely have more carefully scrutinized Kislingbury's emotional state at the time, notwithstanding Kislingbury's outwardly positive guise? The young lieutenant's exuberance was overflowing, and evidently overcame any hesitation or doubts on the commander's part. Greely had not just offered Kislingbury a new adventure and an escape, he was lifting Kislingbury's soul. Greely sympathized with the grief-stricken lieutenant and took him at his word. The reality of that decision would only become clear later on.

Hazen forwarded Greely's request for Kislingbury to General Sherman, where it hit a stumbling block. Sherman, the officer committed to pacifying the northern plains, flatly disapproved the request, declaring that "this officer is needed with his regiment, which is on exposed Frontier duty." Appealing to the Secretary of War, Hazen prevailed, and Kislingbury joined the expedition.[10]

Lieutenant James B. Lockwood was the second commissioned officer assigned to the expedition. Born at the U.S. Naval Academy on October 9, 1852, Lockwood's early years were spent like many a military family, constantly on the move from one post to another. In 1873, he succeeded in joining the U.S. Army as a second lieutenant, 23rd Infantry. Dissatisfied with a series of mundane postings throughout the plains, but with an interest in telegraphic communication, he volunteered and joined the Signal Corps. While stationed in Washington, D.C., he volunteered for the expedition and was accepted. Recommended to Greely as an "officer of sterling merits," Lockwood would be a hard-working, vital contributor who would faithfully fulfill Greely's orders. As

87

an officer though, he was often unsure in a leadership role and noncommittal as a decisionmaker.[11]

Five men with "technical" skills relevant to the expedition's purposes were assigned temporarily to the detachment: Winfield Scott Jewell, a weather observer with the Signal Corps (meteorologist); David C. Ralston, a surveyor with the Signal Corps (assistant astronomer), Hampden S. Gardiner, an "instrument maker" with the Signal Corps (assistant astronomer); George Rice, a Canadian civilian (photographer); and Edward Israel, a recent University of Michigan graduate (astronomer). Dr. Octave Pavy, already in Greenland, would serve as a civilian under contract to the army.[12]

The lion's share of members, sixteen in total, would be Regular Army enlisted men drawn from frontier outposts. Selections were to be made across various stations, so as to minimize the disruption. The heavy reliance upon soldiers recruited from western posts was based on the theory that service at stations in the so-called "high latitudes" of the northern plains, with its attendant extreme winters and isolation, made men better adapted for work in the polar regions. Roaming the Dakota and Montana Territories may have "acclimatized" soldiers to cold weather, in the opinion of the military, but living and working in the High Arctic required different field skills and an emotionally solid frame of mind.

Besides Sherman's objections, more than one naysayer to Greely's plans spoke up in an effort to halt the removal of officers and enlisted men from frontier posts. From the headquarters of the 18th Infantry, Fort Assinniboine, Montana Territory, Captain R. L. Morris voiced his disapproval of the selection of several volunteers from his command: "I do not think it proper that such details be taken from the army. I am of the opinion that good men are needed in the military service as they tend to increase its efficiency and morale."[13]

Recruiting "qualified" soldiers from varied backgrounds and experiences posed other problems at the posts. An advance of one year's pay for officers and four months for enlisted men may have served as an enticement or simply a way out of doleful frontier service for some, including lackluster performers. At Fort Custer, Greely's telegram offering Kislingbury a position with the expedition was

The Lady Franklin Bay Expedition

Members of the Lady Franklin Bay Expedition.

circulated throughout the garrison and quickly became a hot topic of conversation among Kislingbury and potential recruits. So enthusiastic was Kislingbury that he approached at least twenty potential recruits for the expedition. According to his perturbed commanding officer, Colonel John Wynn Davidson, 2nd Cavalry, several zealous but naïve men were "induced to volunteer for the [expedition]" through Kislingbury's actions. Writing to the adjutant general, Davidson remarked that to "try and prevent tampering with the men" he felt compelled to put before them "the difficulties and hardships of such an expedition."[14]

Davidson's sobering address had its effect, and two of the volunteers immediately reneged, thus sparing him of their loss. Davidson's forebodings failed to deter the four members successfully recruited by Kislingbury from Fort Custer: Sergeant David Linn (or Lynn), and Private William A. Ellis, both Company C, 2nd Cavalry; Corporal Daniel C. Starr, Company F, 2nd Cavalry, and Corporal Paul Grimm, Company H, 11th Infantry. (Grimm however deserted before the expedition's departure and Starr would be subsequently sent back).[15]

Little is known of Linn, a Philadelphian, whose rather pointed talent before enlisting in November 1876 was making patterned wallpaper. He had been promoted to sergeant before volunteering for the expedition from Fort Custer. William A. Ellis, at the time also serving with the 2nd Cavalry, was, like Linn, an Indian wars veteran. As a private in the 20th Infantry in June 1876, Ellis was serving in a gatling gun detachment under Lieutenant Low. Though the detachment accompanied Terry's detachment from Fort Abraham Lincoln, difficulties in manhandling the guns across broken terrain and a shortage of serviceable horses left them as non-combatants at the ill-fated Little Big Horn.

Several recruits from other posts were dropped for medical reasons, though three privates from Company F, 9th Infantry, deemed "unfit" by Brigadier General Crook (Privates Jacob Bender, William Whistler and Francis Long (the last of whom was previously assigned to the Howgate expedition)) were subsequently accepted. Born in Friedberg Germany, George Leyerzapf, aka Jacob Bender, trained as an apprentice tinsmith before immigrating to the United States in 1869. Upon his arrival, Leyerzapf adopted his alias for unknown reasons. Bender served in the army in 1872 through 1880 with various frontier units before joining the Lady Franklin Bay Expedition. Whistler, originally from Indiana, likewise was a craftsman and carpenter at the time he enlisted in November 1878. (Coincidentally, Whistler's brother Clarence was a national champion free-style and Greco-Roman wrestler).

Private Francis Long, born in Böhmenkirch, Germany, had emigrated to the United States in 1869, enlisting four years later. Long likewise had a tenuous connection to the Custer engagement. A fanciful tale was so widely publicized in his obituary after his death on June 8, 1916 that it became accepted as fact. According to his friends, Long was with Custer's command near the Little Big Horn, but avoided Custer's fate by volunteering to deliver a dispatch to Major Marcus A. Reno, 7th Cavalry, the day before the engagement. In the aftermath of the battle the story goes that Long was the first soldier on the scene to help identify the dead.[16]

Corporal Joseph Elison, Company E, 10th Infantry, applied with the added vague qualification of having "for the last ten years read of various expeditions to the North Pole and the results obtained." But there was more to Elison's recruitment than having pored over arctic narratives. While Kislingbury was in Fort Wayne, Michigan,

The Lady Franklin Bay Expedition

on his way to Detroit, the two chanced to meet and Kislingbury discussed his arctic plans. Elison begged to go, and according to one newspaper report, though Kislingbury "spoke plainly to him of the dangers and told him he was foolish to go," Elison was undeterred and was accepted.[17]

Private Henry Biederbeck, Company G, 17th Infantry, also applied and was accepted. Biederbeck had studied medicine in Germany before emigrating to the United States and was serving as acting hospital steward at the time of his volunteering.

Private Charles Henry, aka Charles Henry Buck, 5th Cavalry, Fort Sidney, was accepted by Greely upon the highly favorable recommendation of Henry's post captain, George Frederic Price. Price was well known to Greely as Price had been a suitor competing with Greely for the affection of Henrietta Nesmith. Unknown to either Greely or Price, Buck, an imposing, muscular fellow originally from Hanover, Germany, had previously enlisted in the army in 1876, serving with Company G, 7th Cavalry. To members of that outfit, Charles Henry Buck was a well-known rascal. After the return of his company to Fort Buford following the Nez Perce campaign, Buck spent his time forging checks for large amounts on the post traders. Despite his culpability, he avoided punishment. As a clerk at Camp Sturgis (later Fort Meade), he repeated his misconduct and, in August 1878, was dishonorably discharged, court martialed, convicted and sentenced to one-year hard labor at Fort Leavenworth, Kansas. An unscrupulous rogue, he reenlisted in December 1879, just three months after his release, under the name Charles Henry, serving with Company E, 5th Cavalry, Fort Sidney, Nebraska. During the three-month period, he was rumored to have killed a man in a barroom brawl in Deadwood, Dakota Territory. After reenlisting, he volunteered to join the Greely Expedition. His subsequent conduct on the expedition would prove no better.[18]

The selection that would prove to have the most importance to the Greely Expedition was Sergeant David Legge Brainard (1856-1946) of the 2nd Cavalry. Brainard would become the bedrock of the expedition, the fabric that held it together under the most trying of circumstances. At the age of nineteen, flat broke, Brainard had enlisted in the army three months after Custer's defeat. He quickly found himself at Fort Ellis, Montana Territory, with the 2nd Cavalry, still engaged with the Northern Indians. In the fight against the Miniconjou Lame Deer at the Battle of Muddy Creek, Brainard was wounded by gunfire in the right arm and his left cheek, damaging the sight in one eye. Years later, for his action at Muddy Creek, he received the Purple Heart, only one of twelve awarded in the Indian wars. He proved his worth as a dutiful soldier in other heated actions during the Nez Perce War. In 1880, Brainard had been selected for Howgate's disastrous *Gulnare* venture, but when the ship was condemned, like the other recruits, he reluctantly returned to his frontier post.[19]

Heavy snowstorms across the northern plains forestalled Kislingbury's anxious departure east. Greely and Kislingbury communicated by telegraph their respective thoughts about the upcoming expedition, as weather permitted. Greely's preoccupation with geographical exploration was apparent; the pursuit of scientific inquiry was a mere afterthought. Questioned by Greely about his scientific qualifications, Kislingbury admitted that "I make no pretensions near to anything in that direction." No matter, Greely was focused on the British Arctic Expedition of 1875-76 and besting its geographic accomplishments. The monumental expedition, for which £150,000 had been earmarked for its success, marked a renewed British national interest in the Arctic since the fabled expedition in search of a Northwest Passage by Sir John Franklin in 1845. The two steamships of the British Arctic Expedition, HMS *Alert* and HMS *Discovery,* under the command of Captain George Nares, had wintered on the northern coast of Ellesmere Island in 1875-76. HMS *Discovery* had been stationed on the northern side of Lady Franklin Bay, the same location pinpointed by Greely as the location for the Greely Expedition. HMS *Alert* proceeded further northwest to Floeberg Beach on the Ellesmere Island coast, the farthest northern point ever reached by ship.[20]

British sledgers had achieved a number of geographic firsts, including a "Farthest North" (the highest northern latitude ever attained), by means of the strenuous exertions of Commander Albert Hastings Markham and his sledge party in May 1876. Sledge parties led by Lieutenants Pelham Aldrich and Lewis A. Beaumont had achieved "farthests" on the west coast of Ellesmere Island and on the north coast of Greenland, respectively. Greely had carefully scrutinized those accomplishments, making a point of emphasizing them and their locations for Kislingbury's benefit. In contrast to the British who manhauled sledges, both Greely and Kislingbury agreed that dogs would serve as the best means of arctic travel. Drawing upon his frontier experience, Kislingbury suggested to Greely that "it may be possible to learn something from [the Sioux] in regard to this question," and he undertook to do so. Greely had taken Kislingbury under his wing, even soliciting Kislingbury's advice as to additional officer candidates. Kislingbury responded by rejecting several candidates, including the outspoken Lieutenant Gustavus C. Doane. Doane's participation would have been doubtful. Pressured by his wife and disgusted after his *Gulnare* experience, Doane advised the adjutant general in November 1881, that he would no longer volunteer for any further exploratory expeditions.[21]

Finally, Kislingbury managed to make his way to Washington, D.C., fighting fall storms and deep snow, while transporting a mentally unsound soldier and dealing with his own demons. Out of shear grief, he purposely avoided a stay at the homestead that he had acquired with his beloved Jessie. Preoccupied with the rushed arrangements prior to departure, and still captivated with the allure of the upcoming adventure, he may not have fully calculated the emotional consequence of a possible multi-year separation from his children.

During that trip, Kislingbury passed through Fort Keogh with young Douglass and Wheeler. He briefly rekindled his friendly relationship with Major Ilges, the jovial officer who had rushed to relieve him some months before. Ilges found a much different Kislingbury, no longer the lively, animated personality he knew from those bitterly cold days at the Musselshell while sharing venison stew. According to Ilges, Kislingbury "looked haggard and careworn, and the almost boyish and always cheerful expression in the face of former days had given way to a hard and stern look of determination." Kislingbury "talked hopefully of the proposed trip to the Arctic regions," noted Ilges, as if it might serve as a rejuvenation. Kislingbury's forlorn demeanor was no doubt dampened by his separation from his two children. Douglass boarded a stagecoach to travel unaccompanied to relatives in Deadwood, and Wheeler was sent back to the Schofields in St. Louis.[22]

Another curious incident was retold by Jay Stone, private secretary to Robert Todd Lincoln, as to Kislingbury's frame of mind while immersed in those rushed preparations. As recalled by Stone, at the War Department offices the day before Kislingbury's departure to New York, Kislingbury warmly pressed Stone's hand and remarked, "I never expect to return again." Taken aback, Stone replied "Nonsense, you are young, active and vigorous – why should you not return?" According to Stone, Kislingbury confided that a feeling of deep melancholy had "taken possession" of him and he could not shake it. In light of his mental state, Stone urged the despondent lieutenant to withdraw, to which Kislingbury claimed that he would not under any circumstances, but at the same time, he believed that he "would not live out the term of his voluntary exile." Stone was the first stenographer for the military and had been highly regarded as an accurate transcriber. There is no reason to doubt the truth of the story. Curiously, a friend of Kislingbury, J. Lohman, confided to another mutual friend of Kislingbury that Kislingbury "would occasionally complain of being always behind in money matters." When Lohman asked Kislingbury why he was going on such an expedition, Kislingbury replied "for fame, Lohman, and to get away where I can save some money enough to pay my debts." [23]

Relatives and friends were hastily recruited to take care of his youngsters, then between the ages of four and thirteen. After Aggie's death, Frederick's brother John Kislingbury had been given custody of Walter at Frederick's request, so logically Walter remained with that family. Major Schofield, whose wife Alma had died in March 1879, continued responsibility for Wheeler, the youngest of the Kislingbury boys (though the major's brother Reverend James Van Pelt Schofield and his wife, in St. Louis, actually housed, educated and cared for the boy). Major Schofield also agreed to serve as administrator for Kislingbury's financial affairs while away and, in the event of Kislingbury's death, to take charge of Kislingbury's estate and to provide for the support, education and welfare of his children.[24]

The Lady Franklin Bay Expedition

Charles Lamartine Clark between Walter and Harry Kislingbury.

Charles Lamartine Clark (1851-1918), the closest friend of Kislingbury, took responsibility for Harry, the oldest of the boys. Clark also agreed to act as successor administrator of Frederick's estate, should Schofield be unable to serve. The thirty-year-old Clark was a lawyer and insurance salesman in Detroit, with an active interest in anti-temperance societies and women's rights reform. He was a life-long friend of Frederick Kislingbury, the two having known each other from their days in Rochester (Clark had moved to Detroit in 1868). He would eventually take on the heavy responsibility for the welfare of Frederick's children after the untimely deaths of both Frederick Kislingbury and Major Schofield.

Seven-year-old Douglass had been sent to Deadwood with Seth and Martha Bullock, where he was raised in a welcoming family with their three children. Despite their placement within loving families, the separation was trying. Obsessed with the welfare of his children, Kislingbury, who had little savings based on his meagre military pay, wisely took out an insurance policy in the sum of $5,000 (the equivalent of roughly $157,000 in 2025).

Chapter Ten

Seeds of Discontent

FILLED WITH MOUNTING ANTICIPATION, the members of the Greely Expedition assembled in St. John's, Newfoundland on June 22, 1881. In the midst of their high hopes however, Lockwood found the city itself "a queer and forlorn old place; everything about it is antiquated, slow and behind the times in every respect." The reality of their endeavor quickly set in as the transport ship, *Proteus*, a 200-ton converted sealer, prepared for their departure to the North. As second-in-command, Kislingbury had his hands full organizing and stowing the disordered shipments of supplies aboard, as the commander made his way to the *Proteus* by steamship, arriving on June 27. At the time, his admiration for Greely knew no bounds. As he had left Washington, D.C., Frederick had written to his friend Charles Clark that "Greely has thought of everything, in fact, his thoughtfulness, forethought & everything else about him makes me endeared to him as our commander."[1]

Despite the frenzied pace of activity at St. John's, momentous news from the United States captured the attention of Kislingbury and the other members of the expedition. News of the attempted assassination of President James A. Garfield on July 2 had reached St. John's by telegram, leaving Greely, Kislingbury and others in a gloomy state. Follow-up reports over the next two days relayed the more promising news that he was recovering. Unbeknownst to the departing expedition, Garfield would linger for eighty days until his death on September 19, 1881.

Of nearly equal interest to the frontiersmen now-turned-explorers was the report that the revered warrior Sitting Bull and some 200 of his followers had surrendered to the U.S. Army at Fort Buford, Dakota Territory, at the confluence of the Yellowstone and

Missouri Rivers, near present-day Williston. On behalf of his weary people, the legendary leader had concluded that they would be better cared for at the reservation. Here they relinquished their arms and horses in exchange for amnesty. Sitting Bull would be held as a prisoner-of-war for almost two years, until his transfer to Standing Rock Agency, a location Kislingbury knew well. On December 15, 1890, in the midst of his attempted arrest, Sitting Bull and a number of his followers, as well as an Indian policeman, would be killed. The reservation would see more bloodshed two weeks later with the tragic events at Wounded Knee.

There were local events of interest, even in St. John's. By coincidence, while anchored at this port city, the Greely Expedition members chanced to meet members of another polar expedition at this out-of-the-way destination for American naval vessels. The USS *Alliance,* a screw-gunboat of 1,375 tons and the last of the wooden-hulled warships, was on a desperate search for the exploring ship USS *Jeannette*. In 1879, the *Jeannette* Expedition, which had been sponsored by the flamboyant newspaperman James Gordon Bennett, Jr., had departed on a northward course from San Francisco in search of the North Pole. The expedition had entered the icy waters of Bering Strait and had been unheard of since. *Alliance* was one of two relief expeditions dispatched in the fruitless search for *Jeannette*. At St. John's, the *Alliance* had returned unsuccessfully after its relief efforts along the coasts of Iceland and Svalbard. The second *Jeannette* rescue cruise, that of the USS *Rodgers,* had plied the waters of Bering Strait and had likewise returned emptyhanded.

The unexpected appearance of *Alliance,* and the failure of its desperate mission, served as an all-too-grim reminder to Greely's men as to the hazardous nature of their own undertaking. Perhaps for that reason, Lieutenant Greely chose not to mention the encounter in his popular account, *Three Years of Arctic Service,* or even in his official report to the chief signal officer. Ironically, in August 1884, *Alliance* would lead the North Atlantic Squadron into Portsmouth harbor as escort to the rescue ships returning with the survivors of Greely's harrowing expedition.

For Kislingbury, activity on the plains was a distant memory as he acclimated himself to a far different situation under his new commander. While at St. John's, Henry Macdona, correspondent with the *New York Herald* sailing with the *Alliance*, had the opportunity to size up the commander of the Lady Franklin Bay Expedition. The *Herald* newsman was evidently left with a favorable impression of Greely's grit and determination, writing that "his [Greely's] plans as he explained them to me prove him to be no laggard." Interestingly, though Greely intended to faithfully carry out his scientific observations in accordance with the International Polar Year, Macdona confirmed that a competitive spirit of discovery had overtaken the would-be explorer. To Macdona, Greely made no secret of his overwhelming desire to reach the highest northern latitude ever achieved by any expedition. Macdona also harbored no doubts that Greely would achieve that objective. It was one of the ironies of the Lady Franklin Bay Expedition that its leader had engaged in precisely the actions that Weyprecht sought to avoid with the International Polar Year program—individualistic glory-seeking attempts at geographic firsts.[2]

Leaving St. John's, the expedition made for the coast of West Greenland. On the voyage north, Frederick Kislingbury wrote a series of intriguing letters in which he openly shared his innermost thoughts and fears to an unidentified individual with whom he was evidently on affectionate terms. The letters proved an outlet for his overwhelming grief, for expressing the mixed emotions caused by severed home ties, and for hopeful thoughts of a new life "that would run away my troubles." Only extracts of the letters have survived, without identifying the recipient, beyond a handwritten note on the earliest one (dated May 31, 1881) explaining that they were written "to his [Fred's] affianced."[3]

Was Frederick Kislingbury in fact betrothed to another at the time of his departure? Some fragmentary comments circulating among family members may perhaps shed some light on a clandestine relationship. In 1886, well after Frederick's death, John Kislingbury had remarked to Fred's oldest son Harry, that Charles Clark had once revealed to John Kislingbury "something about Fred being engaged to a young lady in Detroit." Clark offered no details beyond her name, a Miss Egelston. By this time John believed it was safe to reveal to Harry more details of the mysterious Miss

Egelston and their alleged relationship, advising Harry that "Fred seemed to place all confidence in her and they were to be married when he returned." It remains an open question whether Fred had in fact become engaged to Miss Egelston within five months after the death of his beloved Jessie. No further details about the possible relationship seem to have survived.[4]

Kislingbury conceded that his principle avowed fear, expressed through multiple letters to his children, as well his "affianced," was the potential effect of the long, dark winter on his mental health, thus acknowledging his shaky emotional constitution. From St. John's he leaned on his unnamed confidant as a pillar of strength and support: "think of me during the dreadful long monotonous night, this I told you before was my dread, pray to God that I may not become restless, impatient for the morrow. . . . But now I am all alone among strangers, please pray for me [redacted name] all the while that I may get strong." The anguish of parting with his children was particularly overwhelming: "Poor little men! When I stop to think how I have torn myself from them; how good, how brave they were, and to agree to Papa going, because he thought it for the best. I almost give way.... I can hardly realize that I am separated from them, everything from Fort Custer to here was done so quickly, with such a rush, and now, it is too much like a dream." In that candid moment of frankness that spoke to his troubled mental state, he also confessed that he had not fully recovered from his terrible grief. He would do his utmost to suppress those feelings, but at times he lapsed into despair admitting that "were it not that my honor, my future, <u>our</u> future is at stake, I would abandon all and come back."[5]

In the face of strong gales that left Greely and several others wretchedly sick in their cabins, the ship reached the village of Godhavn, on the south side of Disko Island. There they brought on board Dr. Octave Pavy and Harry Clay, who had remained there since the failed *Gulnare* expedition the year before. While at Godhavn, some dogs were obtained through the generosity of the Inspector Krarup-Smith. Lacking fur clothing, a must-have for the expedition, Greely was forced to barter for a few items, the only way locals would part with them. Pavy also contributed nine dogs,

Dancing Chief

The Lady Franklin Bay Expedition visits Godhavn (Qeqertarsuaq).

three sledges and 3,500 pounds of dried fish for which Greely was thankful, in light of the difficulties of acquiring supplies not ordered in advance. The Greenlanders extended their usual courtesy to visitors, hosting a well-attended and lively dance in the local carpenter's shed. Kislingbury and Lockwood tried their hands at Greenland waltzes with the locals, while Kislingbury impressed them with an Indian dance. Kislingbury may have been outwardly enjoying their venture, but Greely carped that both his officers, Lockwood and Kislingbury, had set a bad example by "partaking too freely of the various liquors." Greely was also annoyed that Kislingbury spent much of his time alone writing letters. Judging by the number and length of his letters to his children and their caretakers, this was certainly true. Perhaps, in retrospect, it was likewise a sign of gnawing homesickness.

With those ever-present thoughts of his children at home, Kislingbury penned a letter to seven-year-old Douglass on July 17 while in the harbor of Disko Island. On this, his maiden arctic cruise, like many a landsman before him, he had been mesmerized by the natural beauty and magnificence of the North. The bewildering shapes, sizes and colors of the passing icebergs saw him spellbound as he tried to describe them for his absent son: "Passed through immense fields of floe ice which was the most wonderful sight I could ever imagine. The colors were exquisite, of the most perfect hues of blue and green and the shapes of some of the bergs were grotesque in the extreme." The island of Greenland and its "curious Esquimaux" in their sealskin wardrobes were an equal eye-opener. In the midst of this exotic setting, an exuberant spirit now took hold of him, lifting his dark mood. Frederick Kislingbury sounded in an upbeat frame of mind as he closed a letter to Douglass: "I am in perfect health and everything, ice, etc., is favorable for our progress north.... I feel that I shall like the life ahead of me. The night will be my only dread, but I can go through that I think as others have done. God bless my darling Douglass and all at your good home."[6]

To his unnamed intimate friend he echoed that positive outlook, writing that "I am in the most sanguine of spirits and know that all will go well with me." An additional stop was made at the settlement of Upernavik, where Greely was fortunate to acquire ten additional fur-suits. While in Upernavik, Lieutenant Lockwood was ordered to travel by the steam launch *Lady Greely* some fifty miles south to enlist two Greenlanders, Jens Edwards and Frederik Thorlip Christiansen. Lockwood returned with the two men on July 28, along with some additional fur-clothing. Both Greenlanders would serve valuable roles as hunters and dog-drivers. As neither had a strong grasp of the English language, communication with other expedition members would be frustrating at times and was managed largely by means of hand signals and expressions. Rice was taken aback by the emotion they showed on leaving their friends. "They shed bitter tears that fell indeed until their homes were out of sight," he noted.[7]

Leaving Upernavik, the *Proteus* proceeded northward into a dense fog. Greely now faced a navigational dilemma. Should the *Proteus* follow the longer circuitous route along the coast of Greenland, thus minimizing the chances of being beset in the pack ice of Melville Bay, or chance a direct course across Melville Bay to Cape York on the northwest Greenland coast? As Greely stood perched on the deck of the vessel, the near absence of pack ice on the horizon led him to take the *Proteus* through the "Middle Pack" of Melville Bay, a constantly moving mass of floating ice and icebergs that could sound the death knell for ensnared vessels. By

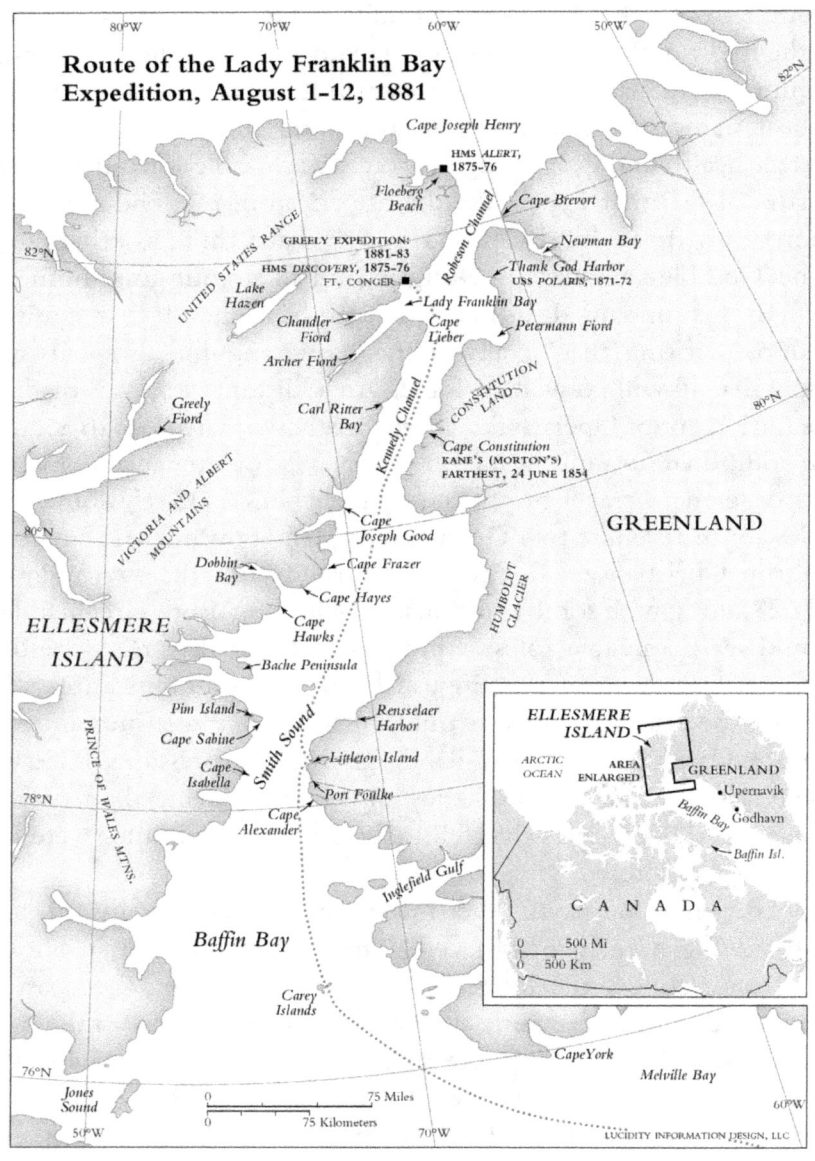

Seeds of Discontent

way of but one example, in August, 1857, Sir Leopold McClintock had gambled on a quick passage, but his *Fox* was frozen in the pack for the next eight months, even with the benefit of steam.

In the remarkably short time frame of thirty-six hours, Captain Richard Pike, with the benefit of a head of steam on the *Proteus*, easily cruised through fragmented pancake ice into Baffin Bay, and reached the so-called "North Water." The "North Water" is a triangularly shaped region with stretches of open water and broken ice (so-called polynyas), extending from the northern end of Baffin Bay into Smith Sound. Sir John Ross in his voyage of 1818 confirmed its earlier and then forgotten discovery by William Baffin. Thereafter, whalers directing their course west through the North Water sailed along the west coast of Baffin Bay to take advantage of the productive whaling grounds. Impacted by the vagaries of wind, currents, tides and ice floes, the dynamic nature of the North Water can cause the breadth of the ice-free area to vary greatly year-to-year.

Thus far the voyage of the *Proteus* had done much to maintain Kislingbury's newly found exuberance. An avowed hunter on the plains, he could barely contain himself in his zeal for truly exotic big game. He also quickly demonstrated that he was one of the best marksmen. While crossing Baffin Bay, at the shout of "polar bear!," donning only his slippers and without any overcoat, he literally leaped over a table where Harry Clay was seated in his quest for the first shot. Sporting a specially ordered Remington rifle, the elusive bear was taken by him by a single bullet through the head. On the same day, Kislingbury also took down a seal and later a walrus; while at a rookery he felled some 400 auks and guillemots by shotgun blasts.

His shooting prowess caused the first discernible friction over Greely's authority. Proud of his big game trophy, Kislingbury boasted to his sons that "I will not deny a feeling of pride when I found I had really killed a white bear.... I had killed nearly everything but a polar bear and I was anxious to tackle one. That I should so soon be gratified was beyond my expectation." The polar bear, fearsome predator of the North, rightly held the top position in the hierarchy of arctic big game hunting. Not surprisingly, Kislingbury sought to keep the hide as a furry souvenir. Greely, however, felt differently, ordering the skin to be turned over as government property. Sadly disappointed, Kislingbury grumbled slightly, but resigned himself to his commander's wishes.[8]

On the heels of the bear incident, several additional events, minor in the overall scheme of affairs, nonetheless reflected a mounting frustration on Kislingbury's part. About the last day of July, Kislingbury sent his already well-used rifle to the enlisted men's quarters with orders that it be cleaned. When it had not been returned, a slightly miffed Kislingbury took up the matter directly with the enlisted men. Those subordinates simply gave the second-in-command the cold shoulder. Kislingbury wrote in his diary that "no one seemed to know anything of the gun and they acted very indifferently about the matter." Later, Sergeant Brainard returned the gun with no signs that it had been cleaned.[9]

At Kislingbury's request, Brainard interceded with the men. Brainard returned with the surprising news that only Private Ellis offered to clean it, which he claimed he had, but refused to do it again. Far from supporting Kislingbury, his senior officer, Brainard bluntly told Kislingbury that "it might as well be understood now that the men considered it menial work to do anything of the sort," and that their position was that "everybody (officers and men), would have to do their own chores." Curiously, however, Private Maurice Connell reported that about the same time, Greely ordered the enlisted men to do the officers' laundry.[10]

Taken aback by the outright rejection of an order by the enlisted men, Kislingbury expressed to Brainard his dissatisfaction with Brainard's failure to exercise his authority. As to raising the matter to Greely, Kislingbury held his tongue, even though the men were also complaining that the officers had been "rambling the hills" while the men did the heavy work, and were grumbling about the allocation of food rations. Evidently, only one month out of St. John's, Kislingbury was growing exceedingly wary of his commander's management. Tellingly, Kislingbury privately remarked in his diary that he would have raised these issues with Greely, but Greely "does not take kindly to anything I say reflecting upon the conduct of the men." More distressing though, Kislingbury had concluded that Greely "does not favorably receive contrary opinions to his own and I have consequently become cautious in this respect." The second-in-command had quickly perceived one of Greely's foremost shortcomings. At the moment, avoiding the ire of his commander, Kislingbury believed it best not to have the commander think that Kislingbury "opposes him [Greely]." That opinion would soon change.[11]

Coincidentally, that same evening, Greely ordered the men to stand to on the deck of the *Proteus* for an inspection of their clothing, and he ordered Kislingbury to conduct the examination. To the humiliation of the men who believed they knew full well how to keep their clothes, Kislingbury made a spectacle of the part, delicately lifting open their shirts and peering as if they were vermin-infested. It was the first and last time Greely issued such an order. Brainard remarked in his diary that "it was the most shameful affair that I ever saw. To submit us tamely to such indignities is too outrageous. It exposed us to ridicule by the sailors." By the "sailors," Brainard meant the rough crewmen of the *Proteus*, who found the affair roaringly laughable entertainment. Corporal Starr complained directly to Greely, remarking that the men had been "particular about washing and changing their clothes." Brainard attributed Kislingbury's theatrics to "pure spite because we refused to clean the guns of the two junior officers and perform menial or the servant duties," but Brainard may have misread the reason for Kislingbury's disdain.[12]

The following morning, while boarding a boat on the hunt for a seal, Lieutenant Kislingbury was ordered by Greely to take two men with him. Kislingbury ignored the order, leaving the men, but in any event the seal had made its escape before departure. When the animal made a second appearance, Greely again ordered Kislingbury to include the two men, but the two were delayed and Kislingbury prepared to shove off without them. According to Greely, Kislingbury "did not relish the instruction, saying that if [Greely] so desired, [Kislingbury] could remain back and let the two men go alone." Kislingbury ultimately relented, but the elusive seal "proved to be another false alarm."[13]

Having made a remarkable crossing of treacherous Melville Bay, Captain Pike and Lieutenant Greely elected to head for the Carey

Islands, an isolated group of rocky islands and islets, some thirty miles off the Greenland coast. On the easternmost island, Kislingbury and Pavy located the cairn erected by Captain George Nares in 1875 and that by Allen Young with the yacht *Pandora* in 1876. Some 3,600 pounds of rations left by Nares were also discovered, and found to be in good shape. Several cans were taken aboard and their contents heartily eaten by a few of the more fearless souls, with no ill effects besides some "griping pains in the stomach," recorded the second-in-command.

A sturdy whaleboat, also left by Nares, otherwise found to be serviceable, became another sticking point between Greely and Kislingbury. Believing that the boat could be of use to the Greely Expedition, both Kislingbury and Lockwood strongly urged Greely that it be taken aboard the *Proteus*. To their surprise, Greely nixed the idea, advising Kislingbury that it might be of use to any passing whalers. Kislingbury was taken aback by the response. Though the expedition was equipped with the steamer *Lady Greely*, one whaleboat and a smaller jolly-boat, the one at the Carey Islands was better built and came equipped with oars and sails. Kislingbury believed that no whaleships ever frequented the area, and "as we need the boat, I am forced to say that I feel Lieutenant Greely is making a mistake in not taking the boat." For his part, Greely claimed they could pick up another at Foulke Point, farther to the north. A slightly perturbed Kislingbury confided to his journal, that "a bird in the hand is worth three in the bush."[14]

Working north into Smith Sound, the *Proteus* threaded its way through the narrow channel between the headlands of Cape Alexander and Cape Isabella. Smith Sound comprises the lower stretch of a waterway known as the Nares Strait, which separates Canada's Ellesmere Island from Greenland and extends to the Arctic Ocean. From the northern end of Baffin Bay into Smith Sound, the Nares Strait opens into the broad Kane Basin, then into the more slender Kennedy Channel (with Lady Franklin Bay near its northwest edge). At its upper reaches, the Nares Strait incorporates the Hall Basin, Robeson Channel and, at its entrance at the Arctic Ocean, the Lincoln Sea.

The so-called "Smith Sound" route, i.e., a northward passage through the Nares Strait, now followed by *Proteus,* had become a favored approach for explorers attempting to reach the North Pole. The prevailing thought was that this pathway offered the potential for a land base at a high northern latitude (at the tip of Ellesmere Island or Greenland) that would reduce the time and distance travelling on the unpredictable drifting ice of the Arctic Ocean on the way to the Pole.

After Sir John Ross had spied the prominent headlands (and named them after his two discovery ships, HMS *Alexander* and HMS *Isabella)*, more extensive journeys through Smith Sound were made by Dr. Elisha Kent Kane in 1853-55 and Dr. Isaac Israel Hayes in the 1860-61. In 1871, the eccentric explorer Charles Francis Hall led an attempt on the Pole through the Smith Sound route. This expedition ended in failure and the death of Hall. Thereafter, the British Arctic Expedition of 1875-76 had journeyed through Smith Sound on its unsuccessful North Pole attempt. With heavy ice and bergs drifting southward, navigation within the Nares Strait poses a serious hazard, as the Greely relief expeditions would later learn. Greely recognized that he and his men were among the earliest explorers to the region, and as Euro-Americans that was true, but Aboriginal peoples had preceded them, in some cases, by several thousand years.[15]

The *Proteus* made a further stop at Littleton Island, a windswept rocky islet just off the Greenland coast, to retrieve mail previously left by *Pandora* for the British Arctic Expedition. Lieutenant Lockwood and a party of four unloaded six tons of coal as a precaution in the event of a subsequent disaster, a task made difficult by the need to haul it some thirty feet above the high-water mark. Kislingbury and four others rowed to a sheltered inlet (Life Boat Cove), a circumstance which served as another stark reminder of the unpredictability of navigation in the North. Here the detachment fell upon the scattered ruins of the expedition ship USS *Polaris*, which had been abandoned near there in 1872. In 1871, the explorer Charles Francis Hall had commanded *Polaris* on its fateful attempt on the Pole, via Smith Sound. Hall died an untimely death on November 8, 1871 under suspicious circumstances (there was evidence he may have been poisoned by arsenic). Sailing Master Sidney O. Budington, taking charge of *Polaris,* attempted a retreat south, but the ship was nipped in the ice and ultimately abandoned to its fate, its survivors rescued the following year.

Remarkably, upon lifting a rock, Kislingbury located a weatherworn prayerbook, a relic from Hall's aborted expedition. Carefully turning its pages, his eyes fell upon "the Prayer at the North Pole." The precious leaves were tucked away by Kislingbury with the thought that should he be fortunate to reach that point, he would "offer the prayer most fervently," he wrote to Douglass. At the same time, he sought to caution his absent son to not worry:

> You must not be anxious about me if [a relief] ship does not reach us next year, as we have fully two years supplies and can get back some way. I am in the very best of health and weigh more than I ever did before. My appetite is inordinate and I am sanguine that I can get through this sort of life successfully and unless afflicted with disease or sickness feel that I should come back a stronger and healthier man than ever.[16]

Proteus made another clear run across Smith Sound during the evening of August 2. In contrast to the decrepit *Gulnare*, Harry Clay highly praised the durability of the *Proteus*, remarking that:

> She was built expressly for ice navigation and was undoubtedly one of the staunchest ships ever put into the Arctic Ocean.... It was wonderful what hard knocks she could receive from the ice with apparent impunity. I have seen her run at full speed into the ice thirty feet thick. I have seen her nipped between two heavy floes that would have crushed the *Gulnare* like an egg shell, but she escaped unharmed.[17]

Kislingbury remarked that their route had been so fortuitous that he believed they "could have run right to the Pole." Their first view of the Ellesmere Island coast was an awe-inspiring view of striking cliffs and headlands. Ellesmere Island is the most northern landmass

**Lieutenants Kislingbury and Lockwood on the Ice Pack.
Latitude 81˚35 North, August 5, 1884.**

in Canada, the country's third largest island and the tenth largest in the world. Its geography is formidable. A series of lofty and precipitous mountain ranges fill the interior. An extensive ice shelf and sprawling glaciers blanket almost half of its landmass. The imposing glaciers snake far back into the interior and have carved numerous fiords that mark the coast. A high arctic climate prevails—cold, frigid winters, and cool, sometimes cold temperatures during the all-too-brief summer. Fogs are frequent, particularly along the coastal zone.

A brief stop was made just north of Cape Hawks, a distinctive rocky headland which Captain Nares of the British Arctic Expedition had compared to the Rock of Gibraltar. Scrambling ashore, Kislingbury and Pavy located a jolly boat left by that British expedition which was taken aboard (though smaller than the one left behind). Another 3,600 pounds of rations left by the *Pandora* were also located and found to be in good shape.

The vagaries of the pack ice of Kennedy Channel, which had been remarkably open, just as quickly closed. After depositing a small depot of bread, pemmican and rum on Franklin Island within Carl Ritter Bay, just a few hours later *Proteus* found itself hemmed in by a wall of ice while situated slightly above Cape Lieber. A mere eight miles from their destination, Lady Franklin Bay, the vessel was barred by ice extending entirely across the channel through which

Fort Conger, headquarters of the Lady Franklin Bay Expedition.

not even the stout *Proteus* could proceed. Kislingbury quickly learned that patience was a necessary virtue when travelling in the North. While idle in his cabin, he continued his letter writing campaign to his children and his intimate friend. Despite the current setback, he still found everyone "happy and jubilant!" As for a possible two-year sojourn, to the novice arctic traveler, the mere thought of the extended stay was "a glorious pleasure for me to look forward to!" In their leisure, Lieutenants Kislingbury and Lockwood even managed to be photographed by Rice on the ice. Certainly, at the moment, any feelings about abandoning the venture were not even thinkable.[18]

On August 12 the ice relented, and twenty-five members of the expedition disembarked from the *Proteus* and set foot on terra firma at Lady Franklin Bay. They prepared to settle in for what would eventually become a two-year-stay on the northeast coast of Ellesmere Island. Their location within Discovery Harbour on the northern shore of the bay had previously been the location of HMS *Discovery* during the British Arctic Expedition of 1875-76. As the expedition was advancing the purposes of the First International Polar Year, no particular concern by the British or Canadian authorities was raised with respect to any territorial ambitions. That would be different for later explorers to Ellesmere Island, such as the Americans Robert Peary and Donald MacMillan, and the Norwegian Otto Sverdrup.

From August 13-18, Lieutenants Lockwood and Kislingbury

closely supervised the unloading of the prodigious cargo from the *Proteus*, alternating four-hour watches. During a break, in a rather prophetic statement made in one of his last letters to his confidant, he opined that "I dare not allow myself to think the ship will not be able to reach us next year. Would not this be too awful? God forbid." But, by now, he was emotionally more settled and feeling buoyant, adding that "I haven't the slightest dread of the future, I feel that everything will be well with me and that I shall succeed and that I shall surely come back."[19]

Keeping to the task at hand, however, the remainder of August was occupied round-the-clock under nearly constant daylight with crews constructing their winter quarters, hunting game for food stocks and preparing for the spring sledge journeys. Their more-than-adequate quarters comprised sturdy wooden barracks some twenty-five-feet wide by sixty-five-feet long and fourteen-feet high. With assistance from carpenters on board the *Proteus*, the structure boasted wooden floors, framed windows and doors, and tar-papered walls. It was also fitted with two large stoves and a kitchen, and even included the luxury of a bathtub. Few winter parties had been fixed with such a pleasurable degree of comfort during the long winter night. The explorer Robert Peary would later deconstruct the building and repurpose its wood for smaller quarters during his North Pole attempts more than fifteen years later. Greely's headquarters were named Fort Conger after the U.S. Senator Omar D. Conger (MI) a strong supporter of the project, and ironically a founder of the American Red Cross.

Chapter Eleven

Fort Conger

WORK MAY HAVE GONE OFF AS PLANNED, but the relationship between Dr. Pavy and Lieutenant Greely would continue to be strained. On August 14, Greely bore firsthand witness to Pavy's headstrong personality. The quarrelsome Pavy delivered a blunt ultimatum to his commander: unless Clay was removed from the expedition, Pavy would leave with the *Proteus*. Pavy and Clay had previously clashed during the long winter in Greenland. In fact, the bad blood between the two was so great that they staked separate lodgings as far as possible from one another in the tiny settlement of Rittenbenk. Possessed of a sense of honor and professional duty, Clay never forgave Pavy for callously halting medical treatment for the child of Mr. K. M. Moldrup, an assistant in the Greenland Trade Service, while they wintered in Greenland. As the boy's illness dragged on, Pavy chose to discontinue treatment rather than face the distraught parents, who pressed him to do more. Ultimately, the poor child died.[1]

Greely "found it trying in the extreme" that a subordinate under his military command should be dictating orders to his commander, but he also realized that the presence of a physician was of vital importance to the expedition. Under the circumstances, Greely felt that his hands were tied and that he had no choice but to surrender to Pavy's terms. As a result, Clay was reluctantly ordered home. Though bitter over Pavy's spiteful behavior, Clay unhesitatingly accepted the mandate and displayed far more professionalism than the vindictive Pavy. Clay even allowed Greely to declare to the men that Clay had broken the deadlock by voluntarily tendering his resignation to Greely, thereby avoiding the embarrassment of Greely's capitulation to Pavy. (Greely also kept up that position in his official report). Ironically, though Clay could not have known it at the time, Pavy's mean-spirited ultimatum may have spared Clay the terrible fate subsequently suffered by almost all of the expedition's members. Ironically, though Clay may have dodged a bullet by leaving the Greely Expedition, on September 22, 1884 he died from a gunshot wound inflicted by a Louisville councilman and barkeeper during a drunken quarrel.[2]

Pavy's insubordination was a toxic ingredient that would soon undermine Greely's authority and exert a negative influence upon the men. For different reasons, two other men were sent back: Corporal Daniel C. Starr on account of his asthma and Private James Ryan, who had suffered an epileptic seizure (though allegations of drunkenness may have contributed to his departure). Kislingbury was pleased to see Starr's departure as he found him a "dissenting spirit" and a troublemaker.

On August 14, according to Greely, Kislingbury was "quite mortified" by the order to report for duty, as Kislingbury "seemed to think that he should have time for letters and not be required with his men all the time." On August 16, further to the call of duty, Greely sought an affirmation from his two officers, Kislingbury and Lockwood, that they were committed to remaining at the isolated post beyond 1883. Greely's plan was to leave at that time, and he wanted the assurance of continuity of command thereafter. For a man previously tortured by conflicting feelings, Kislingbury showed no hesitation in responding, "am devoted to the duties and...I hold myself ready to remain as long as my Government desires me to." A more cautious Lockwood, on the other hand, remarked that it was "too far in the future" to make such a commitment.[3]

At the same time, Greely believed that order and discipline were slacking on the heels of Pavy's insubordinate demands. According to Greely, both Kislingbury and Lockwood, Greely's two highest ranking officers, were setting a poor example. On August 19, Greely reported that both men had slept past noon, well beyond the 7:00 a.m. breakfast call. Once awake, they left their posts vacant all afternoon, while the enlisted men were working fourteen-hour days. On August 21, Kislingbury again rose late for breakfast and lounged in bed until dinner. Lockwood remained in bed until dinner as well, then both went off for a shooting trip to nearby

Muskox Bay. After a similar late sleep-in the following day, Greely reprimanded both of them for "remaining so late and for so many hours in bed at a time when men are working 12-14 hours daily to get matters in shape."[4]

Lieutenant Lockwood apologized for the failure and promised to change his habits. Lockwood even admonished Kislingbury over the incident, directing Frederick "not to make any further trouble." According to Greely, Kislingbury on the other hand, "took the reproof in a very bad part," claiming that he "had been working as hard as anyone." Kislingbury's frustration was more than just a matter of oversleeping. Believing himself slighted, he remarked that he "was treated as one who was in the way" and that Greely was simply ignoring the advice of his second-in-command. The commander advised Kislingbury that his advice had been listened to, "but that as commanding officer he was obliged to consider all things in their various lights and that he was responsible that proper means were followed to attain success."[5]

Kislingbury's misbehavior closely followed on the heels of the frustratingly slow departure of the *Proteus*. Captain Pike had been exceedingly anxious to get the vessel off. Greely had discharged the *Proteus* on the August 18, but newly formed ice in the harbor had stalled the passage. One day later, as Kislingbury and Greely fretted, the transport ship finally got under way, but was stopped only a mile or two from shore, snagged in the rapidly formed young ice. There she sat perched for several more days, displaying slight movements as the ice shifted, awaiting a favorable change. Over that time, Kislingbury watched the *Proteus* poised on the brink of departure with increasing apprehension. On August 25, he spent the better part of the day aboard the ship, while Captain Pike anxiously paced the deck scanning for a watery exit. That evening, Kislingbury advised Pavy that chances looked good for the ship's escape the following day. On the next day, *Proteus* managed to exit the harbor, but remained hemmed in five miles from the encampment at-the-ready for a final opening in the ice.

Coincidentally, with the *Proteus* now poised to break free, on August 26 Kislingbury's discontentment reached a breaking point after yet another squabble over his absence from breakfast.

That morning, he wrote in his diary that "strange what one day will bring forth and how a man's prospects may be suddenly changed." Upon being ordered by yet a third request from Greely to attend the 7:00 a.m. meal at the same time as the enlisted men, Kislingbury surprised Greely by declaring that he would remain in bed and would simply go without breakfast. Greely snapped back, demanding that Kislingbury rise whether he ate breakfast or not. A fastidious Greely towed the line with his second-in-command, advising him that it was a regulation of the expedition and must be complied with, to which Kislingbury responded that he would only do so, "if it was *insisted upon*." Greely bristled at this retort, scolding the young lieutenant, declaring that "this was no place for an officer to say that he would obey an order only if it was insisted on, that cheerful compliance was expected and when an officer could not yield it his usefulness as a member of the expedition was destroyed." Though Kislingbury attempted to get a word in, Greely cut off any further discussion and considered the matter settled.[6]

That did not end the affair. Brooding in his cabin, Kislingbury poured his feelings into his diary, providing a justification for his decision. He believed that "for some time past that Greely inwardly, for some reason best known to himself, would be better pleased if I were not connected as the second officer to the expedition…. On various occasions he has shown a want of confidence in me, and to tell the truth I cannot shake from my mind the thought which passes itself upon me instinctively that it would be pleasing to him if I were not connected to the expedition in the position in which I am."[7]

At noon, Dr. Pavy, acting as messenger, passed a letter to Greely setting forth Kislingbury's resignation in lengthy terms to his commander, reasserting, in his opinion, the right to ignore orders from his commander that he "considered of no practical importance," such as Greely's order to breakfast with the enlisted men. Kislingbury understood that his position flew in the face of strict military protocol that orders are to be obeyed, but his remarks also highlighted Greely's unbending governance under all circumstances and the perceived disregard of his second-in-command as compelling factors in his resignation:

Dancing Chief

In conversation at breakfast this morning, you said, in effect that if I could not agree to certain ideas of yours I "had better go." This I take that my services are no longer desirable to you as a member of this expedition. After receiving such a suggestion or invitation to go, from my commanding officer, because, possibly, I expressed myself too freely, the only thing I feel left for me to do is to ask to be relieved from duty as a member of the expedition and ordered to report to the Chief Signal Officer of the Army. On other occasions you have seen fit to find fault in me over matters in which I may have been lacking or which might have been annoying to you but of no practical importance; and from your final request this morning already stated, it will doubtless be better that I go. You and I disagreed this morning because I differed from you in the matter of early breakfasting. I objected to being compelled or required to breakfast so early. You would have me breakfast when the men do, at 7 A.M. I would not agree that the officers should be required to rise at the same time and breakfast at the same time with the men. You then said that I "had better go" unless I saw fit to do as you required in such matters. If I had been accused of anything of a serious nature, warranting you in telling me this or anything tending to a necessity for a severance of my connection with the expedition, I would act differently in this matter–would, doubtless, resist being relieved; but if such a trivial matter as this morning causes you to express such a wish as you did–*so readily*– I cannot but feel that the comfort, peace and harmony, and even success of the expedition, may be jeopardized if I remain. It is possible that I am at fault, but, if so, it can only be because I have been too candid....

It is hardly necessary to say anything further, *yet I shall leave the expedition in sorrow.* I see many bright hopes ahead. I am become fond of Arctic life.... But I must be in the way or you could not have told me what you did this morning, and rather than be the slightest bar to the present or future success of the expedition, I abandon all my bright expectations, and feel that it would be better that I go before it becomes too late for me to do so. The *Proteus* is still within reaching distance. With the assistance of enough men to help me take my things off the ship I can reach her over the ice.[8]

After dinner, with the resignation in hand, Greely summoned Kislingbury, Lockwood and Pavy outside of the station. Greely made clear that Lockwood and Pavy were not called for their opinions or to help broker a settlement of the matter, but so as to prevent any misunderstanding as to Greely's position. Greely claimed he did not remember telling Kislingbury that he had uttered the words that "he [Kislingbury] had better go," or that he wanted Kislingbury to leave. He added that "when he [Greely] wanted an officer to go, he would plainly say so," and he had not. But the issue as Greely saw it was the noncompliance by an officer with an order that such officer found "unreasonable," which Greely could not accept.[9]

According to Greely, Kislingbury was asked if he continued to believe the order to breakfast with the men unreasonable, to which he responded that he thought so. Greely bluntly advised Kislingbury that "I will put it stronger than the language you said I used this morning and now say not that any officer so thinking and acting had better go, *but that he must go*." Continuing his tirade, Greely barked that he would rather lose every officer than be surrounded by men who were disposed to question orders given. Asked if Kislingbury still wanted to leave as a result, Kislingbury responded "yes, since matters have gone this far."[10]

Kislingbury recorded the conversation slightly differently, but with the same result. Asked by Greely if Kislingbury was prepared to "cheerfully agree to all [Greely's] wishes and obey implicitly [Greely's] orders," Kislingbury replied that "I [Kislingbury] had gone so far now that it was too late for me [Kislingbury] to turn back." Kislingbury essentially believed that to further argue the matter with Greely would be pointless. With that, Kislingbury's official capacity with the expedition was terminated. Greely issued an official order for Kislingbury to return by the *Proteus* to St.

John's and to report without delay to the chief signal officer at the nation's capital.[11]

There was the practical matter of settling financial accounts. Having paid his expenses in advance, rather than over time, Kislingbury had burned through the year's advance pay. He had also outfitted himself at his own considerable expense with suitable clothing and equipment for the venture. Kislingbury would therefore expect the Government "to be at least lenient to me, or thoughtful, considering my pecuniary matters." If by chance the *Proteus* was held over for the winter, he would expect food and antiscorbutics (agents that prevent scurvy) to see him through. And, as for his departure, he asked for assistance to carry his belongings to the *Proteus*.

In retrospect, that attempted, but unsuccessful, last-minute departure by Kislingbury would become one of the most tragic events of the expedition, an expedition that would suffer many fateful consequences. Hastily gathering his belongings together, with the assistance of several of the men, Kislingbury rushed toward *Proteus*, keenly following its billowing trail of smoke as it started to push its way through crumbling ice toward home. Sliding and tumbling about slippery hillocks and slogging through slushy ice along the coast, he reached the location of the ship's anchorage that morning. By now the ship was moving down Kennedy Channel and Kislingbury's diminishing profile, a mere speck within the prodigious landscape, passed unobserved by the retreating vessel. Kislingbury could only watch longingly as the *Proteus* steamed away leaving him behind, and unknowingly sealing his fate. Ironically, as one commentator noted, had Kislingbury shortened that final confrontation with Greely by a matter of minutes, he might have met the departing *Proteus*.[12]

In the close quarters of the encampment, Kislingbury now occupied a very awkward position. Officially, he was no longer subject to Greely's command and could act in no official capacity for the expedition. As he pondered his situation, he asked himself whether he should ask Greely to rescind the order relieving him from duty. For a moment, he thought perhaps he could swallow his pride, and "smother my feelings and go along, if I could be

Departure of the steamship *Proteus* from Lady Franklin Bay.

allowed, as though the trouble had never occurred." In light of his predicament, he waited, believing that even the hard-nosed Greely might reconsider and welcome him back. That hope was quickly quashed as Greely had no intention of extending an olive branch. On the contrary, with the departure of the *Proteus*, Greely immediately modified his order that Kislingbury leave with the *Proteus*, such that Kislingbury was directed to leave Fort Conger "by the first visiting steamship." Thus, he remained an outcast from the expedition, an accidental holdover, and "considered as on waiting orders at this place." In response, Kislingbury confided in his diary, "I know that I was right. If not why such haste in issuing such order?"[13]

From that time forward, for almost three years, Kislingbury remained isolated within a community in which he played no official role. Brainard likened Kislingbury's unfortunate stay as that of "a guest," though Kislingbury surely would have found that characterization too hospitable. Greely never offered to reinstate the lieutenant, nor did Kislingbury ever ask to be returned to duty. Over time, the broken relationship with Greely would diverge even further. The two would be barely on speaking terms, awkwardly sidestepping each other in the close quarters of Fort Conger. Not until their last dying days did Greely approach Kislingbury and offer him his reinstatement and an attempt at reconciliation.

In his widely publicized narrative, *Three Years of Arctic Service*,

Greely defended his actions and his leadership style, holding the lieutenant fully responsible for the circumstances of their falling out. He also added a stinging criticism of Kislingbury's fitness for military service. Referring specifically to Kislingbury's resignation, the commander wrote that "Lieutenant Kislingbury, dissatisfied with the expeditionary regulations, requested that he be relieved from duty with the expedition.... These unfortunate episodes emphasize the necessity of selecting for Arctic service only men and officers <u>of thorough military qualities</u>, among which subordination is by no means of secondary importance. If in all military commands that element is of great importance, it is of predominating weight in Arctic work, where isolation and self-dependence impose rigid and particular conditions." [14]

As a military leader whose mettle was forged by battle-hardened experience in some of the harshest campaigns of the Civil War—Bull Run, Antietam and Fredericksburg—Greely understood all-to-well that obedience to command was fundamental to maintaining order and the efficient discharge of duties. He could be the meticulous taskmaster in his role, even to the point of being overbearing and unreasonable. But was it necessary to press that point to such an extreme under the circumstances? Even he had recognized the need for practicality when it served the best interests of the expedition. As a result, he could surrender to Dr. Pavy's profound insubordination that flew in the face of Greely's claim of unyielding obedience to orders.

Leadership includes a duty to build trust and to be supportive of subordinates. Comradeship and support were especially necessary within the close confines of an isolated polar expedition of extended length. In light of Kislingbury's emotional quandary, perhaps less rigidity and more flexibility on the part of Greely might have convinced Greely to repair, rather than sever, their relationship for the benefit of the expedition.

That rings all the more true by virtue of their joint history. Frederick Kislingbury was the only member of the expedition personally known to Greely before its formation. Kislingbury had long been on friendly terms with both Adolphus and Henrietta Greely, Adolphus's wife. An expression of that relationship was found in one of Greely's last letters home to his wife from St. John's. On July 4, Greely wrote to Henrietta that "Lieutenant Kislingbury sends you his photograph and wishes to be kindly remembered by you."[15]

In the field, Kislingbury had worked hand-in-hand with Greely on the Texas prairie. Greely, in fact, went so far as to claim that Kislingbury had "served under him" in that role. In any event, Greely thought highly enough of Kislingbury to select him for the important role of second-in-command. Having placed his faith in Kislingbury, Greely bore some level of personal responsibility to mend the rift and not give up on the young man, especially after the exit of the *Proteus* and Kislingbury's forced confinement at Fort Conger.

Sergeant Brainard, generally supportive of Greely publicly, not surprisingly sided with his commander in the matter, writing in 1940 in his account *Six Came Back*: "A wise and just, if strict, commander, Greely knew that he would hold the respect of the men only so long as he demonstrated his ability to keep the expedition, including officers, in hand. Kislingbury merely had to admit his shortcomings and promise not to repeat them to have been restored to duty. This he did not do." That musing sounded all well and good, but ignored the fact that the recalcitrant Pavy had also defied the commander in a more disturbing clash and failed to acknowledge his insubordination or to suffer any consequence as a result thereof. Commenting on Greely's rigid military mindset at a later date, Sergeant George Rice aptly opined in his diary that "to manage an Arctic expedition as if it were a body of troops before the enemy seems absurd to anyone." Even Brainard partially acknowledged Greely's over-reaction to the affair, adding in his *Outpost of the Lost* in 1929 that Greely's "trivial" quarrel with Kislingbury over his late rising led to "consequences, which to say the least, seem disproportionate to the issue involved."[16]

Private Maurice Connell, also a witness to the Kislingbury affair and who would later have his own axe to grind with Greely, echoed that sentiment. After his missed rendezvous with the *Proteus*, according to Connell, Kislingbury was ignored by Greely "both as an officer and a man, and treated unjustly." Connell believed that both the officers and the men took Kislingbury's side, and this "dictatorial course" on the part of Greely was the start of the many "quarrels, jealousies and petty dissensions" that would plague the expedition. Connell remarked that Greely's character failed to comprehend that in a venture that undermines the soul through months of loneliness, solitude, and intense cold and darkness, "the idea of companionship should be an ever-moving factor in [the commander's] daily actions and good fellowship the chief desire."[17]

The abrupt change in Kislingbury's attitude since mid-August was completely inconsistent with his dutiful service on the plains. Kislingbury's lethargic behavior and squabbling over seemingly minor matters may have been symptoms of a mental burden that plagued him, that of his young children left behind. The imminent departure of the *Proteus,* and with it, the stark reality of a forced separation from family for possibly two years, left him with one last opportunity to reconsider.

Greely himself found that the protracted departure of the *Proteus*, with its last-chance for withdrawal, was a source of mental anguish over his own loved ones. Greely confided to his diary on August 27, the day after *Proteus* had departed, that its absence "destroys my intense desire to return to my wife and children." It is possible that Kislingbury might have left the expedition under any circumstances, given the weight on his mind. Curiously, the timing of his final "falling out" with Greely did in fact coincide with the final departure of the *Proteus*. Nonetheless, Greely's recalcitrance in light of Kislingbury's troubled state of mind seems to have played an important, if not deciding, factor in that decision.[18]

≈≈≈≈≈

Greely did not waste time over the matter. During the remaining waning hours of autumn daylight, he used the time to establish caches for the spring sledge journeys and to scout for the best potential routes to the north. Although the relationship between Pavy and Greely had been strained from the start, Greely recognized that Pavy's practical experience in arctic travel, coupled with a driving ambition, made him a valuable member of an expedition comprised

Fort Conger

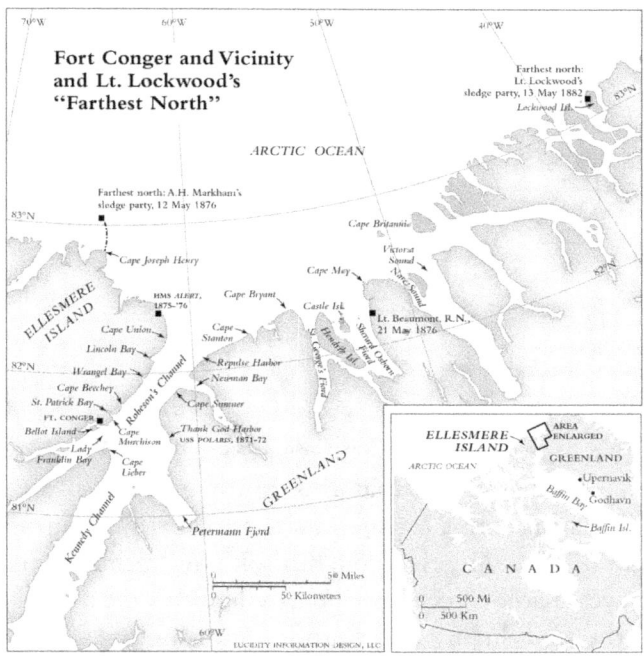

of inexperienced men in northern travel and survival. On August 29, Dr. Pavy, accompanied by expedition photographer Sergeant Rice (who had previously sailed with the *Gulnare* expedition), undertook a sledge journey towards Cape Joseph Henry along the northern tip of Ellesmere Island. Their objective was to scout for a potential route to the north for subsequent sledge journeys and to search for signs of the lost *Jeannette* Expedition. Pavy's medical skills were put to the test when Rice fell ill with acute rheumatism. Pavy ably tended to his ailing companion, carrying his load for miles, and ultimately pushing on solo to obtain help.

Pavy's interest in Cape Joseph Henry is not surprising, as he undoubtedly knew that this location had been the launching point for the record high northern latitude, the so-called "Farthest North," achieved on May 12, 1876 by Lieutenant A. H. Markham of the British Arctic Expedition of 1875-76. As for the *Jeannette,* far from Fort Conger, the vessel had sunk off the Siberian coast three months before, and its commander, George Washington De Long, was making a desperate retreat south with his party.

Two follow-up trips to the vicinity of Cape Joseph Henry

Octave Pavy and Jens Edwards skinning a seal.

confirmed Pavy's opinion that this route was the most favorable approach for an attempt on the "Farthest North." Consumed with the thought of achieving that goal himself, the "monomaniacal" Pavy (in Clay's eyes) had even conceived of villainous means to achieve it. While on the trail during one of those scouting trips, Pavy solicited Private William Whistler to join him in an unauthorized attempt on the "Farthest North" to be made by stealing the expedition's best dog teams. Those dogs had been assigned to Lieutenant Lockwood who had been granted the privilege of leading that all-important attempt after Kislingbury's withdrawal. When Whistler declined to participate in Pavy's mad scheme, Pavy became openly abusive toward him, so much so that Whistler could only settle the recalcitrant Pavy by threatening him with his revolver.[19]

Other excursions included a five-mile trek to the coal seam at Water-Course Bay, where bituminous coal was mined and transported back to the outpost, and a multi-day hike with backpacks led by Sergeant Brainard and two others to the interior and the United States Range, named by Dr. Isaac Israel Hayes in 1861. Interestingly, a group led by a dog-sled driven by Jens Edward, accompanied by Greely and two others, including the now-outcast Lieutenant Kislingbury, ventured to the Bellows, a valley some fifteen miles from Fort Conger, to scout for an inland route to the west coast of the island. With the benefit of Kislingbury's rifle, some ten muskoxen were bagged.

The Greely Expedition had discovered that Ellesmere Island was a haven for the shaggy-haired beasts, which were easy kills when they assumed their defensive huddle. Greely and his men secured twenty-four animals and hundreds of birds that fall, enough to provide each man with about one pound of meat daily through the winter. All told, the expedition is estimated to have killed some one hundred muskoxen during its two-year stay at Fort Conger. Recognizing their vulnerability, Greely made the prescient observation that he feared for the "indiscriminate slaughter" of these animals. His comments foreshadowed the aggressive, large-scale hunting tally of Robert Peary in support of his several expeditions in quest of the North Pole from Ellesmere Island at the turn of the century (more than six hundred muskoxen by one count). The slaughter by Peary's team, and by subsequent explorers such as Donald MacMillian, had a major impact on the reduction of the size of muskoxen herds on the island.[20]

By October 14 the sun had fallen below the horizon, not to return until February 28, a full 137 days later. But even on the darkest of winter days the slightest glimmer of twilight could be briefly discerned on the horizon, and on clear evenings the distant starlight threw off a heavenly glow. For two months during the near total darkness of winter, according to Greely, the time on a watch held close to the face could not be read. Like many newcomers to the polar night, these arctic visitors were awed by the changing mix of colors in the sky through auroral displays, running across the full spectrum. By November outside temperatures reached a numbing 25°F degrees below zero, though the temperature in Fort Conger maintained a mild 55°F to 60°F degrees and at times a balmy 75°F degrees by virtue of coal burning stoves.

Amidst the shortening daylight, on November 1 a final sledge party led by Lieutenant Lockwood, Sergeant Brainard and six others set off for a trip across Robeson Channel to the Greenland coast with a one-thousand-pound sledge to establish a supply base for a spring journey. The party was also tasked with a side trip to Thank God Harbor, the winter quarters of Charles Francis Hall in 1871-72. After a trying effort across nearly insurmountable hummocks they established a depot at Cape Beechey on the Ellesmere Island coast, but failed to cross the partially frozen channel, returning on November 8.

For his part, despite the fallout between the two, Greely permitted Kislingbury's hunting for game and the occasional short sledge journey. Kislingbury did accompany Pavy to establish a cache at Pavy's farthest north at Cape Wrangel Bay in support of Lockwood's party, but remained steadfast from rejoining the expedition. Not surprisingly, Kislingbury was evidently troubled by his purgatory. When important sledge parties returned, Kislingbury was among the first to greet the participants, with a "wistful" look in his eye according to Brainard. The lieutenant left the confines of the station daily, often with Pavy or Rice, and at times on solitary sojourns with just his trusty rifle for safety on the lookout for the occasional game. Alone in the tomb-like silence of the arctic night, he must have pondered the fate of his four young sons and felt a deep longing for home. For amusement, he adopted a pet owl, and later four muskoxen calves, all of which became favorites of the men.

Chapter Twelve

The Farthest North

AS COMMANDER, GREELY UNDERSTOOD that idleness during the monotony of the unceasing arctic winter could be detrimental to the morale of the unaccustomed men. To combat this, he set about a complete plan of scientific and recreational activities. Despite Greely's expressed desire to achieve geographical success, the expedition steadfastly maintained its focus as a participant in the International Polar Year. The lion's share of the responsibility for the scientific observations rested with Sergeant Edward Israel, a highly recommended recent graduate of the University of Michigan and the youngest member of the expedition. Israel had charge of all astronomical, pendulum, meteorological and magnetic observations. Sergeants Gardiner, Jewell and Ralston assisted Israel with the magnetic and tidal observations.

An "observatory" was located two hundred yards from the main building, and with the help of members of the expedition, observations were taken continuously under trying conditions. The magnetometer alone required ten readings per hour, and two readings every five minutes on "term-days," the first and fifteenth of every month. The total number of magnetic, meteorological and tidal observations often exceeded five hundred per day, testifying to the enormity of the effort involved. Curiously, the most serious accident during the first year of the expedition occurred not on treacherous ice fields, but rather during the recording of tidal observations. On November 29, Sergeant Hampden Gardiner lost his step on the icy embankment leading to the tidal gauge, badly fracturing his left leg in a nasty fall. In agony, he managed to crawl his way back to Fort Conger. Though laid up for several months, the bone healed well under Pavy's supervision and he fully recovered.

Dancing Chief

As winter settled in and outdoor activities stalled, more leisurely activities were introduced by Greely to break the monotony, including a tri-weekly education class led by Greely, with assistance from Lockwood. Even the dour Pavy taught a French language class and lectured on African travels. Sunday evenings featured singing of vintage songs and hymns by those so inclined. Surprisingly, Kislingbury, with his fine voice, found the amusement an uplifting diversion, and he was often accompanied Gardiner, Ellis and Schneider.[1]

One novel production involved the short-lived newspaper, *The Arctic Moon*, under Lieutenant Lockwood's editorial hand. Shipboard publications, typically handwritten or typeset, that sought serious and humorous contributions by members were common activities to while away the unending winter night. Unlike its predecessors, *The Arctic Moon* was printed by means of hectograph or so-called "jellygraph," an early form of duplication using a gelatin base that produced "carbon" copies available to everyone. School children of the 1960s would remember its successor, the odiferous "mimeograph" that used a similar roller method.

Theatrical entertainments were also a mainstay of polar exploring parties. However, the Greely Expedition delivered one of the more unique performances, a product of plains experience; nine of the party participated in an Indian war dance. According to Greely, "most of the actors had served in the far West, and some had spent some months continuously in Indian camps, and so were thoroughly familiar with the parts they portrayed."[2]

Thanksgiving was spent in games, foot and snowshoe races, a sledge race between the Greenlanders, Jens and Frederik, and a rifle shooting contest. Heavy bets were wagered using "Durham" and "Lone Jack" tobacco as currency. Rounding out the festivities, all sat down to a sumptuous meal and an extra ration of rum.

Christmas was celebrated in an even more festive manner. Preparations began days in advance, with banners and flag decorations festooning the walls, and a sumptuous multi-course dinner, including a preserved plum pudding of dubious freshness supplied by Mrs. Greely. Gifts and letters from home were surely uplifting but left them longing for loved ones and places far away.

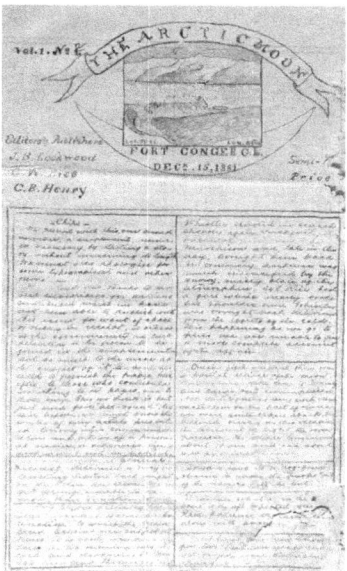

December 15, 1881 Issue of *The Arctic Moon*.

Greely commented that "a number of men, who had lived lives marked with neglect and indifference on the part of the world, were touched even to tears, although they strove man-like to conceal them." For Kislingbury, the Christmas holiday held a special meaning, as he celebrated his thirty-sixth birthday. In the absence of his cherished sons to share both holiday and birthday, the affair no doubt left him in a melancholy mood. After the reading of Christmas psalms by Greely, Kislingbury led a somber hymn and the doxology that much affected the men.[3]

Despite the brief respite for the holidays, the cold, dark, seemingly unending winter left the camp and its residents in a deep malaise. In contrast to the short hours of daylight they were accustomed to on the northern plains in winter, Greely noted that "long-continued darkness [of the Arctic winter] exercised a depressing influence on most of the party." Some men mumbled that they had not signed up for arduous sledge journeys to meet the commander's insatiable plans for geographic triumphs. Adding to the general dispirited state, their countenances took on a pale yellow pallor. Many irritable men fell to carping over even the slightest perceived affront. Even a contested game of checkers could provoke a heated argument. The oppressive gloom of the arctic winter did little to improve Kislingbury's state of mind, and may have exacerbated his mental anguish. Adding to the emotional discomfort, the outdoor temperature fell below a frigid -50°F, freezing the mercury in thermometers.[4]

On December 13, Jens was apparently so mentally affected that he simply wandered off ill-prepared into the night. Rescue parties were hastily arranged, and searched by lantern in directions north and south. In the midst of a snow squall, the searchers managed to fall upon his tracks and overtake the roaming Greenlander. Reluctantly, he returned to the camp unharmed, but Rice suffered a disjointed shoulder after a fall during the escapade and Whistler was temporarily delirious from exposure. When pressed for a reason for his sudden departure in such a fearful state of mind, the Greenlander confessed only that he wanted to make for his home.

The year 1882 opened with the "Great Storm," a violent gale marked by exceedingly high winds and windswept snow which flattened the dog shelter and carpenter's station, and also blew away the anemometers. Reaching the instrument shelter was impossible in the blinding whiteout until guide ropes were laid. Within Fort Conger, though, a tempest of another kind was brewing. Greely was again mightily disappointed in the temperament of his physician, Dr. Octave Pavy, who he believed was the root cause of much of the expedition's internal strife. Greely confided in a homebound letter to his wife that "I am satisfied that he [Pavy] has deceived me in many things and that he is an errant mischief-maker. He has I understand been sowing seeds of dissension and discontent among the men, to no avail however." Greely's informant was Lieutenant Lockwood, who attentively listened, observed and privately reported his intelligence to Greely. Greely's opinion largely rings true, though there had been mild grumbling among the men during the winter who had seen enough of the Arctic and simply wished to avoid a second year.[5]

Lieutenant Kislingbury found a kindred spirit in Pavy, and a shared disdain for their commanding officer. Greely believed that the nefarious Pavy held a powerful influence over the demoralized Kislingbury, confiding in his diary that "I think that Dr. P[avy] has done much to put Lt. K[islingbury] in his present unenviable frame of mind." He further believed that Pavy and Kislingbury were held together by a common bond to frustrate and ultimately break down their commander. Greely's comments echo such personal animosity toward Kislingbury that Greely's own judgment appears anything but objective. Far from attempting a reconciliation, over time his opinions became progressively more severe: "I know that he [Kislingbury] has done everything he can do to destroy Lockwood's chances and work and is eaten up with jealously." Greely claimed that he "despises the man [Kislingbury] and his actions," as well as his "small petty character." Through the long, dark winter, the resentment between the commander and the doctor also continued to fester, but Pavy nonetheless continued to demonstrate that he was an effective physician. He treated a number of maladies, including the most severe, the broken leg of Sergeant Gardiner. Even Greely could admit that as for Pavy's professional medical abilities he found Pavy skilled, for which he gave him due credit.[6]

Kislingbury's unattached position created its own problems for Greely. By Greely's self-admission, Kislingbury was "at his own liberty" and not bound by Greely's command. Nonetheless, Greely was irked by what he perceived as small acts of intentional disobedience by the lieutenant, such as ignoring roll call and sitting down for meals ten to fifteen minutes late. On January 21, 1882, Greely went so far as to "take official notice" in writing of Kislingbury's failure to rise for breakfast by 7:30 a.m. in accordance with expedition regulations. In response, Kislingbury pointedly reminded Greely that he was not enrolled in the expedition, a fact that neither Greely nor Kislingbury cared to rectify. Kislingbury must have looked on with some irony that at the breakfast time each day, only Greely arrived on time. Both Pavy and Lockwood were consistently late. Rather than meting out harsh discipline, excuses were administered. Greely could justify Lockwood's tardiness because he lay in his bed for hours every night before he could get to sleep.

According to Greely, Kislingbury's habit of painstakingly grooming his beard at least six times a day, perhaps done to irritate Greely or perhaps simply a case of self-absorption, particularly grated on the commander. Though Greely believed he had gone

Dancing Chief

out of his way to make Kislingbury feel accepted, he recorded that he found the lieutenant "behaving like a spoiled schoolboy." Within the confines of Fort Conger, Kislingbury barely managed to speak to Lockwood. Long disregarding his rank, Kislingbury was content to simply play cards with the enlisted men. Much to Greely's continued consternation, as he put it, Kislingbury treated the enlisted men "as equals in every way, putting himself exactly on their footing." When those games included poker and stakes for money, Greely stepped in and stopped it. Curiously, on the other hand, Pavy recorded that Greely had played checkers with Julius Frederick.[7]

※※※※※

By mid-February 1882, a glimmer of light on the horizon brought the preparations for the exploring parties and a slight uplifting of spirits. Despite Pavy's insistence on the Ellesmere Island approach to the north, Greely maintained focus on the Greenland coast, an approach for a "Farthest North" that offered the benefit of more extended travel by land rather than upon the vagaries of the drifting ice above Cape Joseph Henry. Greely's original intention was to rely almost completely on dog-driven sledges, limiting man-hauling to short duration trips. However, due to disease ravaging the dogs over the winter, the twenty-seven workhorses procured in Greenland were reduced to a mere fifteen serviceable canines by the spring of 1882.

A first reconnaissance party comprised of Brainard, Lockwood and Frederik Christiansen, along with one dog team, followed the previous track to initially examine the ice east of Cape Beechey. A second party, with the same three men and Jewell, was to cross to the Greenland coast and reach Thank God Harbor. There they would establish a depot and assess the feasibility of Greely's plan for a northern route following the Greenland shore. The travelers departed on a positive note with the formerly absent sun making its first but fleeting appearance above the snow-clad mountains of Greenland. A few malcontents could still carp in spite of the seasonal improvement. Ellis grumbled that he "did not care a damn if he never saw the sun."[8]

The Farthest North

Thank God Harbor was reached in good time on March 3. The site lay in the midst of a sweeping plain fully exposed to the elements, set against a backdrop of low-lying craggy mountains. The abandoned ruins of the *Polaris* observatory and Hall's unadorned grave made for a forlorn setting. The nearby graves of Able Seamen James J. Hand and Charles W. Paul, members of the British Arctic Expedition of 1875-76, who had succumbed to scurvy on their own Greenland excursion, left them in low spirits.

A cold whistling breeze added physical discomfort to the mix. In a doleful frame of mind, Brainard wrote that "surveying the scene, one scarcely wonders that Hall died. I think the gloom would drive me to suicide in a week." Brushing aside their melancholy frame of mind, Brainard's party did locate the cache left by Lieutenant Lewis Anthony Beaumont during the British Arctic Expedition, finding some serviceable food and supplies, as well as some welcome blankets.[9]

Travelling north of Thank God Harbor by retracing Hall's route, they stopped just shy of Cape Sumner by way of Newman Bay, concluding that a serviceable trail could be waged to the north. The one-hundred-thirty-mile trip was managed under severe weather, averaging -40°F degrees, but the use of snow huts added comfort and safety. At their farthest outbound point they were momentarily in a serious predicament as their damp matches failed to light the wick of the alcohol lamp. Facing the daunting prospect of a return trip without the benefit of water from melted snow, a last-ditch attempt succeeded in generating a flame on a cherished love letter that Jewell had carried close to his heart.

Greely was extremely pleased with the success of the venture. He believed it had fully demonstrated that his thorough planning and outfitting, including proper sledges, gear, rations and dogs, had been successful. Matters of organization still proved one of Greely's stronger traits. Always measuring his achievements against those of Hall and the British, Greely was pleased that Lockwood had travelled a route from Thank God Harbor to Cape Sumner in three days, at times held up by storms, that took Hall six days.

Despite their perpetual infighting, Greely recognized that Pavy was an accomplished arctic traveler, and an enthusiastic volunteer for sledge work. At times, they could put aside their headstrong personalities to work together. To aid Lockwood's northern sledge party, Greely permitted Pavy to lead a party to establish a depot on the Greenland shore. The five-day trip by Pavy with Linn and Jens, under difficult conditions, succeeded in establishing a cache below Cape Sumner. Greely would even commend his physician, writing that the trip "reflected credit on Dr. Pavy's energy and determination."[10]

When Pavy insisted, on the basis of his previous journeys, that a northern route could still be advanced from Cape Joseph Henry, Greely permitted him to test his theory, even offering his own dog team in support. Octave Pavy was a dreamer on a quixotic pursuit. The tantalizing glimpse of the fabled open polar sea, thought to have been observed by the physician-explorers Elisha Kent Kane and Isaac Israel Hayes and so eloquently portrayed in their writings, had left a marked impression on the young Pavy, and in his own words, "profoundly moved my imagination." At best, those previous explorers had viewed a regional polynya, an area of open water surrounded by sea ice, not a vast open ocean to the Pole. On March 19, 1882, Pavy, Jens Edwards and Sergeant George Rice left Fort Conger with two sledges and nine dogs. By March 28 they had reached only as far as Cape Union, where they were stymied by ice along the Ellesmere Island coast.[11]

From a latitude north of where William Morton, on the expedition of Elisha Kent Kane, claimed to have seen an open polar sea in June 1854, Pavy viewed the upper reaches of Nares Strait along the Greenland coast. However, the hoped-for-view of the expanse of water so visible to his predecessors was not what now faced Pavy:

> To the south the faint outline of Cape Constitution evoked reminiscences of "The good Christian knight, Elijha [sic] Kent Kane," and set my mind pondering over the now old and nearly forgotten fable of an *Open Polar Sea*. I was standing on the extreme point reached by the poetical vision of Hayes, at the threshold of a once great mystery, that in younger days had so profoundly moved my imagination. Instead of a promised sea I could view nothing but the stern and cold reality of an impenetrable ice pack.[12]

Once a firm believer in the open polar sea, Pavy now just as firmly denied its existence. No doubt, he would have declared the title of Albert Hasting Markham's book, *The Great Frozen Sea,* more appropriate for the ice-obstructed region than *The Open Polar Sea* adopted by Dr. Hayes for his work. After nearly being set adrift in the broken ice, Pavy's party retreated to Cape Joseph Henry and scrambled back to the safety of land. Although the trip did not accomplish its main objective, Pavy had completed a six-week sledge journey of some three hundred miles by dog-driven sledge across some of the most difficult conditions in the Arctic. However, the affair only confirmed Greely's opinion that striking along the northern coast of Greenland offered a better avenue for achieving a "Farthest North." With evident satisfaction and contradicting his own previous opinion, Greely gloated to Henrietta that "Dr. Pavy's failure was always expected. He has always failed, indeed he appears to be quite a Jonah."[13]

On April 3, Greely's highly anticipated attempt on the "Farthest North" commenced. Petty grievances and frustrations were momentarily forgotten amid an uplifting sendoff of pistol shots, flag waving and cheers. Greely could not contain his overwhelming desire for geographical success in order to take what he believed would be his proper place among the most prominent of polar explorers. Possessed of even a modicum of ambition even at this date, Kislingbury must have looked on with disappointment, and perhaps a tinge of jealously, as Greely placed complete command of the enterprise under Lieutenant James Lockwood, Kislingbury's replacement. Lockwood had proven his obedience to orders during the previous eight months. Kislingbury's contribution to the expedition would be to walk ahead of the exploring party and set up camp at the end on the first travel day, a modest though fully appreciated gesture after a hard day on the trail.

Lockwood mustered as many able hands as possible for the attempt. Lockwood and Jewell (who was later swapped for Brainard) would travel by light sled and eight dogs driven by Christiansen. Support parties would manage the heavy lifting; four Hudson Bay sledges would man-haul supplies and food as far as possible. As many as ten men worked the sledges, with a few sent back over time due to illness or sheer exhaustion. Before their departure, three depots had been established on the route, the furthest situated in the middle of frozen Robeson Channel. Warm protective clothing was a mixed bag of wool and skins that would never fully serve the purpose. Most men wore double layers of woolen underclothing and socks, and some a light duck suit outer garment to prevent the wool from absorbing moisture. A handful wore only an outer garment of skins. Footgear was moccasins or canvas boots.

The initial days of travel were done at night to gain the warmth of the sun's rays while resting. From the start, the going was by no means a cakewalk. The top-heavy sledges overturned frequently in the hummocks and uneven ice as they crossed the sound, forcing the time-consuming and frustrating lashing and relashing of the burdensome loads and strenuous use of the ice axe. Harnessing the more mobile dog-sled, Lockwood would circle back to help reduce the loads.

At one point, a raging storm confined them to their camp for several days. The intelligent use of snow-banks and snow huts for shelter offered more comfortable respite than canvas tents, but raised the temperature to a balmy ten degrees, leaving them uncomfortable in water-soaked sleeping bags. Lockwood shared a sleeping bag with Frederik Christiansen but found little sleep, as the Greenlander "groan[ed] like a piece of machinery." In the midst of the hardships, Brainard, more than any other expeditioner, could find curious distractions from their harsh circumstances, such as finding in a gully an American penny with a date of 1858 (apparently from Hall's expedition), and watching the sun momentarily dip below the horizon, only to immediately rise upward again (a "queer thing for the sun to do," he noted).[14]

At *Polaris* Boat Camp, reached on April 10, one damaged Hudson Bay sledge was dismantled. Fully proving their worth, the eight hardy dogs ferried Lockwood and Frederik on a remarkable journey to Fort Conger and back, one hundred miles in fifty-four hours, for additional runners and supplies. The remaining heavier sledges needed to be man-hauled through deep snow in places and even across bare stretches of rubble, gravel and sand, often requiring the men to team-up and double back to assist pulling each sledge. Nerves were more than frayed, and words of discouragement were not uncommon. Brainard mused that "the Anti-Swearing Society was the beneficiary of this day's march, rolling up a large total of fines."[15]

On April 26, after dropping the heaviest sledge, they reached the cache established on the north Greenland coast by Lieutenant L. A. Beaumont of the British Arctic Expedition 1875-76 at Stanton Gorge (found to contain forty "barely eatable" rations and a can of rum marked "Bloodhound," the former name of HMS *Discovery*). A cairn was built and a record placed within. Beaumont's sledge party had left HMS *Discovery* at Lady Franklin Bay on April 6, 1876, crossed Robeson Channel and charted several hundred miles along the northwestern Greenland coast before turning back on May 22, 1876. On the return, less fortunate than Lockwood's party, Beaumont's party of twenty-five suffered from scurvy, with two men dying (Hand and Paul).

On April 29, Lockwood's support party and sledges were sent back while Lockwood, Brainard and Christiansen, with the light dog sled carrying some 750 pounds (25 days provisions), would make a dash "north into the unknown." However, not willing to pull the now heavily-laden sled when it sank in the snow, the dogs simply stopped in their tracks, forcing half of the supplies to be offloaded and recovered on a back trip by Brainard and Frederik. Brainard suffered from snow-blindness, and stumbled about for a day or two. Despite their travelling difficulties, on May 3, a crack in the ice near Cape May offered the opportunity to obtain a sea-depth measure. With cold hands, they sank a six-pound lead weight 820 feet without striking bottom, and in the process lost a valuable length of seal-thong attached to the end of the sounding rope. Shuttling continued by two half loads. But not every minute was an exertion. At one stop, while Brainard awaited the return of Lockwood and Frederik, he whiled away the time reading the humorous British periodical *Puck*.

On May 5, with a high degree of pride, Lockwood boasted that they had reached "land before untrodden by man, and thenceforth everything was new." At Cape Britannia, Brainard and Lockwood climbed the 3000-foot summit to view an imposing scene, a northeast continuation of the coast for twenty-five miles, marked by projecting headland after headland, all separated by deep fiords. Like Pavy, they found that the "Open Polar Sea" was a myth, in reality a broken field of "paleocrystic" (multiyear) ice that extended as far as the horizon. By May 12, they had covered some ninety miles from Cape Britannia in six marches, hugging the coastline while avoiding tidal cracks and leads. Low on rations and with the dogs dropping in their traces, they reached their "Farthest North," on May 13, at Latitude 83°23.8'N., 40°46'W., the highest north ever achieved, exceeding the British Arctic Expedition by a mere four miles.[16]

The accomplishment marked the highlight of the Greely Expedition's geographical achievements. About their feat, in his field notebook, Brainard recorded that "we have reached a higher latitude than ever before reached by mortal man, and on a land farther north than was supposed by many to exist. We unfurled the Stars and Stripes to the exhilarating northern breezes with an exultation impossible to describe." With a touch of humor, Brainard carved the words "St 1860 x", i.e., short for "started trade in 1860 with ten dollars," the advertisement for "Drake's Plantation Bitters," a predecessor to the humorous "Burma Shave" advertisements of another era. The celebration was all too brief, as hunger pangs and a shortage of food compelled a quick retreat homeward bound.[17]

Greely certainly relished the accomplishment, writing in *Three Years of Arctic Service* in a tone that sounds more of jealous boasting of beating the British:

> For three centuries England had held the honors of the farthest north.... Now Lockwood, profiting by the labors and experiences of his "kin across the sea," surpassed their efforts of three centuries by land and ocean. And with Lockwood's name should be associated that of his inseparable sledge-companion, Brainard, without whose aid and restless energy, as Lockwood said, the work could not have been accomplished.[18]

It was strong praise, but it ignored the contributions of Greenlander Frederik Christiansen, the third member of this now

The Farthest North

"Farthest North," painting by Albert Operti.

celebrated party. His efforts, particularly in handling the dogs, were certainly as valuable as those of Lockwood and Brainard. Poor Frederik, even in the "great" painting "Farthest North," by the artist Albert Operti (painted at life-scale, 8 feet high by 12 feet long), which captures Lieutenant Lockwood and Sergeant Brainard verifying their noteworthy location, the Greenlander is given a less-than glamorous role, standing in the rear of the picture tending the dogs.

The achievement of the "Farthest North" did not put an end to Greely's zest for geographic discovery. Also at the top of Greely's to-do-list was the exploration of the inland region of Ellesmere Island, the tenth largest island in the world. A vast unexplored interior remained hidden behind rugged mountain ranges capped by a sprawling ice sheet. Though Greely would not admit as much in his official reports, both Brainard and Pavy claimed that the islands deeply indented bays and fiords had enticed Greely with the thought that they might connect with a continuous water route to the western ocean. Evidently, the lure of a fabled Northwest Passage could capture the imagination as late as the turn of the century. Not surprisingly, that passage failed to materialize, but during several excursions Greely's parties discovered and explored Lake Hazen (the largest freshwater lake above the Arctic Circle) and its environs, discovering an arctic oasis teeming with abundant wildlife and evidence of Thule culture.

Lieutenant Lockwood, Sergeant Brainard, and dog-driver Frederik Christiansen return to Fort Conger June 1, 1882.

Now back at Fort Conger, Greely's relationship with Pavy continued to deteriorate, even after the mutual agreement to renew Pavy's one-year contract, which had expired on July 20, 1882. There was no end to Greely's faultfinding with Pavy, but some of those complaints were justified. The responsibility for cataloguing the expedition's extensive natural history collection was transferred to Lockwood after Pavy simply lost interest in it, continuing his lack of detail first evident during his *Gulnare* experience. Pavy even became delinquent in reporting on the medical condition of the men. Greely was deeply frustrated, but believed that Pavy's services were so "indispensable" that he was constrained from imposing punishment.

Greely aptly summarized his poor opinion of Pavy's incorrigible character in his *Three Years of Arctic Service,* published in 1886: Pavy's "previous Bohemian life made any restraint irksome and subordination to military authority particularly obnoxious." Sergeant Brainard held both men partly to blame for their falling out, a situation perhaps equally true in the case of Greely vs. Kislingbury. Brainard's assessment of the two competing personalities (Pavy and Greely) was likely the more accurate when he stated that "between the cosmopolitan bohemian and the New England puritan, the difference in temperaments had been too great." Interestingly, notwithstanding Greely's opinion, both Pavy and Kislingbury could command the respect of many of the men. By way of but one example, Private Henry spoke for a number of them when he wrote that "kind Kis[lingbury] and his extensive experience made his society equally agreeable and instructive. All enjoy his company and are strongly attached to him."[19]

Matters between Kislingbury and Greely fared no better as the two maintained their standoff. On June 22, Kislingbury requested permission to retain the heads of two muskoxen he had taken. Greely stubbornly declined, advising the lieutenant that the U.S. government had sent them "at great expense" and that he "could exercise no discretion in the matter." Only General Hazen could authorize such a request. Kislingbury pointedly reminded Greely that he did not belong to the expedition, to which Greely replied that he "did not consider him [Kislingbury] as belonging to the expedition, but that he could do as he pleased but he would have to deal with the chief signal officer, under whom he certainly was serving." Their awkward relationship continued. Greely permitted Kislingbury to lead a party of some seven men to retrieve supplies at St. Patrick Bay, and to continue his hunting and scouting trips, at times alone, for one to three hours, for days in succession.[20]

Despite the falling out, through the end of summer of 1882, Greely could view the expedition as successful. They had weathered a first winter in fine physical shape, without suffering the effects of scurvy that plagued the British Arctic Expedition of 1875-76 in the same locale (with credit due to Pavy for his emphasis on fresh meat). Scientific readings, in accordance with the First International Polar Year, had been studiously collected. The expedition's principle geographical accomplishment, the "Farthest North," would stand until 1896, when Fridjtof Nansen and Hjalmar Johansen achieved a higher north latitude by sledge after journeying from the expedition ship *Fram*. Now all the expedition needed was a welcome relief ship from home.

Chapter Thirteen

Season of Despair

AS SUMMER WANED, GREELY EXPEDITION members looked longingly for a break in the ice that would favor the return of the *Proteus*. Their hopes rose as their own steam launch *Lady Greely* made a fine run to Cape Cracroft, viewing an expanse of open water down Kennedy Channel with no visible ice. Fresh supplies for a second year would be welcomed, but in particular, news from the outside world was feverishly awaited. Initially optimistic based on their previous year's experience and their largely unobstructed arrival at Lady Franklin Bay, most men were wagering bets as to the date the ship would reenter the harbor, not seriously considering its failure to arrive at all. Letters had been written to absent loved ones and packages assembled to be sent home, such as photographs, scientific observations and natural history collections. Little did they know that some two hundred and fifty miles to the south the relief ship *Neptune* had become entangled and beset in the unpredictable ice of Smith Sound. After a harrowing week, it managed to extricate herself, but limped home without reaching Lady Franklin Bay. In the midst of its travails, a mere ten days of rations were deposited for Greely's men at Cape Sabine and at Littleton Island.

By mid-August of 1882, by which time the *Neptune* had escaped the death knell of the pack and surrendered its task, Greely's men were resigned to the fact that the long-awaited relief ship would not arrive this season. For Kislingbury, he faced the grim reality of an extension of his unwanted and unwelcome stay at Lady Franklin Bay through a second year. The absent relief ship must have been an almost unbearable disappointment.

An unanticipated overwintering in the far north, especially after having withstood one previously, could be a demoralizing affair. The all-to-familiar surroundings and faces, the unchanging routine, and the oft-repeated stories created a dull monotony and brooding discontentment among the men. Despite Greely's bid to quell "acrimonious" disagreements, petty grievances and complaints which had been suffered in silence under military discipline last year were echoing louder. Even attendance at education classes suffered, though scientific observations went on like clockwork. Compounding that disappointment was some disconcerting conduct. Calling to mind Greely's falling out with Kislingbury, Pavy sardonically noted that Lockwood had been absent at the start of breakfast for eight consecutive days. Pavy also had surmised that Cross had been stealing alcohol from his medical supplies. During one delirious binge, Cross raved insensibly about lassoing an iceberg, and spent the better part of two days sobering up.

Greely did little to foster contentment among the men. Several transgressions at the beginning of October, although minor in their gravity, sparked out-of-proportion disciplinary actions and raw feelings. While Sergeant Linn and two others had been on a walk to nearby Dutch Island they learned from a separate party that bear tracks had been spotted. Returning to the station for a gun, Linn again set off, only to be overtaken by a hunting party led by Lockwood. At Greely's order, Lockwood demanded that Linn turn over his gun to one of Lockwood's party. Returning to the station and incensed over the matter, Linn momentarily lost his temper with Greely. When Greely confirmed that he had ordered Linn to give up his gun, Linn angrily barked, "Well I don't think much of it." After Linn repeated the objection (calling it a "mean trick"), Greely bristled at his outburst, and ordered the poor fellow reduced in rank to a private, declaring that he would have him tried by court-martial after their return. Adding insult to injury, Greely mustered the full command to hear Greely read the order, prefacing his address with remarks "as to the gravity of such an offense," and characterizing the action as a "mutiny." Reflecting the views of most of the men, Rice found the punishment far too disproportionate, and Greely's mutiny characterization "a very strange and strained construction."[1]

The matter did not end there. More disconcerting was Greely's order that all the enlisted men should suffer punishment as a result of Linn's outburst. They were forbidden to travel more than 500 yards without Greely's permission, a demoralizing command that limited their ability to travel to Dutch Island, a retreat which provided quiet time for self-reflection outside the cramped and noisy quarters of the station. In a similar vein, Ellis was severely reprimanded by the commander for taking tobacco in return for cutting the men's hair. The balding Connell, a recipient of one such haircut, was advised by Greely that his close-cropped hair was inconsistent with a military command.

Not unexpectedly, Thanksgiving and Christmas passed off with little excitement in contrast to the previous year. Brainard noted that "the enthusiasm of the party for these occasions has diminished considerably and a celebration, no matter how we strive to make it, becomes nothing more than a mockery." Rather than a time for merrymaking, a glum Private Schneider found the holidays "gloomy." Greely only added to the somber mood by imposing other restrictions viewed as unnecessary by the men. They were not allowed to lie down during the day, a circumstance exacerbated by the shortage of chairs. Greely's address to his troops on Christmas Eve dampened, rather than lifted spirits. According to Rice, Greely "spoke of the possible retreat next year and with it, the possibility of death in its most horrible forms staring the party in its face, in which case, he said, he had no doubt we would all die like men and heroically."[2]

The depressing mood evidently had Greely on edge, who took personal offense at rather benign comments by Kislingbury. On the evening of January 12, Kislingbury complained to the cook that the soup was "very poor, but you cannot be blamed for it! You cannot make soup out of nothing!" Greely was strangely affronted by the remark, believing that as he (Greely) was the only one responsible for the cook, the comment was "a stricture on the commanding officer" that undermined the discipline of the enlisted men. Greely poured out his frustration in two full pages in his journal as to Kislingbury's comments, which he viewed as unbecoming an officer. By now, Greely believed that the attitude of the demoralized Kislingbury had taken a more spiteful turn. Both breakfast and dinner were intentionally taken late after milling about the table, with the cooks forced to tender separate meals. Poker playing with the enlisted men for money continued and Greely believed that Kislingbury took no effort or interest on behalf of the expedition. Greely attempted to defend, or more accurately to rationalize, his own record with Kislingbury, confiding to his diary that he has "always treated Lt. K[islingbury] with the utmost consideration and kindness, that I have given him <u>in all cases</u> preference over my officers, even feeling perhaps I have gone too far at times in my efforts to prevent his appearing as an abused man." Evidently, the thought of making amends and offering to return Kislingbury to duty was not one of those considerations.[3]

As the second winter passed, Dr. Octave Pavy was becoming more and more uneasy about their circumstances. After re-reading the history of the Franklin Expedition, he contemplated whether members of the Greely party were destined to share the same fate. On March 9, he felt compelled to set in writing his concerns to Greely. His letter urged Greely to consider making plans for a southward retreat and suggested that a scouting party (or the entire expedition) be dispatched to Littleton Island to establish a potential line of communication with the absent relief parties. He similarly "*earnestly* recommend[ed]" that early season sledging activities for discovery purposes should be dispensed with to avoid weakening the health or injuring the men in advance of what looked to be an expected retreat from Fort Conger.[4]

Pavy's opinions reflected, in part, a medical man's concern over the men's health and safety and thus fell fully within the scope of Pavy's appointed responsibilities. By this time however, Greely's disdain for Pavy so skewed his judgment that even sound and rationale recommendations were peremptorily dismissed without consideration or discussion. In words that in retrospect seem eerily prescient as well as heedless, Greely declared that "to practically abandon [the field work] and think only of personal safety, especially at a time when there seem possible discoveries which would be valued by the world and creditable to my country, would be difficult for me even under the most adverse circumstances, but now, under favorable circumstances, would appear dishonorable and unmanly."[5]

Anxious about the fate of the expedition and likely urged on by Pavy, one week after Pavy's rejection, Kislingbury approached his commander with a similar proposal. Like Pavy, Kislingbury proposed that the work to the north be abandoned, and in its place, a relief party establish a large depot or two far to the southward. Accordingly to Greely, Kislingbury "suggested sending a party to Littleton Island to leave notice or to remain there and have the vessel land a relief party on the west side of Smith Sound."

Not surprisingly, Kislingbury fared no better with the commander than Pavy. Greely nixed the idea, claiming that such a sledge party would suffer fatal consequences even under ordinary circumstances and a relief party "has no cause to land at Littleton Island." According to Greely, Frederick Kislingbury "very vehemently" opposed Greely's plan for business as usual-more field work. [6]

Unquestionably, Kislingbury pained for home, causing his temper to flare. Touching on Greely's dictatorial manner, the lieutenant snapped back at his commander, remarking that "the voice of one man should not weigh against twenty-four." Not only was Kislingbury fearful of their chances for survival, in a remarkably sagacious observation, he told Greely that he "was confident that the men were depressed over this foreshadowed fate." A hardheaded Greely had closed his mind to contrary opinions, declaring to Kislingbury that "I was only doing the duty in which I had been sent, that I could not abandon the work on a chance of a vessel not coming." To his diary, though, Greely also pondered their fate: "If no vessel comes, I consider our chances desperate. If none come, God help us." For a different reason Greely elected to abandon his own plan to lead an exploration of the interior of Ellesmere Island. He was fearful of leaving "the ill-affected men, like Pavy and Kislingbury, to depress the party." In light of future circumstances, it is understandable why Greely elected to omit these dissenting voices in his work, *Three Years of Arctic Service*.[7]

At Greely's direction and in spite of objections by Pavy in particular, a number of extended traveling parties were conducted without Greely. After laying caches for a northern trek, in late March, Lockwood and party completed a sixteen-day journey along the Greenland coast. They were abruptly stymied from exceeding last year's "Farthest North" by a stretch of open water at Black Horn Cliffs, some fifteen miles north of Repulse Harbor. Lockwood made a push for another northern trip, but Greely finally closed the door, not due to Pavy's and Kislingbury's objections, but due to lack of sufficient provisions and healthy dogs. For his part, on April 14, Kislingbury accompanied the ten-man party led by Sergeant Rice to retrieve the British ice-boat left at Thank God Harbor, an asset for any intended retreat.

By late April, with further attempts at a "Farthest North" now abandoned, several other journeys continued, including Lockwood's successful month-long survey of the interior of Ellesmere Island, reaching the western shore and a large inlet named Greely Fiord. Throughout the course of the various journeys, Greely went out of his way to defend the excellent physical condition of the men of the returning sledge parties, remarks no doubt intended to counter any claims by Pavy. That good health was made possible by virtue of a considerable quantity of game, especially muskoxen that were taken throughout the summer. The course of scientific observations continued. Kislingbury contributed his own scientific efforts, turning over to Greely an extensive collection of lichen, which Greely found to be "very complete and valuable."

Matters again came to a head in July 1883, when Pavy's annual contract was again about to expire. In disgust, Pavy refused to renew the arrangement, blaming his commander for a litany of perceived failures. However, true to his oath, Pavy continued his professional responsibilities as physician. Pavy had made a careful study of his arctic predecessors and his diary reflected accurate recommendations based on those earlier experiences. The well-read Pavy recognized the importance of a fresh food diet from the start. He emphatically jotted in his journal that he was "energetically in favor of the powers of fresh meat as the best antiscorbutic." Anxious to avoid the difficulties suffered by the British Arctic Expedition, which succumbed to an outbreak of scurvy after its first year, Pavy was fastidious about maintaining a diet of fresh meat. His diary reflects the close scrutiny he paid to early symptoms of scurvy, such as swelling of the gums, and the prompt treatment he meted out when faced with potential outbreaks.

When Greely ordered Pavy to turn over that diary in accordance with regulations, likely the last thing Pavy would want Greely to see, the doctor outright refused. Greely had him placed under arrest and subject to court-martial. Recognizing the absurdity of the situation, reminiscent of William Godfrey's "arrest" by Elisha Kent Kane during his arctic expedition of 1853-55, Greely relented and permitted Pavy freedom to wander within the camp. The erudite Pavy confided to his journal that "I have for nearly two years lived in a circle that even the genius of Dante could not have created for the most guilty souls of his inferno."[8]

As the battle between Greely and Pavy played out, a drama of another sort was taking place in the ice-strewn passage of Smith Sound. Unbeknownst to the men at Fort Conger, a series of ill-advised decisions, from the top brass down, led to the failure of the relief expedition of the summer of 1883. The steamer *Proteus* that had ferried Greely and his men without incident two years before had been requisitioned for the task. The USS *Yantic* would accompany as a support ship with some 7,000 rations, but was precluded from advancing above Littleton Island. Lieutenant Ernest A. Garlington, 7th Cavalry, a West Pointer and veteran of the Indian wars, accepted command of the expedition. Secretary Lincoln's suggestion that a navy officer command what was essentially a naval operation was quelled by Hazen, a stubborn departmental attitude that would play a role in the fiasco. In words that would prove prophetic, the brash Hazen even went so far as to write to Clay, a persistent advocate of a relief party, that "the military plans 'were sufficient against any calamity to Lieutenant's Greely's party.'"[9]

After a series of frustrating delays, *Proteus* finally bored its way to Cape Sabine on Pim Island (named after the British officer Lieutenant Bedford Pim), jutting out from the Ellesmere Island coast, where Garlington personally inspected the stores deposited by the British Arctic Expedition of 1875-76 and those deposited by *Neptune* the year before (1882). Remarkably, Garlington elected to leave no others, believing they were sufficient. In a rapid turn of events, in a mere four hours, the unrelenting ice had severely damaged *Proteus,* crushing the ship off Cape Sabine. Garlington, Pike and crew scrambled to Cape Sabine, where they deposited 500 rations (enough food for barely three weeks for Greely's men), then set about their own safety. The shipwrecked mariners crossed Smith Sound to Littleton Island, and made their way south. The *Yantic*, with its 7,000 rations, reached Littleton Island, but it too headed south leaving nothing for Greely's party.

Greely's orders compelled him to abandon Fort Conger no later than September 1, 1883, if the 1883 relief vessel failed to reach him by then. He was to lead his party south by boat along the Ellesmere Island coast until the relief vessel was met or Littleton Island was reached. By late August, that relief was a foregone hope, and Greely ordered a withdrawal. Optimistically, he hoped to reach Littleton Island and perhaps get as far as the Carey Islands, where at either location he believed that relief supplies would last them through the winter.

Spirits were not necessarily high, comfortable as they were at Fort Conger. Some men (perhaps nearly all) would have preferred to simply remain and await salvation rather than to work for their own deliverance. They all understood fully that Greely was gambling with their lives by blindly accepting that the relief ships had deposited sufficient stores. "We are basing our hopes on the assumption that a ship has succeeded in passing the barriers of Melville Bay. What will become of this party of poor wretches on reaching Littleton Island with nothing to subsist on," Brainard confided to his diary. A stickler for instructions, Greely would not hear of remaining at Fort Conger. For Kislingbury, the opportunity, dangerous as it was, lifted his heart, as he was now looking forward to reuniting with his "darling sons." Though the difficult trip would ultimately manage to tax his tenuous relationship with Greely close to the breaking point, Kislingbury could write at the start that "I must jot that there is lots of fun in all this tough sort of life and work."[10]

With the twenty-eight-foot steam launch *Lady Greely* towing three boats (and a one-man dinghy), the twenty-five men took their chances on the vagaries of the shifting ice of Kennedy Channel toward Smith Sound. A sense of uneasiness fell over the men as Greely arrived on deck resplendent in his dress uniform, sword and half-cocked revolver, attire more appropriate for a ceremonial parade than a desperate retreat. Despite the large flotilla, the party

Dancing Chief

Abandoning Launch *Lady Greely*, Sept. 10, 1883. Watercolor by Greely.

carried rations for only forty days, a severe deficiency in hindsight. With the addition of a cache stocked with some twenty days of supplies at Cape Hawks, this was considered by Greely more than adequate for the journey, assuming the relief parties had managed to cache the anticipated supplies. No one expected that the retreat would be an easy one.

Although good progress was made during the first few days reaching opposite Crozier Island, they were soon stalled by fogs and "an impenetrable pack," parallel to the location where the *Polaris* was beset. Although a confident and self-assured landsman at Fort Conger, tormented by the unpredictable drifting ice and swirling currents at sea, Greely was out of his element. As an uncertain leader, he was easily angered and hurled insults and abuse that only exacerbated the situation. With no real idea of how to navigate the situation, Greely's ignorance was quickly detected by the men, who lost confidence in his handling of the boats. Elison confided a comment in his diary, one likely shared by all: "I am afraid our commander will get us in a scrape yet through his ignorance." Cross remarked that "our two worthy's [Greely and Lockwood] stand on the forecastle and give contrary orders at the same time. Neither of them knows as much about working a boat as a boy around twelve years old around our docks." Kislingbury similarly

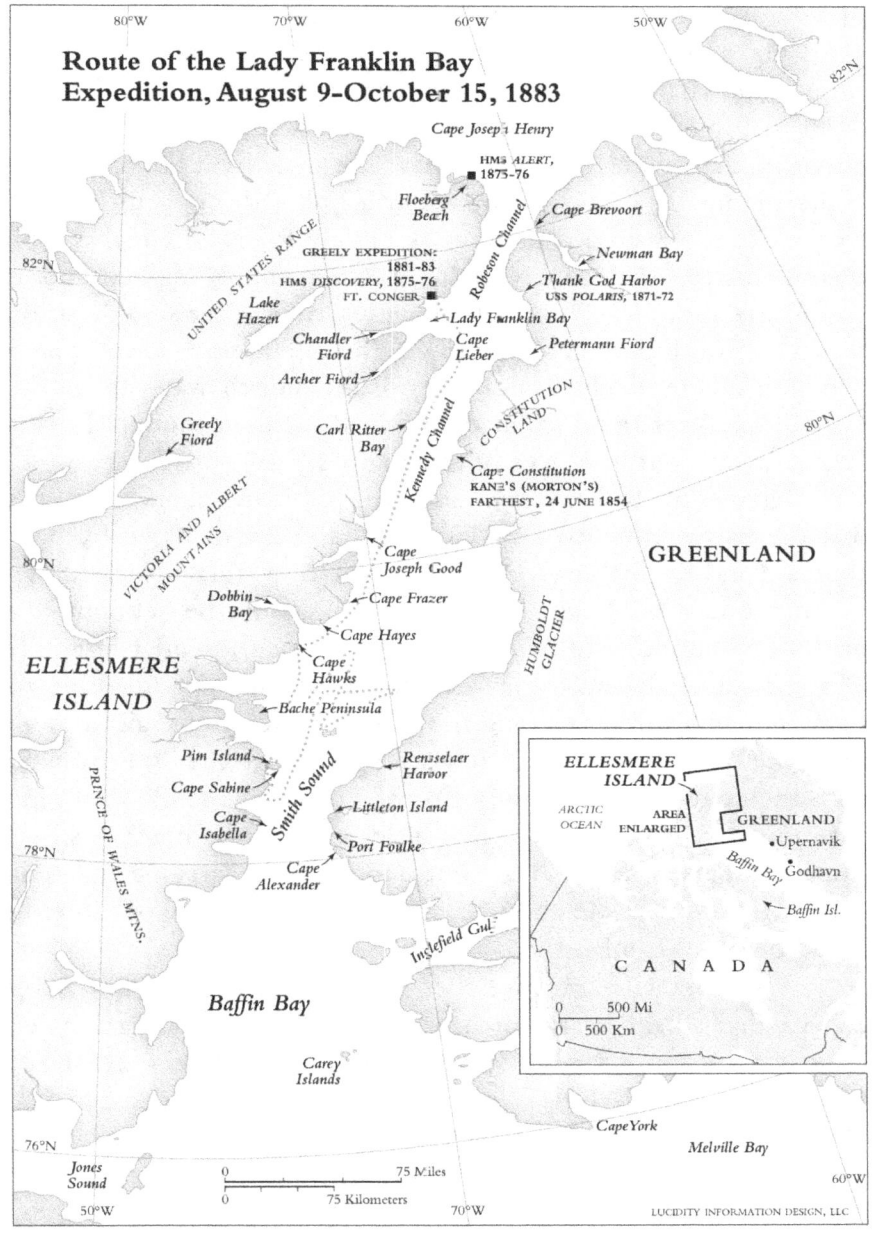

bemoaned Greely's hardheaded failure to acknowledge his complete lack of experience amidst the constantly shifting ice and suggested that the navigation be turned over to Rice.[11]

One particularly disturbing event occurred as Cross, while laboring down below on the boiler, failed to heed or to hear Greely's order to come forward. According to Cross, Greely snapped at him, declaring that "when he [Greely] gave me an order if I did not obey it the instant <u>he [Greely] would put a bullet through me</u>." Cross was not exaggerating, as the remark closely followed Greely's own account of the incident. Nonplused, Cross simply replied "do as you please about it." Though frequently drunk, Greely understood that there was little he could do with the intemperate Cross whose handling of the mechanical aspects of the launch was vital to the expedition. After the third alcohol fueled incident though, Private Frederick was put in charge of the engines.[12]

Delayed by bad weather and ice, some members suggested that the party return to Fort Conger (an opinion shared by both Brainard and Kislingbury), but that proposal was abruptly shutdown by an intractable Greely. Such an action would be "contrary to orders," he confided to his journal, ignoring an essential principle of arctic travel, the need for flexibility. Kislingbury's suggestion to the commander that they hug the shore or attempt to sail through the center of the sound was likewise dismissed by Greely. Frustrated with their progress along the coast of Ellesmere Island, on several occasions Greely floated the radical idea of abandoning the steam launch and hauling the boats onto an ice floe, carrying but ten-days of rations, and somehow drift towards the vicinity of Littleton Island off the Greenland coast.

As for Brainard, in a weather-beaten, pocket-sized notebook that carried all the marks of hard wear in the field, he scribbled his vehement objection. Brainard characterized the scheme simply as "disastrous," and "little short of madness," pointing to the fate of the *Polaris* crew and those of the German *Hansa* expedition, both of which had cast crewmembers about aimlessly on ice floes. Greely's potential plan evidently did not sit well at all with any other expedition members either, and quickly fomented further discontent. Brainard went on to record that on August 15, "Dr.

Season of Despair

P[avy] has insinuated (subrosa) his intention of declaring the C.O. insane should the attempt [to reach Littleton Island] be made & Lt. K[islingbury] will assume command if Lt. L[ockwood] will not assist him. Will place him [Lockwood] under arrest."[13]

In light of his own feelings on the matter, Brainard must have carefully considered Pavy's proposal. Any such realistic plan for a "mutiny" would have required Brainard to report such misconduct to his superior commissioned officer. A failure to report such an action would be punishable in the same manner as the act itself. However, at the time, he recorded no reaction to Pavy's "insinuation," and the matter passed without being carried out as Greely never issued the objectionable order. In the surviving copy of the fragmented notes from Pavy's diary, Pavy makes no mention of this plan. It is a surprising omission for a man who preferred to share his "closest thoughts and feelings" for the sake of posterity. Neither did Kislingbury nor Rice, both more fully later implicated in the story by Brainard.[14]

In Kennedy Channel, the ever-shifting ice made for the occasional open lane, only to be as quickly closed. In but one example, on August 21, in the face of a dangerously pressing pack 500 yards away, a restless Greely ignored the advice of his men and ordered a move on. The boats were pressed upon the icefoot between the shore and the ice, and only by "superhuman" efforts, according to Kislingbury, was the pressure relieved and the boats steered into a cove. Kislingbury spoke for all the men when he wrote, "if [Greely] would take the advice and heed the warnings of those who understood there would be some encouragement, but as matters stand we are liable to be ruined most any moment. There is serious dissatisfaction amongst the men. Poor fellows, they cannot be blamed. They behave manfully, patient and sensibly through all.... More better and cheerful men under the circumstances could not possibly be found." Cross echoed similar remarks, stating, "he [Greely] has ill-treated and abused some of the best and most willing men that ever was [sic] in the Arctic and they have put up with it...." Greely's prancing with a self-cocking pistol, as if to encourage work and prevent mutiny, only exacerbated the situation. Without a formal role, Kislingbury made himself as useful as he could, largely hunting, scouting and hauling the boats, and later manhauling sledges. He became a stalwart member on the retreat, invigorated perhaps by thoughts of home. So far, the trip was too his liking. After downing a half pint of seal blood, he boasted that "I am in tip top health and spirits."[15]

On August 27, by which time they had travelled some two hundred miles, the ice-pack closed completely. Even turning back to Fort Conger was no longer a viable option. Brainard noted that "I do not think that ever before did an exploring party meet with as many adversities as we have on their retreat." For himself, Greely was harboring doubts, believing they were in a critical situation, as no record of any relief party had been found at the British cache at Cape Hawks. On September 3, while lying in his sleeping bag, the commander overheard Kislingbury speaking to Connell and others, carping that the party had made no effort to move for almost two days. Jumping out of his sleeping bag, Greely bristled at the perceived affront to his leadership. He scolded Kislingbury, remarking that "Lt. Kislingbury are you aware what you are doing? You are an officer of the US Army and are holding forth to enlisted men language that in the mildest judgment cannot be calculated to cause otherwise than discontent, and in the opinion of many officers would be considered as inciting to mutiny." (Cross, by the way, found "mutiny" to be Greely's favorite word). They were strong words, but the lieutenant, "in wonderment" by the outburst, replied that he had no such intention. Greely advised Kislingbury to speak directly to Greely if he had anything to say, to which Kislingbury advised him that he was tired of making suggestions as his comments were simply ignored. On the contrary, blurted Greely, in his opinion Kislingbury's comments "were of no account and would have had poor results," to which Kislingbury responded that "I can remind you [Greely] of half a dozen suggestions I've made to you which were wise ones and proved correct." Here the matter ended, but Kislingbury confided to his diary that he found Greely's public dressing down in front of the men in poor taste and undignified.[16]

The vagaries of the swirling ice in the sound, at times driving the party toward Greenland, and at other times toward Ellesmere Island, left Greely utterly unsure as to how to proceed. Finally paying more heed to the considerations voiced by the men, Greely called a conference with his officers and several enlisted men. When asked his opinion, Kislingbury suggested abandoning the steamer *Lady Greely* and the jolly-boat and proceed to Cape Sabine with sledges, two remaining boats, rations and supplies. Greely curtly dismissed the suggestion, but issued essentially the same order a week later. Showing more confidence in Kislingbury, the lieutenant was even placed in command of the six-man sledge with five men (Greely commanded the twelve-man sledge). For all, it was backbreaking slogging for several weeks, loading and unloading supplies as they hopped from floe to floe toward land.

They were fully at the mercy of driving winds and currents, and occasional violent storms that rapidly eroded their nightly ice floe bivouacs. Although a few seals were shot and even a walrus, they were unable to retrieve the carcasses before they sank or drifted away. Truly disheartening was the instance in which a dispatched walrus floated within several feet but could not be grappled by poles and retrieved. Compounding their woes, a number of men suffered from diarrhea. With rations running low, all remained anxious to learn whether a cache had been left by a relief ship on the west side of Smith Sound.

Chapter Fourteen

"Here we are dying like men"

FROM AMIDST THE FLOES, the members of the Greely Expedition watched as they haplessly drifted south of Pim Island, raising the fear that they would lose any chance of reaching terra firma again. With no choice but to make a desperate trek over the broken and slushy ice, they somehow managed to make landfall below the rocky outcropping by the end of September. Their destination had been reached in an exhausting fifty-two days, a circumstance that left them with a meager 35-40 days of rations. Shelter was Greely's immediate concern, and he decided that three structures would be built to house the men, in three equal groups. It was back-breaking work, excavating large rocks and moving them in place to form walls which were then sealed with ice, moss and dirt. Tempers flared under the strain. Even mild-mannered Israel complained, carping that Brainard had made an unfair distribution of supplies and equipment. Greely chastised the emotionally shattered astronomer. In Greely's mind, Sergeant Maurice Connell was viewed as the villain, who had "been talking violently" and undermining the moral of the men, even the most loyal ones. Publicly humiliating Connell, Greely announced a severe punishment—a reduction in his rank from sergeant to private. The disgraced Connell matter-of-factly remarked that "there is no love lost between us," and in mumbled tones swore at Greely. Conversely, Greely told Brainard that he had "implicit faith in his fairness, equity and impartiality." That evening, Greely informed Lockwood that he planned to bring charges of mutiny against Connell, Pavy and Kislingbury when they reached home.[1]

Anxious to learn if the relief parties had left supplies at the appointed location at Cape Sabine, Rice and Jens volunteered to make the trek there. After a rough journey, they managed to reach the rendezvous point, where they recovered written messages left by the relief parties. They returned to the Greely camp with what Rice characterized as "good and bad news," though as Greely read the reports, it seemed more bad than good. In the summer of 1882, after being stalled by ice on an attempt to reach Lady Franklin Bay, Major William Beebe, on the *Neptune,* had left a paltry 250 rations at Cape Sabine. To make matters worse, it was learned that during the following summer of 1883, the *Proteus*, the transport ship that had cruised into Lady Franklin Bay in 1881, had been nipped and crushed in the ice in the summer of 1883. Fearful for their own lives, the crew had abandoned the ship, leaving a mere 500 rations near Cape Sabine as they scurried to safety at Littleton Island (though the actual ration deposit was less). Brainard found those relief efforts, "a flawless record of misfortune and blundering."[2]

Greely now faced the near certainty that a relief ship would not reach them before winter. With the addition of some stores left by the British Arctic Expedition, he calculated that he could collect slightly more than 1,000 total rations, enough for six weeks at best, leaving him to face "a winter of starvation and probable death." The specter of the tragic Franklin Expedition hung heavy on Greely as he pondered whether his own expedition was bound to share the same fate.[3]

Despite having nearly broken his men while building winter quarters, Greely decided to backtrack some twenty miles to the vicinity of Cape Sabine, rather than retrieve the food and supplies from that location. After another difficult trek, they established their quarters on Pim Island, named Camp Clay by the commander after Pavy's now absent companion, Harry Clay, a circumstance that must have irked Pavy to no end. The camp sat perched on a rugged finger of land protruding from the island, some three miles south of Cocked Hat Island. Pim Island is separated from Ellesmere Island by Rice Strait, and is a mere eight miles long and some four miles wide.

Though affording an unobstructed view of Kane Basin, the rocky, glacially-scraped outcrop lies in a region less frequented by marine mammals and is largely devoid of seabird colonies. One benefit of their location was a fresh-water lake formed by the melting of a nearby glacier. The circumstances of the miserable stay at Camp Clay have been documented in full detail by numerous researchers. Over the course of the next nine months, seventeen expedition members slowly died of starvation and malnutrition.

They hastily set to constructing one "permanent station," rather than three separate quarters. Stones were again hauled and formed into a three-foot-wide foundation for a structure measuring some 25 by 15 feet. To cut down on drafts, the walls were chinked with snow and mud and sealed with a layer of ice. An overturned whaleboat supported by oar blades and covered with a tarpaulin and a layer of snow formed a precarious roof. Their barren and dismal location was all the more depressing, with the men's misery increased by thoughts of their dire situation.

To make matters worse, in early November Kislingbury suffered a painful ordeal and near fatal experience. While manhauling the sledge, he suffered an abdominal strain, nearly causing an internal rupture. The injury left him writhing in "excruciating agony," he confided to his diary, and utterly helpless. Fearful that the injury might be fatal, a concerned Pavy managed to tightly bandage his patient and confine him to bed. After ten days confinement, Kislingbury could finally manage to crawl out of his bag though it was some weeks before he could claim to be himself.

Faced with little prospect of rescue before the spring of 1884, on November 1 Greely ordered rations reduced to a mere fifteen ounces per person per day, so as to stretch their remaining food stocks to about April 1. Even when supplemented with occasional game (largely dovekies and the occasional fox by this point), the limited caloric intake left the men slowly starving to death. Along with this, complaints of thefts of food and unfair division of rations abounded. Among the first was a drunken Schneider, who was relieved of his position as cook after accusations of stealing food. Vocal discord was also not uncommon. According to Greely, Pavy engaged in "mutinous" conduct for suggesting that if Pavy's advice had been followed, the party would have remained at Fort Conger. Despite the dreary circumstances, Greely initiated a series of lectures and readings.

"Here we are dying like men"

Christmas passed with little fanfare, but with bright hopes for the future. Extra rations left the men with fuller stomachs, a rare treat. Songs livened the spirits, including some Danish ones by the two Greenlanders. Kislingbury celebrated his thirty-eighth birthday with constant thoughts of home and children. As gifts, he presented each member of the party with a cigarette. The new year was now looking somewhat positive as the days inched closer to the expected relief. However, at the same time, the men were growing weaker and closer to death. Attempts at stealing food from the commissary by unknown actors were becoming more frequent. Brainard pointed the finger at Connell in his diary, but was reluctant to voice his opinion publicly.

The first of the deaths, Sergeant William Cross, whose constitution may have been weakened by his drinking habit, occurred on January 18, 1884. His funeral ceremony was an almost macabre event. A gloomy Brainard deemed it a "ghostly procession of emaciated men moving slowly and silently away from their wretched ice-prison in the uncertain light of the Arctic night, having in their midst a dead comrade about to be laid away forever in the frozen ground." Previous to Cross's death, poor Elison was incapacitated by frozen extremities after a trip to Cape Isabella with Linn, Rice and Julius Frederick, and was near death.

On February 2, carrying backpacks and firearms, the indefatigable Rice and Jens made an attempted excursion to cross the sound to Littleton Island, optimistic that any Inuit at Etah could provide some assistance. With warm handshakes and prayers they left on a daring and desperate mission, but returned abruptly four days later, stopped in their quest by open water.

With fuel for lighting at a minimum, it was February 22, 1884 (or three months), before Kislingbury could again take pen to his journal. Longing for home, at the top of his list was the documentation of a lasting record for his boys. "I am extremely sorry I've not been able to keep a daily record of each day's events. It is a duty I owe to my darling boys, because if I do not survive this ordeal it will be a sore disappointment to them," he wrote. He had nothing but complimentary comments about the resilience and noble courage of his comrades: "If the world could see the charmingly cheerful spirits throughout all it would yet be more surprising." On the same date, he also proposed to Greely that he (Kislingbury) and a party of the ablest men cross to Littleton Island for game or help. After discussion among the group, Greely nixed the idea, viewing this proposal as "an abandonment to their fate of the weak of the party."[4]

In March, Kislingbury took a fall through the ice while hunting, nearly drowning in the ordeal. With no warm clothes to change into or a fire to warm him, it took a miserable five days for him to dry out. His spirits were still high, as he noted that "my heart is buoyant cheerful, the body is unable to respond." He suffered a setback when he reinjured his groin pulling a sledge up a glacier; after two weeks, he could crawl out of his bag.[5]

Much credit is due Rice and Brainard for ingeniously rigging large dip nets to enable the men to catch shrimps or "sea-fleas" to stretch their dwindling food supplies. The so-called "sea-fleas," *Onisimus edwardsi*, are small crustaceans, the size of a grain of corn according to Kislingbury, found in the cold waters of the arctic regions. As scavengers, they could be attracted in large numbers by baiting with animal skins or flesh. One study concluded that 43% of the caloric requirements for the Greely Expedition between March and June 1884 were derived from *Onisimus edwardsi*. The food seemed to satiate the hunger pangs of the men, at least temporarily, and the nourishment certainly extended their lives.[6]

The conditions were pitiable. With no fires or light, except during mealtime, they huddled together sharing sleeping bags, warmed only by the heat of their own bodies. The poorly sealed roof vented what little heat rose from inside. With little space to move, and largely in darkness, with their stiff backs pressed against stone walls covered in frost, they had little choice but to watch each other waste away. Rations were reduced to twelve ounces per day, leaving them gnawing with hunger. What little conversation was spent dreaming of favorite foods, feasts and overindulgences, broken by the occasional bickering over allocations of rations. With time on his hands, Brainard devoted nine pages in his diary to a list of "epicurean delights."

Death by starvation was a painfully slow process. As the body

"Here we are dying like men"

marshaled energy from muscle and tissue, limbs weakened and organ systems began to fail; the mind became clouded and at times delirious; the lethargy could be overwhelming.

Most of the men still faithfully adhered to the commander's orders, however. But as food became scarcer, allegations of theft came to the forefront, with bacon becoming a particularly sought after item. In late March, as food supplies continued to dwindle, Henry was spotted by Jens making off with food. Protesting innocence, Henry was given up after vomiting the contraband into a can. Though a number urged violent retribution, Greely withheld severe punishment at the moment. The affair came on the heels of another near fatal circumstance. On March 24, while cooking breakfast, a number of the men lost consciousness as a consequence of the failure to remove the shelter's vent plugs. Dragged from the hut, to his credit Pavy worked "like a Trojan" to aid them. Though dazed, they were all revived.

In early April, a godsend was delivered when they managed to hunt down a polar bear caught wandering near the station. Ravenous, all enjoyed an ounce of the animal's uncooked fat. But this sustenance did not come soon enough for Christiansen, Lockwood, Linn, and Rice, who succumbed beforehand, followed by Jewell shortly thereafter. They were laid side by side and covered with stones, the men too weak to provide a proper burial. As days dragged on, the failing health of all was readily apparent, as Kislingbury noted that "we are all very weak and a breath will almost brush most any of us away. We are all skin and bones." Remarkably, even in their most dire circumstances, staring death in the face, Kislingbury could look on the bright side, writing "Yet, our spirits are good, away up in fact. How we shall think of this life in the future!"[7]

With Lockwood's death, on April 9, Greely took the astonishing step of ordering Kislingbury to officially report for duty as second-in-command of the expedition. The issuance of that order immediately after Kislingbury's unsuccessful withdrawal in August 1881 would have quite possibly altered the dynamic of the expedition these last several years. Belatedly, Greely seems to have come to grips with his falling out with the lieutenant and sought to make amends. Kislingbury recorded verbatim Greely's contrition in his diary:

Dancing Chief

> I [Greely] consider it proper and my duty under the present circumstances and also in justice to you to restore you to the position of a member of the expedition. There is no telling what may occur in the future and it would be better understood in the event of my death that the command would devolve upon you. I will say that your conduct both at Fort Conger and since up to the present time has been upright, commendable and manly under all circumstances. In fact you have proven yourself since we left Fort Conger a noteworthy man in many respects. I shall when I return to the United States make this report to the proper authorities giving you full credit for your creditable behavior throughout the time we have been together and will soon as a more convenient opportunity affords writing issue the necessary orders.[8]

It is worth noting that Biederbeck's contemporaneous diary entry corroborates Greely's candid admission:

> He [Greely] extremely regretted to have lived on so different a footing for nearly three years, and with what pleasure he had seen Lt. K. behave himself in every way as a thorough gentleman and more than a man, to have done his work, especially since our retreat from Ft. Conger, and during this eventful winter, and that he would be sure that whatever might happen he would see that due credit so amply carried should be given to him.... Lt. G. said besides that Lt. K. had behaved while at Fort Conger like a man and more than a man, and that he, Lt. G., was materially wrong.[9]

Upon later reflection, in his *Three Years of Arctic Service*, Greely could not bear to admit his contrition and any suggestion of his own failing in the matter of his relationship with Kislingbury. Greely even downplayed the praise he had heaped on Kislingbury in person. Instead, he offered up a begrudging thanks for Kislingbury's

"Here we are dying like men"

assistance in organizing supplies for the retreat from Fort Conger, while also ignoring his complimentary remarks about Kislingbury's conduct at Fort Conger: "I complimented Lieutenant Kislingbury highly on his labors the preceding autumn, when he had spared neither strength nor exposure to collect our scattered supplies, and had overworked and seriously strained himself." Sergeant Brainard, in his *Six Came Back*, published well after the availability of Greely's book, similarly echoed Greely's remarks, stating that Greely "eulogized [Kislingbury] in the highest terms for his efficient assistance in the retreat from Fort Conger."[10]

On April 14, 1884, five days after Greely had reinstated Kislingbury, the commander had an abrupt change of mind and countermanded the order. According to Greely, Kislingbury had taken a turn for the worse, and "shows very decided mental derangement." Greely recorded that the lieutenant was rambling "like an infant" and could scarcely move about. Greely had no choice but to appoint Brainard as his successor in the event of Greely's death.

By late April, even though eye-catching patches of green were making an early spring appearance, all hope was beginning to fade. The remaining men were fastidiously making wills and writing last letters to loved ones in contemplation of their deaths. Greely gave his instructions to Brainard, advising him that his priorities were gaining Brainard's commission, his daughter's career as an "analytical chemist," and for Mrs. Greely to be awarded a special pension.

On May 6, Greely himself was evidencing unhinged conduct. In the heat of an extended argument with Pavy over increasing rations, according to Ralston, both Pavy and Bender refused to "hold their tongues when ordered to by the commanding officer." When that failed after four admonitions, Greely attempted to grab Long's rifle, claiming that a "mutiny seemed imminent" and declaring that he would shoot Bender if he did not cease; as for Pavy, if he were not the doctor Greely admitted that he would have shot him as well. Pavy had been bickering with several of the men. Even Kislingbury, once Pavy's closest comrade, had his own gripes with Pavy, including several loud arguments over undisclosed subjects. Kislingbury scribbled in his diary that "the doctor is irascible and has made himself mean and disagreeable and has done me great injury in various ways."[11]

Dancing Chief

With food thefts now at issue, Biederbeck confided to Greely that Pavy had stolen Elison's bread rations last fall, together with four cans of beef extract. On April 23, Elison made his own complaint to Greely of Pavy's theft of Elison's bacon. On April 27, Kislingbury found Henry in a drunken stupor having improperly doubled up on his alcohol ration. On May 3, Whistler was found by Bender and Henry to be "ravenously" eating uncooked bacon and shielding two pounds of it in his coat.

Curiously, as allegations of theft continued to abound, the commander himself was partaking more than an even share. Biederbeck wrote in his diary on April 15 that "Lt. Greely told me today confidentially, that after hearing from Dr. Pavy the weak condition of Lt. Kislingbury and after a great deal of mental worry, he had allowed himself an extra allowance of a small quantity of pemmican and hard bread, as he saw the necessity of keeping himself up for the well of the party." Greely himself admitted that he had taken extra rations for "a few days," and that the dates could be found in Brainard's diary. Beginning on April 13, several other survivors, including Brainard and Long, were given extra rations, in light of their heavier duties as hunters. Jens was one of them, but sadly he soon died in a drowning accident, a severe blow to their hunting efforts. At this point of time in the expedition, when even a small number of calories meant the difference between life and death, the implication was obvious.[12]

Lieutenant Kislingbury was coherent enough to add a stirring entry on April 23, in words that echo those of Robert Falcon Scott's *Message to the Public*, some twenty-seven years later, as Scott awaited his own death (Scott wrote, "Had we lived, I should have had a tale to tell of the hardihood, endurance, and courage of my companions which would have stirred the heart of every Englishman"):

> We are all very weak and a breath will almost brush most of us away. What a study our poor wasted frames would be for the physicians. We are nothing but skin and bones, the later protruding almost through the former. Yet our spirits are good, away up, in fact. How we shall think of this life in the future! It is a simply a dream now.... When

the world hears the story as told us by our noble Frederik, I venture that few will learn of it who will not wonder, and whose hearts will not swell with deep emotion. But there are many things for them (the world), to learn, and wonder about. Oh, the heroes! Rice, who actually died, sacrificed his life for us and in the performance of his duty trying to do what he did for the slightest increase of our very limited allowance of food. I desire so very much to be able to give the details of these two noble men to the world.... Great God help that the tale of their noble deeds can be told that they may shine forth in all their lustre that others may profit by their noble example.[13]

Through the month of May, five more perished: Jens, Ellis, Ralston, Whistler, and Israel. Like the others, Kislingbury's health continued to falter. On May 1, Brainard had recorded that Kislingbury threw himself on the sledge outside and, weeping like child, said "it is hopeless, I cannot fight longer!" On May 11, Kislingbury recorded another conversation that was telling. Outside of the station, Greely approached Kislingbury with his hand extended, and stated:

> Kislingbury, I wish to say to you that you and I the past three years have misunderstood each other, for that is what it was. You were standing, when we finally fell out, simply for your rights. I was cross as I am too frequently. I can not now blame you and I ask now if it is too late in the day your forgiveness for the unkindnesses to which I've treated you. Your conduct has been manly and commendable throughout.[14]

Bender was a witness to Greely's statement and recorded that "Lt. Greely acted the man for once in his life and spoke to Lt. Kislingbury and asked him to forgive him for not putting him on duty sooner." The astonished Kislingbury thanked his commander and asked that Greely include those remarks in his official order restoring him to duty, that he may send it to his children. According to Kislingbury, Greely "readily consented and promised to give me the order at the first opportunity." Kislingbury was still skeptical of the commander's reasons, believing it "the first act of civility and kindness he has shown me since August 26, 1881, day I was relieved."[15]

Sadly, Kislingbury's last entry in his diary was the following day, May 12, in which Kislingbury politely reminded Greely of his promise to officially memorialize the order, which Greely immediately denied. Kislingbury was particularly angered by Greely's backtracking on his promise to "relieve and exonerate me from all blame at Conger and since we left there and he would pay me the compliment and give me the credit I deserved." According to Kislingbury, in response, Greely "cut me short, flew into a passion, and called me, in a loud, insulting (highly so) manner, 'a Liar,'" denying that promise and promising only that he would write to Hazen. Both Bender and Henry confirmed the remarks, with Henry noting that Greely "calls Kis[lingbury] a liar and apologizes to enlisted men."[16]

Though acknowledging the conversation and apologizing for "improper and ungentlemanly language," Greely defended himself in his official report, noting that "I look back on that personal episode in the three years' experience as the only one for which I have an abiding regret. Though my statements were strictly accurate, I should have remembered Lieutenant Kislingbury's weak mental state and enfeebled physical condition. I can only plead in extenuation great physical pain, and the resultant mental condition from my severe illness. Lieutenant and I were fully reconciled prior to his death."[17]

Kislingbury lingered until June 1. Just prior to his death, he assembled a tin box from a fruit can in which he placed Jessie's ring, and a collection of plants and minerals. His last words were reciting the doxology, in a weak voice as he slipped back into this sleeping bag. News reports carried the romantic line that he spoke, "Aggie, Aggie," oddly the name of his first wife, but no support for that poignant statement is found in the various diaries. Maurice Connell may have been a malcontent in Greely's eyes, but in an 1890 letter to John Kislingbury he offered an account of Frederick Kislingbury's last moments and a commendable elegy:

> [Kislingbury] was a natural born leader, besides being a loving father, a true patriot and a sincere Christian

gentleman. I shall never forget his last breath unto death chanted in as loud a tone as he was capable of, the hymn, "Nearer My God to Thee." His death was a noble example of the Christian soldier. It is well that the children of Rochester should commemorate such a noble character as he proved himself to be. His life was a succession of heroic deeds. He was noble and unselfish to the last. Were his mind on the sole subject of self-preservation, instead of solicitude for the preservation of the lives of his fellows, undoubtedly he would be among the survivors. But no; he disdained life for his own sake. He felt he had a responsibility resting on him to preserve the lives of others, and so he, the noble soul, died for his companions, may his soul ever rest in heaven.[18]

His death was followed by seven others in the month of June: Salor, Bender, Pavy, Henry, Gardiner, and Schneider. Private Henry's death came at the hands of a marksman, not starvation. He was repeatedly warned against stealing food and ordered shot if he repeated the act. After again admitting to a theft of sealskin thongs he was shot. His execution was carried out by three of the most trustworthy men—Brainard, Long and Julius Frederick (two of them actually fired one shot). On his person, Henry was found to be hording sealskin boots and thongs, as well as stolen knives and a watch. Ironically, though thoroughly disreputable and written off in history, Henry was one of the most expressive of expedition diarists. Besides lengthy remarks on natural phenomena like the aurora and glaciers, even in the worst of times on May 28, he could wax romantically:

> The majority of us fourteen have given up all hope of seeing our friends again but a few still have a chance of at the conclusion of this terrible tragedy, to be welcomed with universal acclamation as worthy frontiersmen of Uncle Sam and as men who have made themselves immortal by a splendid victory and innumerable sufferings hitherto incomparable in the annals of arctic exploration

and against all laws of nature, as Tennyson truly sings: 'and there they lay till all our bones were bleached and lichened into colour with the crags.'[19]

In December 1883, back in the states, the wheels had begun to turn, albeit slowly, on behalf of another relief expedition for the following spring. William E. Chandler, Secretary of the Navy, prodded President Chester Arthur to propose a resolution approving the funding for the relief mission. Once proposed, Congressional approval of the hoped for expenditure was by no means a forgone conclusion. Debates about spending limits, the use of volunteers, and a general aversion to the whole idea of polar expeditions, initially stalled the bill in the Senate. But on February 11, 1884, the funding for the Greely relief expedition was finally approved by both houses of Congress, and signed by the President.

Chandler had not waited for final action. Banking on Congressional approval, he had informally arranged for the purchase of two sturdy sealers, *Bear* and *Thetis*. A third rescue ship, the *Alert*, was graciously loaned by the British Government. Commander Winfield Scott Schley (1839-1911) was offered the command by Chandler. Schley, widely hailed later as the hero of the Battle of Santiago during the Spanish-American War, was an experienced navy man with piercing eyes, a receding hairline and a distinctive thick mustache and narrow chin whiskers. His instructions were simple: find and rescue Greely and his comrades at all cost. Recognizing the publicity value to the Navy associated with a successful rescue, there would be no hesitation this time.

After a brief refitting for arctic service, the three ships departed for the North. By June 21, an unprecedented early season traverse of the North Water found the *Bear* and *Thetis* off Littleton Island. With no word of Greely, Schley gambled on a quick run across an open Smith Sound to Cape Sabine off the Ellesmere Island coast. In less than four hours, the squadron had crossed the sound and approached Cape Sabine. On Brevoort Island, just south of Cape Sabine, a record was located by a search party providing the useful

"Here we are dying like men"

The Greely tent at the time of rescue.

information that Greely was at Cape Sabine. Though informative, the note, dated October 31, 1883, sent a shiver up Schley's spine as he pondered whether Greely's men could have survived the winter and early spring at this desolate location.

At Cape Sabine, seven men sat idle in their tent in a sorry state, all thought of self-salvation gone. Their meagre food stores consisted of boiled sealskin and lichen stew, and fragments of their own pants and boots. The tent was crumpled atop of them after the tent-pole had collapsed and none had strength enough to upright it. As Schley approached Cape Sabine, the *Bear* sounded three long whistles. Unsure of the source of the unusual sound, and despite his skepticism of a rescue party, Greely sent Brainard and Long to investigate. Brainard returned to the tent convinced that the wind whistling through some empty cans had been the source of the noise. Long, however had lagged behind. He spotted the cutter from the *Bear* with its crew gesticulating wildly. Upon touching shore, Lieutenant John C. Colwell, a veteran of the aborted *Proteus* relief party one year before, and James Norman, first mate on the same ship, grasped his hand. Their first question to Long was "How many are left?" Long could only feebly respond: "Seven-seven left alive!" Reaching the disheveled tent, it was cut open with a knife. Greely raised his head from his sleeping bag and responded, "Yes, Yes, seven of us left, here we are dying like men. Did what I came to do, beat the best record." It was a remarkable statement in light of Weyprecht's stated objectives of the IPY and his disdain for vainglorious personal geographic achievements. Only seven men were still barely alive, though in wretched condition. One of them, Elison, died shortly thereafter.

Upon Greely's return, he was left to deal with the circumstances surrounding the execution of Private Henry, as well as more detestable affairs.

Chapter Fifteen

Home Again

An unprecedented celebration greeted the survivors of the Greely Expedition when they arrived in Portsmouth, New Hampshire. Thousands of persons had gathered along the shores of New Castle, New Hampshire, and Kittery, Maine, the small communities spanning either side of the Portsmouth harbor entrance, just to gain a fleeting look at the incoming relief ships. The naval procession was led by the escort vessel, USS *Alliance*, the ship that had met the expedition transport *Proteus* in St. John's on its outward-bound voyage when spirits were still high. The rescue ships USS *Thetis,* USS *Bear* and HMS *Alert* followed, with Greely and five other survivors aboard *Thetis*. From the deck of the flagship USS *Tennessee* anchored in the harbor, high-ranking officers viewed the procession: Secretary of the Navy William E. Chandler, Chief Signal Officer William B. Hazen, and Rear Admiral Stephen B. Luce, commander of the squadron. The nearby USS *Tallapoosa* ferried Henrietta Greely, her relatives, and Greely's mother to the awaiting *Thetis*. More watched from the shore, while a multitude of vessels of all sorts— barges, yachts, steam launches and fishing dories—crowded the harbor. The well-wishers voiced loud cheers and waved white handkerchiefs, while smartly-dressed naval officers and sailors lined the decks and rigging of the ships.

The joyful reunion of Adolphus and Henrietta Greely was widely publicized. Lieutenant Greely was aware Henrietta was making her way to Portsmouth from their hometown of Newburyport, Massachusetts, but was not informed when or where she would be present. Asked to step into Schley's cabin, he made himself comfortable, after which Henrietta entered unannounced, accompanied by Schley. According to the one newsman permitted on board, "with a loud cry that was more like a gigantic sob half smothered, or such a sound a dumb animal might give if overcome with delight, Lieut. Greely bounded from his chair with his eyes half standing from their sockets in joy of the sight that gladdened him." To Adolphus's surprise his mother was also present. Few words were exchanged between the two beyond hugs and tears. Fearful of the shock to Greely's constitution, Commander Schley felt the need to intervene and "direct the conversation to less emotional channels."[1]

Relics from the fateful expedition were displayed on board the *Thetis* for any who wished to view; the wooden oar wrapped with shabby cloth that served as a distress signal, the reindeer skins that served as sleeping bags, and a broken-down sledge. In a somewhat macabre exhibition, the "sarcophagi" (as described by one newsman), fashioned to hold the remains of the dead were also displayed by Schley. These specially made, "hermetically sealed" iron caskets, painted black and securely riveted, would preserve the remains for "public health purposes," a measure that would raise some eyebrows. Metal name plates attached to the weighty five-hundred-pound caskets were still blank at the time, as if avoiding any mention of the dead. A more standard pine funeral box was placed within each metal casket, adding to its weight. The bodies themselves had been preserved in alcohol and tucked away on the *Bear*, with instructions that no one could view them. Following the ceremony, the press was invited to board the steam launch *Wentworth* for a celebratory meal. In a rather awkward statement that stands out in light of the dreadful fate of the expedition, one reporter remarked that "a magnificent dinner was served to the hungry writers."[2]

August 4 was another day filled with more ceremony, as some fifteen thousand people watched as a procession of two thousand marchers proceeded downtown opposite the stately Rockingham House for a grand review. Every street was festooned with flags, bunting and decorations for the ceremony that stretched for hours. That evening, more persons assembled in Portsmouth's Music Hall, where a congratulatory meeting was held to honor the rescuers and survivors. Long tributes were paid by religious, civic and military leaders. Though respects were paid to the dead, with the

Home Again

U.S. Navy coordinating the rescue and the ceremony, much credit was paid to the rescuers, spinning what had been a disaster into a remarkable deliverance. In light of the tragedy that so marred and overshadowed the expedition, the scale of the multi-day revelry seems oddly overdone.

Charles Clark, Kislingbury's close friend, had managed an interview with Greely while the commander was recuperating at Seavey's Island, part of the Portsmouth Naval Yard. Still bearing the marks of his travails, Greely was weak and appeared "bloated" and was unable to stand upright without the aid of a chair. According to Clark, Greely had nothing but kind words for Kislingbury. Greely remarked that "Kislingbury was a brave and noble man, who did his duty on every occasion, and did it well. He never flinched, while he could he took even more than his share of hardships." There was no ill will between the two, in fact, so said Greely. Kislingbury fully supported Greely, and Kislingbury was one of his favorite officers. Kislingbury and Connell did most of the hunting as they were the best shots. These kind words masked the reality of the situation.[3]

In separate ceremonies, the dead were also honored. In the tiny hamlet of Godhavn, Greenland, the body of Frederik Thorlip Christiansen had been carefully escorted by officers and sailors of the USS *Bear* to the local church. After a brief memorial service, he was interred in the local cemetery, overlooking the ice-filled Disko Bay. Simple white wooden crosses and bright flowers brightened the setting. A memorial service was also graciously held by the citizens of St. John's, Newfoundland, prior to the expedition's return to the United States.

As the sad news reached distraught relatives of the dead, heartrending stories emerged, and so it was with the children of Frederick Kislingbury. On July 24, a reporter for the *St. Louis Republican* rushed to the home of Reverend and Mrs. Schofield seeking comments from the foster parents of young Wheeler Kislingbury. Instead, the aggressive newsman garnered a surprising interview with the blonde, blue-eyed, eight-year-old boy himself, the spitting image of his father. The child had already suffered an unimaginable share of grief, having lost his mother as an infant (Aggie) and one stepmother (Jessie) as a child. Spotting Wheeler arising from a nap, the eager reporter quickly sharpened his pencil and pushed for an interview. The accommodating Schofields granted one, but chided the newsman to "be cautious of what you say to him, we are very anxious to keep the news from him." The young boy, fair-haired with beaming blue eyes, tearfully recounted that "I told papa he ought not to go on the expedition." He continued, asking "do you think he will come back soon to me and send me to sleep again telling me fairy tales."[4]

In New York City, the bodies of eleven of the dead were received in proper military fashion. A twenty-one-gun salute was raised from fortress Castle William on Governor's Island, New York Harbor, as the caskets were removed from the *Bear* to the *Catalpa*, a waiting tug. From there, *Catalpa* conveyed them to the post hospital at the army headquarters on the island. An honor guard, four companies of the 5th Artillery, presented raised swords draped in black. The military band, its drums shrouded in black, struck up a mournful dirge. An artillery caisson that served as a funeral car conveyed the bodies to the post hospital. The somber procession was followed by family and friends of the deceased, Secretary of War Robert Todd Lincoln, Lieutenant General Philip Sheridan, Commander Winfield S. Schley, and Major General Winfield Hancock, and several battalions of light artillery and officers of the army, navy, marines, and citizen mourners. No other public military ceremonies were conducted.

John and William Kislingbury, brothers of the explorer, with fifteen-year-old Walter Kislingbury, and Charles Clark, were also present at the solemn ceremony. Among the more heartrending sights was young Walter, who had burst into tears as his father's casket was placed on the caisson. If news reports can be believed, every dignitary seems to have had a hand in consoling the sobbing boy. The *Sun* reported that as Kislingbury's body passed, Commander Schley put his arm around the boy "and held him up as he seemed about to fall." The *Herald* reported that as the casket was raised General Hancock took "the orphan's hand and patted it and spoke encouragingly to the boy." Even Secretary Lincoln was moved by the teary-eyed boy. According to the *Tribune*, as the heartbroken boy walked between his uncles, John and William Kislingbury, the secretary "took him by the hand and tried to comfort him, leading the little fellow tenderly the rest of the way to the hospital." Following the ceremonies, Frederick's body was placed in the care of the Kislingbury brothers, who, with the teenage Walter, escorted it to Rochester.[5]

Though individual ceremonies were held locally for some of the dead, none perhaps was as impressive as that for Lieutenant Frederick Kislingbury. His final resting place in the city of Rochester only came about after a few unusual turns, however. With the breaking news of Frederick's death, John Kislingbury, Frederick's oldest brother, had made an application in Superior Court, Monroe County, New York, for appointment as administrator of Frederick's estate and to assume guardianship of Walter, then living with John's family. This action was unbeknownst to Charles Clark, Frederick Kislingbury's close boyhood friend. Clark, who had managed Frederick's affairs during the preceding three years, and held a letter testifying to Frederick Kislingbury's wish that Clark handle his estate in the event of his death, filed an application in Detroit for appointment as administrator and guardian at about the same time.[6]

Privately, with both Clark and John Kislingbury holding strong emotional connections with Frederick Kislingbury and his four young boys, not surprisingly the matter became contentious between the two. At the urging of John Kislingbury, his lawyer fired off a demand letter to Clark threatening Clark with "a scandal" if John was required to enforce his "natural rights" to be named as administrator and guardian. With lawyers retained on each side, a face-to-face was held in Detroit to settle the matter. In light of Frederick Kislingbury's letter of instruction in favor of Clark, John Kislingbury was reluctantly forced to recognize the validity of Clark's appointment and withdraw his claim. In a spirit of cooperation, Clark had acceded to John Kislingbury's request to permit John and his wife to continue to retain Walter under their care. Clark also acceded to the request that Frederick's burial be held in Rochester. Though Frederick's two wives had been laid to rest in Sandwich, Ontario, Canada, both Kislingbury and Charles Clark could agree that Frederick's service to his country justified a burial in the United States.[7]

On August 9, the body of Frederick Kislingbury arrived in

Rochester in its sealed iron casket after 11 p.m. An honor guard and band escorted the casket to the rotunda of the city's stately courthouse, which was ornamented with a mournful black and white bunting for the ceremony. An honor guard posted around the black-draped bier within the rotunda remained on duty all evening and the following morning. Old-time companions from the 54th National Guard Regiment, who had served with Kislingbury twenty-years before, presented a touching display of flowers bearing his Company "E." John Kislingbury's volunteer fire unit contributed handsome floral arrangements. Despite the late hour, in an outpouring of sympathy, a continuous procession of citizens slowly filed past the coffin all night. By late morning, more than 20,000 persons had paid their last respects to one of their own.[8]

For those fortunate to obtain a spot within the courthouse, the Reverend Edward Bristol delivered a brief, but moving farewell to the young lieutenant. After the reverend's address, Civil War veteran and poet, Colonel D. Richardson, read the following poem:

> From out the frozen death land a mourning cortege comes;
> The bells of grief are tolling to beat of muffled drums.
> The nation bows in sadness as moves the funeral train;
> The bravest of Columbia are numbered with the slain.
>
> When duty called, they answered-no shirking at the task;
> They gave their all-we could no grander offering ask.
> The loyal gift accepted, the altar bears to-day;
> The sacrifice of heroes whose flame shall burn for aye.[9]

The Rochester quartet closed with a song, "Peacefully Asleep." A funeral carriage drawn by four chestnut-colored horses transported the remains to Mount Hope Cemetery, followed by a multitude of civic and military organizations in a scripted order of march. Throngs of residents accompanied the procession and lined the streets all along the route. The attendance nearly equaled in size the more festive semi-centennial of the city two months previously. "So were consigned to their last resting-place the mortal remains of one to whom it was the city's melancholy pleasure to render just honors," remarked the *Rochester Democrat and Chronicle*.[10]

Home Again

Funeral of Lieutenant Frederick Kislingbury, Rochester, New York.

    The body did not remain long within that resting place. Even as the Kislingbury funeral cortege had wound its way to Mount Hope Cemetery, disconcerting rumors were circulating. John Kislingbury had managed to speak with several of the sailors on the relief expedition, who advised him that members of the expedition had turned to cannibalism of their dead comrades as a last resort. He wrote to Charles Clark that those navy men informed John that they "know just about how things were found and that Fred was wronged." In an age of "sensational" reporting, newspapers clamored for the "skeleton in the closet" of the Greely Expedition. Home offices of the northern papers were telegraphing their news hounds to confirm the cannibalism rumors and gather explicit details. Comments by Schley and others present at the rescue may have attempted to temper that narrative. On August 13, in response to a reporter who questioned him on the subject, Schley immediately replied "in great indignation," that "there is not a word of truth in that story. You need not show it to me, for I have read it. It has been manufactured out of the whole cloth.... I do not think there was any cannibalism practiced by Greely or his men." Surprisingly, another report in the *New York Herald,* a publication that did not shy from sensationalism, tendered a defense, stating that "there is not the slightest evidence to prove that this flesh was eaten by the dead man's comrades; and it has been suggested that the flesh was used for bait to catch the shrimps upon which the survivors subsisted for so long a time." Adolphus Greely was also quick to defend his expedition from the tawdry claim, remarking that he was unaware of any such conduct.[11]

In Rochester, almost immediately following the funeral, the Kislingbury brothers were approached by William Mill Butler, city editor of the *Rochester Post-Express*, seeking to have Frederick Kislingbury's body exhumed. Butler claimed that the Kislingburys were initially opposed to the exhumation, but Butler "labored long and earnestly" to obtain their consent. Once in agreement, the brothers would claim that their interest in examining the body was not due to reports of cannibalism, but rather concerns as to whether the body was actually in the casket. Specifically, there were concerns that the family had been the victim of a deceitful mock ceremony. Based on conversations with the survivors, the Kislingburys advanced the opinion that the expedition had fragmented into two fractions, with one group led by Greely forcibly preventing the other from food supplies. Pavy and Kislingbury, out of favor with Greely, were members of that excluded group. Rumors (later proven untrue) that Kislingbury had killed a bear three days before his death would seem to contradict Greely's account that Frederick had fallen victim to starvation.

Not everyone in Kislingbury's circle favored the public exhumation. In Deadwood, Seth Bullock, guardian of young Douglass Kislingbury, was livid over the action. Writing to Charles Clark, he remarked in strong words:

> I hardly expected any reply as I wrote him [John Kislingbury] very plainly what I thought of his actions and now since the ghouls have disinterred poor Fred's remains. I don't want to hear from them or see them [the Kislingbury brothers]. I only rec'd yesterday the Eastern papers with an account of the revolting and inhuman scene. It is the most sickening and heartless epistle in this whole miserable business. What a pity they could not have been at Cape Sabine instead of poor Fred, the idea

of their making an exhibition of the poor fellow's remains in order that they might gain a little notoriety. They are little knaves or fools. I hope Walter can be induced to leave them. I also hope you will try and influence his return. I don't think they have brains enough to care for themselves let alone the boy.... I am too angry over the shameful and cowardly outrage to think of anything else; it was damnable.[12]

Bullock's heartfelt interest was in seeing both that the boys were set on the proper course and that they received a helpful guiding hand. A self-made man, Bullock believed that the boys needed some guidance but he confided to Clark that "boys that expect to be taken care of all their lives don't as a general thing have much self-reliance and without this they cannot make their way in the world."[13]

The Kislingbury's correspondence with Charles Clark reveals that their true interest in the exhumation was part of a campaign to publicly discredit Greely, who they believed had besmirched Kislingbury's character. Their vehemence knew no bounds. William Kislingbury wrote to Clark, that Greely was a "craven, scheming man, incompetent to command the respect of his own men. Do not hesitate to let us use [information from Kislingbury's diary] in our efforts to vindicate the character and memory of a brother dear to us as life itself." In another missive, contrary to Clark's demand to cease the public criticisms, Kislingbury bluntly remarked to Clark, "It is no use to talk caution or quiet to me in this matter. Greely has been shown in more ways than one a deceptive intriguer.... He [Greely] knows he was wrong in this dispute with Fred."[14]

Unable to afford the cost themselves, the *Rochester Post-Express*, sensing an exclusive scoop, paid the expense of the exhumation on behalf the Kislingburys. In a remarkably rapid sequence of events, governmental approval for exhuming the body was hastily obtained and the body exhumed on the morning of August 14, four days after its initial interment. Borne by five men with the aid of the undertaker, Lemuel W. Jeffreys, the coffin was carried to the cemetery chapel. The fifty-two bolts were loosened and the lid carefully lifted by undertaker Jeffreys in the presence of two

Kislingbury brothers (John and Frank), Dr. Charles Buckley, and Dr. F. A. Mandeville, who performed the autopsy, and the superintendent of the cemetery. Also present was William Mill Butler of the *Rochester Post-Express*.

Reaching his hand into the coffin and through the layer of white cotton packing, Jeffreys exclaimed "he is there," quickly putting an end to the rumor that no body had been present. A blanket wrapping the body was slowly and "reverentially" removed. As if to mount the tension, the *New York Times* reported that "there was a suppressed cry of horror on the lips of those present." What they saw left them aghast. The body was a mere skeleton, fully confirming evidence of starvation. The gruesome description, almost too sensational to repeat, fills a full three columns of the *Times*. Identification of the body was made by means of a missing tooth and the scars from the injury to Frederick's right toe while a prison guard in Elmira. The coroner's report highlighted that large portions of skin and muscles of the abdomen, back and thigh had been dissected or cut down to the bone, and that in their opinion "the flesh removed was cut away with some sharp instrument." For Frank Kislingbury, however, the autopsy put to rest his stated concerns. He told the *Times* that he "was quite satisfied" with the result, namely that the existence of the body proved the remains were in the casket.[15]

The *Times* found a more outspoken Kislingbury. John Kislingbury continued to voice a more problematic opinion, namely that in their separated struggle to survive, those not in favor with the commander, including Kislingbury and Pavy, were compelled to die so that others might live. More fodder for that conclusion was drawn from the shooting of Private Henry, who was supposedly on the outside of the Greely group. A quote published in the *New York Sun* added the further comment by John Kislingbury that "we have proof that Fred was eaten, in spite of the assurances that his remains were in good condition and recognizable."[16]

Outraged by the publicity and looking to quell the storm of allegations, both Greely and Charles Clark stepped forward. In Portsmouth, Greely was interviewed amid the report of a hostile split and provided an adamant rebuttal, while at the same time incorrectly suggesting that it was business as usual for Kislingbury after the *Proteus* sinking. Greely remarked that:

> In regard to the story of two factions, with Lieutenant Kislingbury in charge of the opposition, I will say that that rumor is totally false, having no foundation whatsoever. The trouble between Kislingbury and myself occurred in 1881, the first year of the expedition. He desired to be relieved from duty, and I, not wishing to retain a man against his will, although I had the power to do so, gave him his liberty. It is my impression that he desired to return to the United States. He went southward, but the *Proteus* was sunk, and he returned to duty. I treated him as though nothing happened, and recently, when Lockwood died, I gave him the second place on the expedition.

At the same time, Greely added that as for cannibalism, "I [Greely] can but repeat that if there was any cannibalism, and there now seems to be no doubt about it, the man-eating was done in secrecy and entirely without my knowledge and contrary to my discipline."[17]

In an interview carried by the *Times,* Clark too went out of his way to quash the rumor that Greely and Kislingbury had a falling out, noting that the two were on "most cordial" terms and that stories otherwise were "untrue." As for cannibalism, he added that "if brought to such a point of starvation, I think the unfortunate men would have been thoroughly justified in doing what they did. It may be that before he died Lieut. Kislingbury was forced to do likewise. It is, to say the least, cruel to criticize, in the manner it has been done, the unfortunate party on the return from the horrors of their exile. The friends of Lieutenant Kislingbury made a mistake, in my judgment, when they permitted the body to be exhumed."[18]

The tempest, particularly over alleged cannibalism, continued to make the rounds in the press for several weeks, but quickly became old news. The secretary of war declined to order a court of inquiry. The military preferred that the whole tawdry matter simply be dropped and the matter considered closed. Schley's *Official Report,* which was released in late October of 1884, acknowledged the near-surgical removal of flesh but avoided the conclusion of cannibalism, remarking that six of the bodies (including Kislingbury's) "had been cut, and the fleshy parts removed to a greater or less extent." Curiously, in the version of the *Official Report* published by the Government Printing Office in 1887, Schley added the deduction that had been floated early on by the *New York Herald*. He concluded that the six bodies "had been cut and the fleshy parts removed to a greater or less extent with a view no doubt to use as shrimp bait."[19]

Clark believed he had legitimate reasons to quiet the Kislingbury brothers. As a fiduciary, Clark's responsibility was to the estate and the four orphans, a responsibility he more than upheld in the face of obstacles placed by the Kislingbury brothers. On their behalf, Clark dogged Frederick's deadbeat debtors (mostly frontier soldiers who had purchased his equipment and supplies), successfully wrangled with the government over Frederick's back-pay and collected on his insurance policy with New England Life. With those monies, he established trust funds for the welfare of the boys and their education, and made sure they were fitted with all their necessaries. Through tutors and political influence, he pushed for Harry's entrance to the U.S. Naval Academy. On behalf of the boys, he pursued a pension claim in Congress, lining up the backing of several prominent Congressmen.

Instrumental to the pension award and helpful to Harry's potential Academy admission were favorable recommendations from Lieutenant Adolphus Greely. Thus, Clark had every reason to maintain cordial terms with the commander. Besides his public show of support, he contacted Greely directly, voicing his outrage with the conduct of the Kislingbury's brothers. In an October 7 letter to Greely he wrote that he "regretted exceedingly the narrow, misguided and bigoted course the Lieutenant's relatives in Rochester have taken all through this matter and know could Fred but speak, he would be terribly mortified at their sayings and doings. I hope they will not push this investigation business further and so advised them they have already prejudiced official circles and the public mind against themselves enough. I want the boys to be helped and pensioned if possible." He added that he could never forgive the Kislingburys for the "outrage they perpetrated" for "exhuming his

[Frederick's] body and dragging it before the public for some beastly news mongers to no fool purpose." At a later date, half jokingly, Clark even went so far as to add that "I think Robt. T. Lincoln should 'be investigated.'" On the heels of Clark's admonition, Greely penned a strong letter of support, and with it, a pension of $10 per month to each child (payable until reaching adulthood), was approved by Congress on March 3, 1885. Greely's intervention was not as successful for Harry's Academy appointment. Though Greely opened a door to the secretary of the navy and had enlisted both Hazen and Schley on Harry's behalf, Harry's age barred him by law from admission (he would have exceeded the maximum of age 18 by his earliest possible date of enrollment).[20]

Chapter Sixteen

Aftermath

EVEN THOUGH PUBLICITY MATTERS regarding the Greely Expedition had largely subsided by early 1885, the Kislingbury brothers were not prepared to let go; they were still pushing for an investigation of Greely's conduct. At their insistence, extracts of Kislingbury's diary were published by editorial supporters at the *Rochester Democrat and Chronicle*, thus advancing their position. The entries quoted by the Rochester paper referenced Greely's restoration of Kislingbury to duty on April 9, 1884, with Greely's favorable comment that Kislingbury's conduct "had been manly and commendable throughout," and Greely's request for forgiveness. Also reported was Kislingbury's request to include those positive comments in the order restoring him to duty, to which Greely had agreed, but later denied calling Kislingbury "a liar." Greely was characterized as incompetent and inefficient, and the cause of the death of the men at Cape Sabine. Though the story was reported by a number of papers, it did little to reignite the flames of controversy, and failed to spark an investigation.[1]

Another expedition member, the demoted Private Maurice Connell, was prepared to come forward to tell his side of the story, and it was to be a far different recollection than Greely's version. Connell had remained in the army after the expedition, retaining his position as a second-class private in the Signal Corps. Unlike his surviving messmates who held or had advanced to higher ranks, Connell's sought-after promotion, which would have placed him "on the same footing with the others" was rejected outright by the chief of the Signal Office. Connell was flatly told that he was not competent enough to take charge of a Signal Office station. To add to the sting, Connell believed that some severely disparaging

Aftermath

comments about his character made by Greely had also caused his removal from his preferred Signal Corps post in San Francisco to the less desirable station in Los Angeles. A bitter man, now intent on resigning, Connell advised Greely on June 27, 1886 that he believed his removal "was for other and different motives." Those "motives" struck a chord with Greely, and within a week Connell found himself seated at his desired location in San Francisco. Sensing vulnerability and concern on Greely's part, shrewdly, in what amounted to a threat, on July 8 Connell demanded re-enlistment as a first-class private and a permanent station in San Francisco. Connell intimated to Greely that if Greely "was aware of the pressure brought to bear on me to talk of certain subjects and which pressure I have so far resisted as far as I was able to resist, then under the circumstances you would think differently about my conduct." Both Greely and Hazen scrambled to push him to re-enlist and quash any such talk by Connell, but by then the request had fallen on deaf ears. Connell refused to sign the tendered re-enlistment papers and left the service on July 24. He told John Kislingbury that, now freed from the service, in the interest of "truth and justice" and an undisclosed personal profit motive as well, Connell could now write a tell-all book about the expedition.[2]

On July 18, prior to his resignation, Connell had gone so far as to meet with a reporter from the *San Francisco Chronicle* to prep the public and stimulate interest in his forthcoming work. As soon as his resignation became effective the next week, Connell would tell the suppressed but 'true' story of the Greely Expedition. The *Chronicle* gave a sample of the more sensational content that was to come:

> The truth has never been published and there are many important facts which have never seen daylight. There are some facts relating to the dissension between the officers, the cruelty of some of the men and the reported cannibalism which have never been made known. There is also the fixing of the responsibility of the fate which befell the expedition, for if the advice of some of the officers had been taken the calamity would never have happened.[3]

Retired from the service, on July 25 Connell felt free to launch a more detailed trial balloon about the expedition, and in particular the failings of its commander. In an interview arranged by the *San Francisco Chronicle* editor George Meek, Connell provided harsh criticism of Greely and his "dictatorial course." According to Connell, Greely mistreated Kislingbury, Pavy and other members and claimed that he was "weak, vain, overbearing and pompous," and unwilling to listen to his subordinates. The falling out with Kislingbury was just the first of many "dissensions and quarrels." Besides those criticisms of Greely, Connell vehemently disagreed with the shooting of Henry. He raised the factually accurate point that others besides Henry (namely Pavy and Whistler), had also stolen food but had not been shot. Connell also disputed the observations that placed Lockwood at the "Farthest North," a claim that was sure to cause the most angst on Greely's part.[4]

One expedition member who was evidently spooked by Connell's words was Sergeant Brainard, who wrote to Greely that "I think that Connell must be effectively silenced." In general though, Connell's newspaper interview evidently garnered more criticism than praise. Julius Frederick and Francis Long, both survivors, quickly responded publicly to the statements, denying their accuracy largely in full (though they agreed others had stolen food). Both blamed Connell's statements on mere jealousy, having been demoted by Greely during the expedition and labelling Connell an "obstructionist." In any event, besides the outright contradiction by Connell's companions, the passage of two years since Greely's return certainly had a bearing on the limited response to Connell's missive. Although newspapers carried Connell's story rather extensively, many viewed it as carping, especially after Frederick's and Long's vehement contradictions. The *San Jose Evening News* likely spoke for many with its blunt headline, "Let it Rest."[5]

Stung by the backlash, Connell wrote to Charles Clark that he had dropped his book plans. He advised Clark that his remarks "have been unkindly received by the public, and I denounced as a falsifier and a slanderer. I hope therefore that you will appreciate my motives in keeping silent in this whole matter hereafter when I tell you in my weak constitution I have suffered much already and

Aftermath

cannot afford to suffer the slings and arrows of outrageous fortune any longer. Although I have finished my book, I am not inclined to have it published for no other reason than my ease of mind." Ironically, though Julius Frederick had publicly stood by Greely, privately he confided to Lieutenant Doane that Doane would have been the better choice for command.[6]

Perhaps other reasons caused Connell's reticence at book authorship. After the *Chronicle* interview of July 25, Hazen wrote Connell "to reconsider the whole matter and not do it." Connell had the re-enlistment in hand, and now through Hazen's immediate efforts, was accepted, promoted to first-class private, and then a coveted position as sergeant. With leverage in his favor, he even garnered a transfer to Eureka, California, where he preferred to serve. Connell therefore turned over to Mrs. Pavy his draft work and other papers he had assembled.

At the same time, however, Charles Clark now viewed matters involving Greely quite differently. By mid-June 1886, Greely's *Three Years of Arctic Service* had been heavily advertised and was widely available. About the falling out between Frederick Kislingbury and his commander, Greely had this to say:

> On the 25th Lieutenant Kislingbury spent the day on the *Proteus* and the next day, dissatisfied with the expeditionary regulations, requested that he be relieved from duty with the expedition. He was relieved and ordered to report to the Chief Signal Officer. Unfortunately, the *Proteus* got under way just as Lieutenant Kislingbury was leaving the station, and he was obliged to return to Conger. He remained consequently at Conger, doing no duty, and with no further requirement than that he should conform to the police regulations of the station. He at no time requested to return to duty as an officer of the expedition.... These unfortunate episodes emphasize the necessity of selecting for Arctic service only men and officers of thorough military qualities, among which subordination is by no means of secondary importance.[7]

Dancing Chief

Its stinging rebuke of Frederick Kislingbury, namely the reference to the lack of "thorough military qualities," and Greely's curt characterization of the falling out, cut Clark and the Kislingbury brothers like a knife. With Greely's support of Kislingbury's children now a foregone fact, an unrestrained Clark now approached Sergeant David Brainard looking for an ally in support of Frederick Kislingbury. With his promotion to commissioned officer pending, and strongly supported by both Greely and Hazen, Brainard quickly quelled any suggestion that he would cross wires with his former commander. In a letter to Clark, he wrote:

> I cannot blame you for feeling indignant at the manner in which the world has construed poor Fred's trouble with Greely at Fort Conger, but I think that you are wrong in attributing to Lt. Greely any suppression or mischaracterization of facts concerning that unfortunate affair. So far as my knowledge of the matter extends, it occurred precisely as Lt. Greely stated it on his return from the North, and as he has also explained in his book *Three Years of Arctic Service*. Of course there might have been other differences between them, but if there was I know nothing of them.... He [Kislingbury] applied to be relieved from duty and was at once granted the request, but the steamer moved before he could get on board, and much against his inclination he was forced to remain.[8]

Either intentionally or as an oversight, Brainard's trite response avoided any of the circumstances or surrounding context leading to Kislingbury's resignation. The most Brainard would proffer to Clark was that "the only cause ever assigned for Fred's application to be relieved from duty with the expedition is the one Lt. Greely has made and which will also be found in his official report." Brainard was prepared to make available his journal to Clark for such information as Clark might require. Evidently, Clark was formulating plans to publish Kislingbury's journal from the expedition. Curiously, Brainard had advised Clark that Kislingbury did keep a diary, but that Kislingbury had advised Brainard that it contained entries only

Aftermath

through Kislingbury's resignation and, being bulky and of little value, was left at Fort Conger.[9]

With the Kislingbury boys' pensions firmly established by law, Clark could take a far more aggressive and direct tack with Greely. On July 2, 1886, he wrote to him indignantly demanding to know why the government had denied him the return of Kislingbury's papers and personal effects for months while they made use of them. More pointedly, however, Clark claimed that both Greely and Hazen "accuse Kislingbury of many things" without providing any specifics. He demanded that "if you [Greely] have anything against him in his record that you wish to tell me, I can stand it and at the same time be impartial as to my friend's faults...." The normally reserved Clark added a final caustic rebuke, advising Greely that "for your own good" he would advise Greely to hire sober agents to peddle his book (*Three Years of Arctic Service*), as the agent who approached Clark in Detroit was intoxicated.[10]

On July 27, 1886, just two days after Connell's exposé in the *San Francisco Chronicle*, in a likely coordinated launch, the *Detroit Free Press* published extracts from Kislingbury's journal. According to the paper, a few days prior to the publication Clark had managed to obtain some seventy-seven closely-written pages of an unbound diary kept by Kislingbury, and two and one-half pages from another. Evidently, Brainard had been wrong about, or had withheld from Clark the knowledge of, its existence. The entries quoted by the *Free Press* referenced basically the same complimentary entries of Frederick Kislingbury that the Kislingbury brothers had published in the *Rochester Democrat and Chronicle* the year before. Like Connell, the article was carried by a number of newspapers, but quickly faded without a splash.

At about the same time, Clark also pushed Brainard to produce a work on the expedition, perhaps believing Brainard would be favorably disposed to offer up a "true" account of the expedition. By now, as the recent beneficiary of a promotion to a commissioned officer, second lieutenant, Brainard boasted to Clark that "I stand on independent ground now, and can write and say just what I please—as I have always done," a statement that certainly stretched the truth of the matter. Nonetheless, Brainard knew where his bread was buttered, and declined the request citing the need to focus his attention on meeting the requirements required of a Regular Army officer. However, he had no hesitation in promoting further action, noting that "I see no harm in going ahead with what you have—with Mrs. Pavy's notes—and prepare the book now. What I could say would not materially add to the value of the publication." Privately, however, Brainard was more circumspect. Having received a list of questions directly from Lilla Pavy about her husband Octave, Brainard confided to Henrietta Greely that he believed that Lilla Pavy's objective was to "magnify and distort everything in her publications in such a manner as to deceive the public." Brainard would respond guardedly in his answers to Mrs. Pavy to protect Adolphus Greely, noting that Greely's "interests are my own."[11]

The Kislingbury and Pavy families had remained united in the deaths of their relatives on the expedition. Lilla Pavy, as the widow of Dr. Octave Pavy, had already published two articles in the *North American Review* defending her husband. Like the Kislingbury family, she too had believed that Greely had discredited Octave Pavy. She was hellbent on redeeming her husband's name. In furtherance of that objective, she approached Clark and the Kislingbury brothers with a proposal to publish a biography of Pavy drawn from Pavy's diary, together with a biography of Kislingbury with extracts from his diary. The work never came to fruition, though Clark turned over the Kislingbury diary to her and she vowed to the Kislingburys that "she would do justice to all concerned."[12]

Lilla Pavy was not prepared to give up on Brainard. She wrote to Clark that Brainard might be open to reconsideration. She stated that "we know not the influence behind the throne," i.e., Greely, and the extent to which Greely may have been the cause of Brainard's hesitance. If Greely failed to receive his coveted appointment as chief of the Signal Corp, she believed that there was a chance that Brainard would agree to publish his diary. Lilla Pavy understood how influential Brainard was with the other survivors. If Brainard had acceded and offered up his diary, she believed that others would follow. Greely, however, would receive his promotion and the publication of Brainard's diary would be delayed almost thirty-five years, and even then, it would be largely supportive of Greely.[13]

Aftermath

For his own part, the unrestrained Clark wrote a series of strongly worded telegrams to Senator Thomas W. Palmer (MI) opposing Greely's nomination as chief of the Signal Corps. A similar letter in opposition was sent to Senator Omar D. Conger (MI), though Conger had no desire to thwart Greely's promotion. The irony was certainly not lost on Clark that Conger was a proponent of the expedition and the namesake of Greely's headquarters on Ellesmere Island (Fort Conger). Clark also found an outlet in the *St. Paul Globe*, calling for a postponement while an investigation into Mrs. Pavy's charges of mismanagement by Greely were heard. Mrs. Pavy appeared before the Military Committee of the Senate to oppose Greely's nomination until the charges were addressed. But her lobbying was wholly ineffectual as the nomination was never in doubt. Greely's nomination was unanimously approved in March 1887.[14]

Over time and with fading memories, some antagonists were prepared to let bygones be bygones. In early 1887, William Kislingbury advised Clark that "my views on the Greely affair have changed from animosity towards the commander to that of leaving for a higher power to deal out." William even went so far as to support Greely's appointment as chief signal officer (much to his brother John's consternation), writing to President Grover Cleveland that Greely's selection "ought to be preferred" based on his experience as a scientist. However, he maintained that in his conduct towards his officers and men Greely showed prejudicial feelings and lack of judgment. Mrs. Pavy was not of such a forgiving nature. William wrote that "she is not in same frame of mind regarding "G" [Greely] as I. I don't wonder at it. Time may change this. A wronged woman, she deserves our aid and sympathy." Unfortunately for Lilla Pavy, she never did manage to publish a book defending her husband. In 1887, she retreated to Europe for a year to regain her health. Within several years, she had remarried and, by all evidence, seems to have finally put the affair behind her. But John Kislingbury never buried the hatchet. As late as August 1887, he was still meeting with survivors of the expedition on an unsuccessful campaign to open an investigation.[15]

Charles Clark had his own personal troubles that hindered his responsibilities to Kislingbury's children. He suffered from an undisclosed illness, likely cancer, that forced him to reluctantly turn over guardianship of Douglass and Wheeler, neither of whom could remain with their host parents, the Bullocks and Schofields, respectively. The Bullocks were pained by the surrender of Douglass, but Seth was supervising a mining business, and he and his wife believed the school-age Douglass could receive a better education back east. As for Wheeler, with both Lieutenant Colonel Schofield and his wife Alma (a Bullock sister) both dead, Reverend Schofield and his wife were reluctant to provide indefinite care for the boy. For the time being, Clark retained his guardianship over Harry and maintained his enrollment at the Michigan Military Academy in Detroit.

Adding to Clark's troubles was the irascible John Kislingbury, who insisted on absolute custody of both Wheeler and Douglass though he already had custody of Frederick's son Walter, and four of his own children. Only after some tense and bickering correspondence did Clark manage to reach a settlement by which Douglass was placed with John Kislingbury and his wife Marion, and Wheeler with William Kislingbury and his wife. Walter had already been in John Kislingbury's care for several years. Clark always believed that John Kislingbury was a poor choice for guardian, more concerned with receiving the financial support from the position than any real love for the boys. Clark had less angst in turning over guardianship of Wheeler to William Kislingbury and his wife. Though Clark would have preferred to retain at least Wheeler, he believed that William and his wife at least had the true interest of the boy at heart.[16]

The boys themselves shared a very close bond with Clark, who fulfilled his responsibilities to Frederick Kislingbury not out of duty, but out of fondness for his friend. Over the years, his guardianship over the boys had struck an appropriate balance between discipline and self-sufficiency, tempered by his own desire to help them without spoiling them. Well beyond their guardianship, "Uncle Charlie" as he was affectionately referred to, received letters from the boys filled with love and gratitude. Seth Bullock, also deeply troubled by the transfer of guardianship to the Kislingburys, declared to Clark with poignant regret that "the poor little fellows seem destined to be cast upon the sea of life without having a home. As fast as they form attachment for persons and places something surely happens to send them adrift." However, at the age of nineteen, Bullock believed that Harry was at the age by which he "must earn his own living."[17]

All four of Frederick's sons nonetheless successfully found their way in life, though the road had quite a few turns. Harry remained under Charles Clark's guardianship and graduated from the Michigan Military Academy in 1886. Unable to qualify for an appointment at the U.S. Naval Academy, he tried his hand at a sea-faring career, initially training for the merchant marine service. A miserable five-month voyage aboard the clipper ship *St. Mark* from New York to San Francisco discouraged him from a career at sea. For a brief time, he did well running the shoe department at Newhall's Sons & Co. in San Francisco. He found his passion as a locomotive engineer, initially for the Santa Fe, then the Zuni Mountain Railroad and later in Panama as a locomotive engineer on the canal project. One newspaper account reported that he served as an engineer for the National Railroad of Mexico. In one hairbreadth escape, it was said that he almost lost his life when a train he was running ran off a bridge that had been demolished by rebels. Harry only saved himself by jumping out as the engine was falling and before it reached bottom. He married his first wife, Annie Hawks, on July 11, 1891, and had one child. Records show a subsequent marriage to Catherine Christman on April 14, 1910. He died on March 1, 1943 at the age of seventy-five.[18]

In contrast to Harry, Walter lived a far shorter life. He attended the Cass School in Detroit until 1883 and thereafter lived with John Kislingbury's family in Rochester through 1889. Like his father before him, he enlisted in the military. From 1890 through 1894, he served with the 4th Infantry in Fort Sherman, Idaho. Like his brother Harry, following his discharge Walter became a well-regarded railroad employee, working for the El Paso & Southwestern and others in the southwest. Married to Laura Coburn, he had three children, but the two divorced shortly before his death. Sadly, a newspaper reported that two of his daughters had visited him in El

Dancing Chief

Douglass Kislingbury at age thirty.

Paso, begging him to return to his home in Winslow, Arizona. He declined, and met his death in El Paso—suicide by opium several hours later at the age of thirty-three.[19]

Douglass Kislingbury sought to follow in the footsteps of his father to the North. Like Frederick Kislingbury, he was an expert marksman and hunter, and an avid outdoorsman. He once claimed to have hiked fifty miles, and the same day climbed the summit of a fourteen-thousand-foot mountain. At the age of seventeen, the young man sought to join Robert Peary's 1891 polar expedition for North Greenland, which was then organizing. He had thoughts of visiting his father's station at Fort Conger on Ellesmere Island to retrieve records relating to his father believed to have been left behind by Greely. Douglass made his request to Peary in secrecy without informing his guardian, John Kislingbury, no doubt fearing John would refuse. Upon learning of Douglass's plan to join, John initially acquiesced. However, upon intercepting Peary's telegram to Douglass announcing that "You are accepted. Report to me at once in Washington," the reality of the situation caused him to withhold Peary's reply from Douglass. Disappointed from what he perceived as a lack of response, Douglass did not learn of the acceptance telegram until four years later, when on his twenty-first birthday,

Aftermath

John Kislingbury tendered the acceptance as a souvenir, a rather bitter one at best.[20]

Douglass did make the personal acquaintance of Peary, and Peary returned several artifacts of Frederick Kislingbury to him retrieved by Peary from Fort Conger. Douglass settled in a comfortable position as a sales representative for a large Ohio candy manufacturer, the Catawba Candy Company (later the Planters Nut and Chocolate Company), headquartered in San Francisco.

In 1928, one newspaper report claimed that Douglass was seeking a position on Admiral Richard Byrd's expedition organizing for the South Pole. Nothing seems to have come of that, though he did volunteer for an expedition with the arctic explorer Donald Macmillan in 1932, which also came to nothing. For Douglass, the northern plains where his father served held as much appeal as the arctic. He made several visits to Fort Custer, the site of his father's station in the 1870s. In 1931, he visited Mandan, North Dakota, as a guest of the Sioux. In a traditional ceremony he was given the name "Bear Looking Back," a recognition as much for his father as for himself. Douglass was also presented with an elaborate beaded and buckskin saddle bag and gun case, fashioned by a Sioux woman. He married Lillie Mae Kislingbury, the daughter of John Kislingbury. The couple had several children and ultimately settled in San Francisco. Douglass Kislingbury died on November 20, 1946.[21]

Wheeler, the youngest of the Kislingbury boys, was also committed to the memory of his father. He married Catherine Wahl on October 20, 1896 and the couple had three children. Like his brothers, the railroad held a special attraction. Wheeler served as a brakeman on the so-called Albuquerque division, in the American southwest. As a member of the national guard for five years, he held all the shooting records from "marksman" to "distinguished expert." In 1913, Wheeler contracted with Frank L. Mulgrew to publish a biography of his father Frederick Kislingbury. Mulgrew, a prominent newspaper man in the San Francisco area, had arranged to sell the rights to the feature to *Harper's Magazine*. Wheeler sought no money from the project. He simply wanted to correct the record and to "show Greely that there is still one of the Kislingburys left yet that will make him sit up and take notice," he told his former guardian Charles Clark. However the project was abandoned after John Kislingbury claimed to hold the original diary and demanded compensation for the work. Adding to the frustration, Mulgrew disappeared with the deposit paid by Wheeler, and any monies paid by *Harper's Magazine*.[22]

Wheeler did meet Greely, a principle topic of that unpublished biography. Wheeler recounted for Clark that while in Los Angeles in 1906, a local newspaper announced that Greely was staying at the stylish Van Nuys Hotel in Los Angeles. Anxious to meet his father's commanding officer, Wheeler waited in the lobby while Greely had his breakfast. As Greely exited the dining hall, a clerk pointed him out to Wheeler, who rushed over to introduce himself. Wheeler held out his hand, but rather than shaking his outstretched hand, "He [Greely] merely touched it, asking me to excuse him as he was going out on the sidewalk to have his picture taken," he told Clark. Wheeler followed him thinking he would have the courtesy of returning to speak to him, but instead Greely reentered the hotel from another door and dashed off, with Wheeler adding, "that was the last I ever saw of Gen. Greely—and I don't wonder now since I have read father's diary. It's a good thing I hadn't read it before." Wheeler died in San Francisco on March 10, 1952.[23]

Notwithstanding the travails of the Lady Franklin Bay Expedition, time and the military were kind to Greely. In June 1886, he was promoted to captain. Less than one year later, on March 3, 1887, with the backing of President Cleveland, Greely was appointed chief of the Signal Corps and with it a promotion to brigadier general. As longtime leader of the Signal Corps and an innovator, during a career which ran from 1886 to 1906, Greely instituted the use of modern scientific instrumentation for weather measurement and communications, and pushed for advances in military aeronautics and the use of wireless. (His Signal Corps introduced the first governmental use of the telephone.) Under his supervision, between 1901-03, a telegraph system of some 2,000 miles was established in Alaska, a difficult task through harsh terrain and severe weather. On February 10, 1906, Greely was promoted to major general and was reassigned from the Signal Corps to command the Pacific Division in Fort Mason San Francisco. Two months later,

Aftermath

while Greely was headed east for his daughter's wedding, the San Francisco earthquake and firestorm had engulfed the city. After Brigadier General Frederick Funston instituted martial law and took active efforts to contain the fire, Greely returned to command the relief effort. Greely retired from the army in 1908, at the age of sixty-four. He received the Medal of Honor for a lifetime of service on March 27, 1935, shortly before his death on October 20, 1935 at the age of 91.

Appendix

The Transformation of David L. Brainard's LFBE Account

ONE UNANSWERED SIDE NOTE TO THE GREELY EXPEDITION bears mention due to Kislingbury's alleged involvement and the seriousness of the allegation. Over the years, the affair has been largely accepted without question by commentators. Brainard's conversation with Pavy on August 15, 1883, later dubbed a "mutiny," by those commentators, evidently haunted Brainard despite the scant attention it merited in his field notebook at the time. Over the years, Brainard felt obliged first to suppress, and subsequently to elaborate upon the matter.[1]

Brainard diligently maintained more than ten field notebooks during the expedition, recording his remarks contemporaneously, day-by-day, as they occurred, including a reference to the so-called "mutiny." Brainard also authored a three-volume quarto-sized journal, transcribing in ink the scribbled pencil entries from those field notebooks (the so-called "ink journal"). A handwritten note dated October 19, 1885 on the front fly leaf of the second volume of the "ink journal" (evidently in the hand of a Signal Office clerk) states that Brainard's entries after August 8, 1883, the day before their abandonment of Fort Conger, were completed by Brainard after the volumes were "filed" with the office of the Signal Corps. Accordingly, it is clear that unlike the field notebook entries, the entries in the ink journal for events after leaving Fort Conger were not completed by Brainard until after the rescue and return of the surviving members to the United States and prior to October 19, 1885.[2]

In light of their fortuitous rescue, Brainard could look with some optimism to his future career within the military. He had shown his commander loyalty, hard work and dedication to their

Appendix

purpose, without insubordination. All these were favorable aspects which spoke of potential further advancement, hopefully as a commissioned officer. Thus, after their salvation and return, a more discerning eye was applied by Brainard to his entries in the three-volume journal, principally those involving the circumstances of their retreat and the trying times at Fort Conger. Particularly disparaging criticisms by Brainard of his commander that were scribbled in his field notebooks in the heat of the moment were suppressed by Brainard. It is obvious why he would prefer that the notebook entry on August 19, 1883 would not see the light of day: "All that ignorance, stupidity, and an egotistical mind without judgment can do in the injury of our cause is being done." And that of 21 August: "Why will the United States government persist in sending a fool in command of Arctic expeditions when competent men can be obtained?" Curiously, however, besides suppressing the stinging criticisms of his commander, Brainard chose to omit completely from his "ink journal" his private talk with Pavy in regards to the "mutiny."[3]

Evidently, the complete suppression of the Pavy affair from the "ink journal" did not sit well with Brainard, who continued to ruminate about the troubling conversation with Pavy. In a separate handwritten memorandum by Brainard dated January 19, 1890, while he was posted at Fort Bidwell, California, Brainard felt compelled to offer up a detailed confession of that dramatic conversation and meeting with Pavy on August 15, 1883. That memorandum, set forth here in full, was placed in Brainard's "ink journal" after the date of August 15, 1883:

Fort Bidwell, California

January 19, 1890

Nearly six years having elapsed since the rescue of the surviving members of the Lady Franklin Bay Expedition at Cape Sabine. I have concluded to enclose a statement of fact which, for obvious reasons has never been mentioned

Appendix

by me until this time. All the actors in this affair, except Connell who knew of it but did not actively participate, are dead, and no one can be injured by making public an episode of life in this very camp (latitude 80°44" north) which might have had a very tragic ending but for the firmness and opposition of myself, egotistical as such a statement may appear. From the time the party left the station to begin the retreat, Lieut. Greely kept the men in a state of great anxiety owing to his desire to abandon the launch and put the boats on the floe and drift southward to Littleton Island. Scarcely a day would pass without his mentioning this, and at one time it was proposed to abandon all but twenty days provisions and go on the floe with the boats, and trust to Providence to accomplish our salvation. Such an act would be little short of madness, and everyone, except Greely, realized the dangers that would result from such a course, and fought hard to discourage it. The episode referred to occurred August 15, 1883 and was as follows:

Lieut. Kislingbury, Dr. Pavy and Sergt Rice came to me with a most extraordinary proposition as follows: Dr. Pavy would examine Lt. Greely and pronounce him insane and therefore incapable of maintaining longer the leadership of the expedition. This he (Dr. Pavy) said, would not be difficult to do, as the frequent outbursts of passion, without provocation, on Lt. Greely's part, evinced insanity of an emotional type if not something more serious, and he did not doubt his ability to establish the legitimacy of such professional action before a court of inquiry should we ever reach our homes. As soon as Lt. Greely was deposed, Lieut. Kislingbury would assume command of the expedition by virtue of his rank and return with the party to Fort Conger for the winter. In the spring we would retreat southward.... Lieutenant Lockwood was to be placed in arrest if he refused to acknowledge Lt. K[islingbury]'s authority or did not concur in his plans for the good of the expedition. Rice very strongly urged that I join them as the men would all go with me and that it was the only means of saving the party from certain destruction. While I was (or thought I was) perfectly familiar with the dangers that beset us, and was almost certain that disaster was inevitable should Greely follow his plans, I told them that I could not recognize any other than Lieut. Greely as commander of the expedition, and that I should resist with my life any attempt to force the command from him and further, that I knew with the exception of one or two men, the entire party would stand by me. This was the first and last time I was ever asked to engage in the mutiny-for it was nothing else-but frequent allusions to it were made by the chief actors mentioned above who never quite gave up the idea though they well knew its impracticability under the present circumstances. I did not mention the affair to Lieut. Greely at the time because I well knew his obstinate nature and feared he would immediately put in execution the plans... Had their plan been consummated, it would be interesting now to note what a great change such action would have made in the history of the expedition. It is not at all improbable that every man would have escaped with his life.[4]

Why Brainard felt compelled to retell the full affair in 1890, seven years after the fact, with added actors and with additional, and even modified, details is unclear. Brainard's justification, that the principal actors were dead, was as true when he composed the ink-journal entries as it was in 1890. Moreover, there were significant differences between his original field notes and the 1890 memorandum that make the later retelling a far more serious and nefarious affair. Brainard's notes from the original conversation referenced only one individual, Dr. Octave Pavy. Kislingbury, Rice and Connell were not participants, or even witnesses. In 1890, rather than a lone disgruntled malcontent, Pavy's plot had the backing of an officer and several enlisted men. Moreover, Brainard originally wrote that Pavy had "insinuated (subrosa) his intention" to declare Greely insane, meaning perhaps merely a suggestion, rather than having reached a firm decision. Most importantly, in the original notes, that action (to declare Greely insane) was conditional, meaning that Pavy would make the insanity declaration <u>only if</u> Greely issued the extraordinary order to take to the floes, a fateful order which never came to pass. In 1890, Brainard dropped that contingency so that the "mutiny" was then immediately at hand.

It was not until 1929 that Brainard published what he claimed was his own journal from the expedition, entitled *The Outpost of the Lost*. In that book and in his 1940 work *Six Came Back*, Brainard repeated the affair in nearly similar terms as the 1890 memorandum. Thus, in 1883, what had been one man's word (Pavy), by 1890 and thereafter had Brainard standing face-to-face with four expedition members hellbent on removing the commander immediately.[5]

In any event, why did Brainard see the sudden need to fully document the affair in 1890 in a manner different than in his field diary? Did he, in fact, wish to take credit for quashing the act and bolster the appearance of his own loyalty, especially if he was considering publication at some date? Was it because he had omitted completely the details of the "mutiny" from his "ink journal" and feared that someone might later discover the omission as a suppression? Oddly, Brainard also seems to contradict himself as to the consequences if the change in leadership and retreat to Fort Conger had come off. On the one hand, Brainard noted that his intervention may have prevented a "very tragic ending but for the firmness and opposition of myself," but on the other hand, in closing, he noted that had the action taken place, "it is not at all improbable that every man would have escaped with his life."

Why identify additional actors Kislingbury and Rice, neither of whom were alive to refute the facts? A review of the surviving diaries of the expedition members, including those of Pavy, Kislingbury, Rice, and Connell, all fail to find any mention of the affair at all. Since Brainard chose not to divulge the event at the time to his commander (itself a violation of duty), only Brainard's word as to its accuracy, and even its occurrence, stands.

Curiously, in another 1890 handwritten memorandum, while still biding his time at Fort Bidwell, Brainard also chose to share the details of a separate event that occurred in the early stages of the expedition. This memorandum was written on February 3, 1890,

Appendix

less than one month after his elaboration of the "mutiny." In his field notebook, on April 10, 1884, in the midst of their dreadful plight at Cape Sabine, the fading Whistler made a death-bed admission. Brainard simply recorded in his field notebook: "Whistler made a statement to both the Commanding Officer and myself, of which the conduct of Dr. Pavy in the field in the fall of 1881 of which I must question him further on our return to the U.S."[6]

Brainard did not elucidate as to that disclosure until the second 1890 memorandum. In that note, Brainard described an almost implausible story of the villainous means that Pavy considered to make a name for himself in the North:

> Fort Bidwell, Cal.
> February 3rd, 1890
>
> The 'disloyal conduct' as stated by Whistler, was to this effect. In October 1881, he [Dr. Pavy] left Fort Conger with party of Private Whistler and Jens, Eskimo dog driver, taking a dog team and sledge with provisions for a journey to Cape Joseph Henry. While on this journey, Whistler states that Dr. Pavy tried to induce him to join in an expedition to the north the following year, with the intention of making the highest latitude ever attained, and, further that Whistler should join him in stealing the only remaining dog team at the station so that the Greenland Party (Lieutenant Lockwood and Sergeant Brainard) could not travel so far, while the Doctor's party would be enabled to go much farther north. Whistler says that on his refusal to aid the Doctor in such a scheme, the latter became angry and abusive, whereupon Whistler drew a revolver. D.L.B.[7]

Though Greely was identified as a witness to this conversation, Greely makes no mention of it in his diary or elsewhere. In this case though, Brainard at least made a contemporary though brief mention of a conversation with Whistler in his field notebook. Like the "mutiny," why Brainard chose to elucidate its details remains a mystery. Brainard did reference the affair along the lines of the 1890 memorandum in his work *The Outpost of the Lost*.[8]

Brainard made other omissions and alterations in his "ink journal" and published works, though they were less significant in their import. For example, on April 27, 1884, he wrote in his field notebook that "Henry is a born thief as his 7th Cavalry name will show-a perfect fiend." The fact of Henry's previous 7th Cavalry service would suggest that Brainard and very likely Greely were aware of Henry's previous criminal history associated with that service, though neither mention it. Perhaps Brainard did not wish to publicly admit to knowledge of Henry's past, which surely would have reflected poorly on Greely's judgment in selecting him in the face of that knowledge.[9]

What can be drawn from these clarifications beyond an attempt to alter or correct the record remains a mystery.

Chapter Notes

Abbreviations

AG	Adjutant General
AAG	Assistant Adjutant General
AGO	Adjutant General's Office
ACP	Appointment, Commission, Personal
ALPLM	Abraham Lincoln Presidential Library and Museum
ARCIA	*Annual Report of the Commissioner of Indian Affairs*
EC	Explorers Club
FCLA	Fort Concho Library and Archives
KFP	Kislingbury Family Papers
LFBE	Lady Franklin Bay Expedition
MSU	Mississippi State University
MSUL	Montana State University Library
NA	National Archives
NSHS	Nebraska State Historical Society
LOC	Library of Congress
OIA	Office of Indian Affairs
RSC	Rauner Special Collections
SHSND	State Historical Society of North Dakota
UMI	University of Michigan

Chapter One. A Respectable Young Gentleman (Pages 1-6)

1. *Dutton, Allen & Co.'s Directory*, 285; Saxton, "Sport and Leisure in East Ilsley," 1.
2. Frederick Kislingbury, birth record dated December 16, 1845, no. 287,

Chapter Notes

East Ilsley Registrar District. Though his birth record states December 16, Kislingbury always marked his birthday as December 25. See Greely, *Three Years of Arctic Service,* 2: 215. Kislingbury's given name was Foster Frederick Kislingbury, but from a young age he was known as Frederick.
3. Saxton, "Lieutenant Frederick Kislingbury," 1; "Insolvent Debtors," *The Jurist,* 340.
4. Schmitt, "Rochester's Frederick Douglass," 13.
5. Farrington Campbell, Endorsement to Kislingbury application, September 11, 1872, Kislingbury Papers, ACP Files, NA (quotation).
6. Statement of Service, August 7, 1878, Kislingbury Papers, ACP Files, NA.
7. *The History of the Dewitt Guard*, 181-82 (quotations); "The Second in Command. Lieut. Kislingbury's Mutilated Body Disinterred," *New York Times,* August 15, 1884. Kislingbury was reported as "on surgeon's sick list" from October 21, 1864 until his mustering out November 11, 1864, perhaps due to this toe injury. Statement of Service, August 7, 1878, Kislingbury Papers, ACP Files, NA.
8. Statement of Service, August 7, 1878, Kislingbury Papers, ACP Files, NA; Kislingbury to Grant, September 10, 1872, U. S. Grant Papers, MSU. On October 22, 1865, his Company D, U.S. 4th Infantry, was transferred to Detroit. Powell, *A History of the Organization*, 63. Kislingbury's enlistment was for three years, expiring June 3, 1868. He re-enlisted as a private on July 3, 1868, and was reassigned to the U.S. 4th Infantry.
9. Gaspar and MacLeod, "A Case of Mistaken Identity," 6; George B. Jenners to Charles Clark, August 26, 1884 (informing Clark how Fred met Aggie), Clark Papers, UMI. George Bullock's family moved to Sandwich in about 1851 (the city of Sandwich was amalgamated into the city of Windsor in 1935).
10. Roosevelt, *The Happy Hunting-Grounds*, 158 (quoting Theodore Roosevelt).

Chapter Two. With the Pawnee Scouts (Pages 7-17)

1. Affidavit of Mary A. Harris (draft), Clark Papers, UMI; Powell, *A History of the Organization*," 65.
2. Kislingbury to "My Dear Mother," October 13, 1867, KFP (quotation).
3. Ibid. (quotation); Kislingbury to President U. S. Grant, September 10, 1872, U. S. Grant Papers, MSU.
4. Van De Logt, *War Party in Blue*, 241-44.
5. Ibid., 13, 32-33. For a history of Pawnee cultural and military prowess, see Ibid., 11-36.

Chapter Notes

6. Cody, *An Autobiography*, 185 (quotation).
7. Van De Logt, *War Party in Blue*, 122.
8. Carr, "Report of Operations," 825-26, Sheridan Papers, LOC; Cody, *An Autobiography*, 191; Bruce, *The Fighting Norths*, 72; Hyde, *Life of George Bent*, 332. See Van De Logt, *War Party in Blue*, 130-31, for a discussion of who had killed Tall Bull.
9. Cody, *An Autobiography*, 190 (quotation); North, *Man of the Plains*, 118-19.
10. Townsend, E. F., Fort Sedgwick, July 1869, Post Returns, NA (quotation).
11. Bruce, *The Fighting Norths*, 72. Other reports state that Tall Bull and his followers had been delayed in crossing the South Platte River due to high water at the time they were attacked. Hyde, *Life of George Bent*, 331.
12. Van De Logt, *War Party in Blue*, 16, 244.
13. Royall, "Report of the Operations," 865, Sheridan Papers, LOC (quotation).
14. Fisher, "The Royall and Duncan Pursuits," 299; Van De Logt, *War Party in Blue*, 136.
15. Duncan, "Operations of Republican River Expedition," 871, 876, Sheridan Papers, LOC (quotations).
16. Carr, "Report of Operations," 828, Sheridan Papers, LOC (first quotation); Duncan, "Operations of Republican River Expedition," 876, Sheridan Papers, LOC (second quotation); Warren, *Buffalo Bill's America*, 112; Van De Logt, *War Party in Blue*, 140.

Chapter Three. "The Most God-Forsaken Part of Uncle Sam's Dominions" (Pages 18-31)

1. Kislingbury to Grant, September 10, 1872, Kislingbury Papers, ACP Files, NA (quotation). On February 2, 1870, Kislingbury had re-enlisted and was assigned to the headquarters of the Department of the Lakes. On February 1, 1873 Kislingbury was discharged as chief clerk in the Department of the Lakes to become paymaster clerk to Major Valentine C. Hanna, but still residing in Detroit. Kislingbury to the Secretary of War, May 26, 1873. Ibid.
2. Miles, "Fort Concho in 1877," 31.
3. Leatherwood, "Llano Estacado."
4. Miles, "Fort Concho in 1877," 31 ("hovel"); Hooker, *Child of the Fighting Tenth*, 104; Grierson, *The Colonel's Lady*, 72, 81.
5. John Grierson to Benjamin Grierson, November 23, 1874, quoted in Grierson, "The Colonel's Lady," 71.

Chapter Notes

6. Matthews, *Fort Concho*, 24.
7. Benjamin Grierson to Alice Grierson, May 2, 1875, Grierson Papers, ALPLM.
8. Grierson, *The Colonel's Lady*, 75-76; Benjamin Grierson to Alice, May 6, 1875, Grierson Papers, ALPLM (quotations).
9. "Scouting on the 'Staked Plains,'" 541 (quotation); Fort Concho, September 1873, Post Returns, NA.
10. Greely, *Reminiscences*, 19 (quotation).
11. Ibid., 16 (quotation); Mitchell, *General Greely*, 49; Fort McPherson, June 1869, Post Returns, NA (noting Greely's arrival at Fort McPherson on June 3, 1869. The Republican River Expedition left the fort with Pawnee Scouts on June 9). That Greely discovered the Indian trails leading to Summit Springs is in Greely's "Statement of Service," AGO Letters Received by the Commission Branch, G702-CB1865, NA.
12. Mitchell, *General Greely*, 51-52.
13. *Annual Report of the Chief Signal-Officer for the Year 1876*, 119 (quotation); Greely, *Reminiscences,* 153; Fort Concho, May 1875-March 1876, Post Returns, NA; Greely to Chief Signal Officer, April 4, 1876, Greely Papers, LOC.

Chapter Four. The Great Sioux War (Pages 32-40)

1. Hedren, *Rosebud*, 62-65, 72.
2. Watson, "A History of Fort Yates," 27-28.
3. Carlin to Ruggles, September 27, 1877, Fort Yates, Letters Sent, Sept. 1877-Oct. 1878, NA (quotation).
4. Burke, ARCIA 1877, 39 (Burke quotations); Carlin to Ruggles, September 27, 1877 (Carlin quotations), Fort Yates, Letters Sent, Sept. 1877-Oct. 1878, NA; Hedren, *Rosebud*, 72.
5. Watson, "A History of Fort Yates," 8.

Chapter Five. Indian Scout Leader (Pages 41-48)

1. *Report of the Secretary of War for the Year 1876*, 537 (quotation).
2. Carlin to Ruggles, September 27, 1877, Fort Yates, Letters Sent, Sept. 1877-Oct. 1878, NA.
3. Ibid.; Fort Yates, October 1876, Post Returns, NA; "Indians Disarmed," *New York Herald*, October 27, 1876; "The Sioux: Disarming and Dismounting

Chapter Notes

the Standing Rock Agency Indians," *Daily National Republican* (Wash., D.C.), October 27, 1976; Clow, "General Philip Sheridan's Legacy," 465-66.

4. Carlin to Ruggles, September 27, 1877, Fort Yates, Letters Sent, Sept. 1877- Oct. 1878, NA.
5. Booth, "Crossed Arrows," 112-15; "The Standing Rock Agency," *Madison Daily Democrat* (Madison, WI), July 27, 1876.
6. Carlin to Ruggles, September 27, 1877, Fort Yates, Letters Sent, Sept. 1877-Oct. 1878, NA; Kislingbury to Post Adjutant, December 8, 1876, U.S. Army Indian Scouts, SHSND; Fort Yates, November and December, 1876, Post Returns, NA.
7. Kislingbury to Post Adjutant, December 26, 1876, OIA Letters Received 1824-1881, Standing Rock Agency, 1875-80:1877 NA (quotation).
8. Ibid. (first quotation); Carlin to Ruggles, September 27, 1877, Fort Yates, Letters Sent, Sept. 1877-Oct. 1878, NA (second quotation).
9. "Sitting Bull and the Sioux," *Columbus Evening Dispatch*, February 13, 1877 (quoting letter to the *Chicago Daily Tribune*, January 11, 1877); see Special Orders Nos. 145, 148, 156 and 168, dated December 1, 5, 13 and 29, 1876, respectively, Fort Yates, NA.
10. Kislingbury to Post Adjutant, December 3, 1876, U.S. Army Indian Scouts, SHSND; see also Booth, "Crossed Arrows," 113 and Van De Logt, *War Party in Blue*, 17 (contrast between military and Indian ponies).
11. Crook, General Order No. 19, March 6, 1873, *Army and Navy Journal*, April 5, 1873, 532.
12. Clow, "General Philip Sheridan's Legacy," 466-67; Anderson, "A History," 467; "The Sioux," *Chicago Daily Tribune*, December 26, 1876; Carlin to Ruggles, September 27, 1877, Fort Yates, Letters Sent, Sept. 1877-Oct. 1878, NA.
13. "Indians: Sending Sioux Ponies from Standing Rock to St. Paul," *Chicago Daily Tribune*, February 1, 1877 (quotation); Carlin to Ruggles, September 27, 1877, Fort Yates, Letters Sent, Sept. 1877-Oct. 1878, NA.
14. Carlin to Ruggles, September 27, 1877, Fort Yates, Letters Sent, Sept. 1877-Oct. 1878, NA (first two quotations); Carlin to Kislingbury, May 18, 1877, Fort Yates, Endorsements Sent, June 1875-Sept. 1881, NA (third quotation); Special Order No. 21, February 5, 1877, Fort Yates, NA; Forrest, "Dismounting the Sioux," 13; "Indians: Sending Sioux Ponies from Standing Rock to St. Paul," *Chicago Daily Tribune*, February 1, 1877.

Chapter Notes

Chapter Six. Fort Yates (Pages 49-60)

1. Kislingbury to Post Adjutant, June 13, 1877, U.S. Army Indians Scouts, SHSND; Forrest, "Dismounting the Sioux," 11.
2. Forrest, "Dismounting the Sioux," 12-13.
3. Carlin to Ruggles, Sept. 27, 1877, Fort Yates, Letters Sent, Sept. 1877-Oct. 1878, NA.
4. Terry to Senator William B. Allison, January 26, 1877, OIA Letters Received 1824-1881, Dakota Superintendency, 1861-80:1878, NA.
5. Kislingbury to "Captain," November 26, 1877, OIA Letters Received, 1824-1881, Dakota Superintendency, 1861-80:1878, NA (quotation).
6. Terry to McCrary, December 13, 1877, OIA Letters Received, 1824-1881, Dakota Superintendency, 1861-80:1878, NA (quotation).
7. Kislingbury to Post Adjutant, November 17, 1877, OIA Letters Received 1824-1881, Dakota Superintendency, 1861-80:1877, NA (quotation); Special Order No. 175, October 18, 1877, Fort Yates, NA. For an earlier and more brief report, see Kislingbury to Post Adjutant November 11, 1877, Fort Yates, Letters Received, 1876-77, NA.
8. Kislingbury to Post Adjutant, November 17, 1877, OIA Letters Received, 1824-1881, Dakota Superintendency, 1861-80:1877, NA (quotation).
9. Ibid. (quotation).
10. Ibid. (quotations); "Educating the Indians," *Chicago Inter-Ocean*, December 6, 1877.
11. Carlin to Terry (first three quotations), November 18, 1877, and Sheridan to AG, December 4, 1877 (fourth quotation), OIA Letters Received 1824-1881, Dakota Superintendency, 1861-80:1877, NA.
12. "Kislingbury's Experiences," *Deadwood Pioneer-Press,* December 3, 1877 (Carlin quotation); see also, "Lieut. Kislingbury," *Army and Navy Journal,* December 1, 1877, 260. A far more exaggerated account of the encounter, possibly by the interpreter Allison, appeared in the *Cincinnati Enquirer* years later. "Kislingbury, Hardy, Honest and Brave," *Cincinnati Enquirer,* March 28, 1885.
13. Hackett, "*Along the Upper Missouri*," 50 (quotation).
14. AAG to Carlin, June 26, 1877, Fort Yates, Letters Received, 1876-77, NA (quotation).
15. Carlin to AAG, August 23, 1877, Fort Yates, Endorsements Sent and Received, June 1875-Sept. 1891, NA (quotation). Carlin had made an earlier request, in March 1877, that was likewise approved. Carlin to Terry, March

Chapter Notes

11, 1877, Fort Yates, Letters Received, 1876-77, NA.
16. Carlin to AAG, February 19, 1878, Fort Yates, Endorsements Sent and Received, June 1875-Sept. 1891, NA.
17. Brown to Commanding Officer, July 10, 1877, Fort Yates, Letters Received, 1876-77, NA (quotations).
18. Kislingbury to Captain Poland, July 10, 1877, Fort Yates, Letters Received, 1876-77, NA (quotations).
19. Clow, "General Philip Sheridan's Legacy," 467; Anderson, "A History," 471-74.

Chapter Seven. Dancing Chief (Pages 61-71)

1. "Standing Rock," *Army and Navy Journal*, January 19, 1878, 372.
2. Special Order No. 67, May 21, 1877, Fort Yates, NA (quotation).
3. Hedren, *After Custer*, 28, 57.
4. *Annual Report of the Chief Signal-Officer for the Year 1879*, 224 (quotation).
5. Huggins to Commanding Officer, April 6, 1880, OIA Letters Received 1824-1881, Montana Superintendency 1864-1880: 1880, NA (quotation).
6. Fort Custer, March, April, July and August, 1880, Post Returns, NA; Report of Brigadier General Terry, in *Report of the Secretary of War for the Year 1880*, 1:63; Ruggles to Davidson, June 4, 1899, in "Complimentary Mention in General Orders," *Helena Weekly Herald*, July 1, 1880 (quotation).
7. Butler, "Lieut. Frederick Kislingbury," 665 (quoting an unnamed soldier). Butler was editor of *The Pythian Knight*.
8. Hanson, *The Conquest of the Missouri*, 397, 400.
9. Fort Custer, December, 1880 and February, 1881, Post Returns, NA; Colonel J. W. Davidson to AAG, November 1, 1880, Fort Custer, Letters Sent, 1877-1898, NA; Kislingbury, Musselshell Account. Kislingbury's account of the Musselshell incident appears to be a sketch prepared by Charles Clark from Kislingbury's journal. Harry to Clark, May 7, 1913, Clark Papers, UMI.
10. Kislingbury, Musselshell Account (quotation).
11. Ibid. (quotation).
12. Thomas, *Bíilaachia-White Swan*, 50-51.
13. Kislingbury, Musselshell Account (first quotation); Davidson to AAG, November 11, 1880, Fort Custer, Telegrams Sent, June 10, 1880-Nov. 16, 1881, NA (second quotation); see also Davidson to AAG, November 12, 1880 (quoting Kislingbury's request for aid), OIA Letters Received 1824-1881, Dakota Superintendency:1861-1880: 1880, NA; Fort Keogh, January 1881, Post Returns, NA.

Chapter Notes

Chapter Eight. Trying Times (Pages 72-78)

1. Lieutenant Colonel Guido Ilges, "To Kislingbury's Relief," *St. Louis Globe*, July 21, 1884 (quotation).
2. Ibid.; Reed to AAG, November 16, 1880, Letters Received 1824-1881, Montana Superintendency 1878-80: 1880 (reporting that Yanktonai returning to Poplar Agency had a "skirmish" with Indians on the Musselshell); see also Fort Custer, December, 1880, Post Returns, NA (noting that "a stealing party of Yanktonias" attacked Kislingbury's group). The passage of time may have altered Ilges's memory slightly of the event. In an interview by a reporter from the *St. Louis Globe* in 1884, Ilges added that "one of the attackers named 'Big Foot' was killed by Kislingbury and his body tacked to a tree." Ilges, "To Kislingbury's Relief," *St. Louis Globe*, July 21, 1884. According to Kislingbury, it was the scouts who accounted for the deaths.
3. Ilges, "To Kislingbury's Relief," *St. Louis Globe*, July 21, 1884 (quotation).
4. Kislingbury, Musselshell Account (quotation).
5. Ilges, "To Kislingbury's Relief," *St. Louis Globe*, July 21, 1884 (first quotation); Kislingbury, Musselshell Account (second quotation). Pursuant to field orders dated December 2, 1880, Kislingbury was, in fact, relieved of duty of the command by the district commander. KFP (extract copy of field orders).
6. Kislingbury to Greely, January 13, 1881, Greely Papers, LOC (quotations).
7. "Died," *Army and Navy Journal*, December 18, 1880, 402; Davidson to AAG, December 9, 1880, Fort Custer, Telegrams Sent, June 30, 1880-November 16, 1881, NA.
8. Kislingbury, Musselshell Account (quotation); *Army and Navy Journal*, May 14, 1881, 851.

Chapter Nine. The Lady Franklin Bay Expedition (Pages 79-95)

1. Howgate, *Polar Colonization: Memorial to Congress*, 15-17.
2. Kislingbury to Greely, January 13, 1881, Greely Papers, LOC.
3. Endorsement of W. T. Sherman, May 5, 1880, Gustavus C. Doane Papers, MSUL (quotation).
4. Greely to the Secretary of War, June 8, 1880, Greely Papers, LOC.
5. Lilla May Pavy to Octave Pavy, n.d. (quotations), Lady Franklin Bay Expedition, EC.
6. Endorsement of W. T. Sherman, March 12, 1881, AGO Letters Received

Chapter Notes

(Main Series), 1881-1889, NA (quotation).

7. Hazen to General A. H. Terry May 6, 1881, AGO Letters Received (Main Series), 1881-1889, NA (quotation).
8. Kislingbury to Greely, January 14, 1881, Greely Papers, LOC (quotation); Greely to AG, March 12, 1881, Kislingbury Papers, ACP Files, NA. See also William Kislingbury to Charles Clark, January 5, 1887, Clark Papers, UMI (William quotes a letter in which "Greely urges Fred to go on the expedition"). In his *Three Years of Arctic Service*, Greely had voiced the opinion that Kislingbury "had a fine reputation for field duty." Greely, *Three Years of Arctic Service*, 1:39.
9. Kislingbury to Greely January 13, 1881, Greely Papers, LOC (quotation).
10. Endorsement of W. T. Sherman March 14, 1881, Kislingbury Papers, ACP Files, NA (quotation).
11. Greely, *Three Years of Arctic Service*, 1:39 (quotation). For a biography of Lockwood, see Lanman, *Farthest North*.
12. See Urness, *Twenty-Five Brave Men*, for details on the backgrounds of the members.
13. Morris to AAG November 28, 1881 and January 2, 1882, AGO Letters Received (Main Series), 1881-89, NA (quotations).
14. Davidson to AAG April 16, 1881, AGO Letters Received (Main Series), 1881-89, NA (quotations). Only after the fact did Greely advise Kislingbury that he preferred that the offer be kept secret, to which Kislingbury remarked that "I'd like to see anybody keep anything a secret at a military post." Kislingbury to Greely February 11, 1881, Greely Papers, LOC. To that point, Captain Davidson admitted to the assistant adjutant general that he had seen an "extract" of the telegram from Greely. Davidson to the AAG, April 16, 1881, AGO Letters Received (Main Series), 1881-89, NA.
15. AG to Commanding General, Military Division of the Missouri, April 8, 1881, AGO Letters Received (Main Series), 1881-89, NA.
16. "Francis L. Long, Weather Man Dies," *The Sun* (New York), June 9, 1916.
17. Crook, Special Order No. 33, Headquarters of the Department of the Platte, April 19, 1881 (copy in Greely Papers, LOC; Elison to Greely April 20, 1881 (first quotation), Greely Papers, LOC; "Dr. Pavey [sic] of the Greely Expedition," *The Buffalo Daily Republic*, August 14, 1884 (second quotation).
18. "Private Henry a Bad Fellow," *Reporter and Farmer* (Webster, N.D.), September 4, 1884; "Enlisted Men Sentenced to Confinement," *Army and Navy Journal*, January 11, 1879, 385.

19. Stein, "General David L. Brainard, U.S. Army."
20. Kislingbury to Greely January 13, 1881, Greely Papers, LOC (quotation).
21. Ibid. (quotation).
22. Lieutenant Guido Ilges, "To Kislingbury's Relief," *St. Louis Globe*, July 21, 1884 (quotations).
23. "A Presentiment Fulfilled," *The Evening Mail* (Stockton, CA), July 19, 1884 (first four quotations); Lohman to Charles Clark, December 29, 1884, Clark Papers, UMI (fifth and sixth quotations).
24. Declaration of F. Kislingbury, June 10, 1881, Clark Papers, UMI; Appointment of John Kislingbury guardian of Walter Kislingbury, July 22, 1880, Kislingbury Papers, ACP Files, NA.

Chapter Ten. Seeds of Discontent (Pages 96–111)

1. Lanman, "Farthest North," 64-65 (first quotation); Kislingbury to Clark, May 29, 1881, Clark Papers, UMI (second quotation).
2. Macdona, "The Arctic Search: Arrival of the *Alliance* at the Port of Reikiavik [sic], Iceland," *New York Herald,* July 31, 1881 (quotation).
3. Kislingbury to an unnamed correspondent, June 15, 1881 (quotation), KFP.
4. John Kislingbury to Harry K., April 19, 1886, Clark Papers, UMI (first and second quotations); Extracts from a total of twelve letters have survived: May 31, June 6, 10, 15, 17 and 21, July 6, 7, 16, 29 and August 12 and 19, 1881, KFP.
5. Kislingbury to unnamed correspondent, June 21, 1881 (first and third quotation); June 6, 1881 (second quotation), KFP.
6. Kislingbury to Douglass Kislingbury, July 17, 1881, Orin Grant Libby Papers, SHSND (quotations).
7. Kislingbury to unnamed correspondent, July 29, 1881, KFP (first quotation); Rice, Journal, July 27, 1881, Rice Papers, RSC (second quotation).
8. Kislingbury to Douglass, August 8, 1881 (quotations), Orin Grant Libby Papers, SHSND.
9. Kislingbury, Journal, August 1, 1881, KFP (quotation).
10. Ibid. (quotations); "The Greely Party. Revelations of Sergeant Connell," *The San Francisco Chronicle*, July 25, 1886.
11. Kislingbury, Journal, August 1, 1881, KFP (quotations). Curiously, a December 1886 article appearing in *The Pythian Knight*, a Rochester, New York publication (unnamed but likely written by Frederick's brother John),

Chapter Notes

claimed that the falling out between Greely and Kislingbury began as early as late June 1881. While in St. John's organizing the supplies, Kislingbury felt obliged to advise Greely that the fur-clothing was inadequate and should be acquired before leaving St. John's. Unable to take even the slightest hint of criticism, Greely "took a violent dislike to the plain outspoken second officer," according to the unidentified writer. When Greely finally acknowledged that additional furs were needed while in Upernavik, Greely selected Lockwood in place of Kislingbury to take the steamer *Lady Greely* to Proven, Greenland for the two Greenlanders and for the needed items, thus "marking the beginning of Greely's deliberate purpose to supplant Kislingbury by Lockwood." "A Pythian Hero," 3.

12. Brainard, Journal, July 31, 1881, LFBE Records, NA (Brainard quotations); Greely to Henrietta, July 31, 1881, Greely Papers, LOC (Starr quotation). Francis Long found Greely's clothing inspection the only order to which he found complaint. "Connell's Charges," *St. Louis Post-Dispatch*, July 26, 1886.
13. Adolphus Greely to Henrietta Greely July 31, 1881, Greely Papers, LOC (quotation).
14. Kislingbury, Journal, August 1, 1881, KFP (quotation).
15. Dick, *Muskox Land*, 37.
16. Kislingbury to Douglass, August 8, 1881, Orin Grant Libby Papers, SHSND (quotations).
17. Apple, "In Search of a Star," 19-20 (quoting the *Memoirs of Henry Clay* in the Susan Clay Sawitzky Papers, privately held).
18. Kislingbury to Harry and Walter Kislingbury, August 17, 1881, Clark Papers, UMI (quotations).
19. Kislingbury to an unnamed correspondent, August 12, 1881 (first quotation) and August 19, 1881 (second quotation), KFP.

Chapter Eleven. Fort Conger (Pages 112-126)

1. Wamsley, "The Arctic Exploits of Dr. Octave Pavy," 9.
2. Ibid., 10. In a letter to Henrietta, Greely claimed that Pavy had finally agreed to let Greely decide whether to keep Clay, and that regardless of Greely's decision, he (Pavy) would remain. Adolphus to Henrietta, August 14, 1881, Greely Papers, LOC. For the details of Clay's death, see "Harry Clay Shot," *Times-Picayune* (New Orleans), September 23, 1884.
3. Adolphus Greely to Henrietta Greely, August 15, 1881 (first two quotations),

Chapter Notes

Greely Papers, LOC; Kislingbury to Greely, August 16, 1881 (third quotation), and Lockwood to Greely, August 16, 1881 (fourth quotation), AGO Letters Received (Main Series), 1881-89, NA.
4. Greely, Journal, August 22, 1881, Greely Papers, LOC (quotation).
5. Lanman, *Farthest North*, 93 (first quotation); Greely, Journal, August 22, 1881, Greely Papers, LOC (remaining quotations).
6. Kislingbury, Journal, August 26, 1881, KFP (first quotation); Greely Journal, August 26, 1881 (second and third quotations), Greely Papers, LOC.
7. Kislingbury, Journal, August 26, 1881, KFP (quotation).
8. Kislingbury to First Lieut. A. W. Greely, "Appendix No. 10. Lieutenant Kislingbury's request to be relieved, August 26, 1881," in Greely, *Report of the Proceedings*, 1:112.
9. Greely, Journal, August 26, 1881, Greely Papers, LOC (quotations).
10. Ibid. (quotations)
11. Kislingbury, Journal, August 26, 1881, KFP (quotations).
12. Todd, *Abandoned*, 3.
13. Kislingbury, Journal, August 26, 1881, KFP (first and fourth quotations); Greely, "Orders No. 5, Appendix No. 11" (second and third quotations), in Greely, *Report of the Proceedings*, 1:113.
14. Greely, *Three Years of Arctic Service*, 1:85 (quotation).
15. Adolphus Greely to Henrietta Greely, July 4, 1881, Greely Papers, LOC (quotation).
16. Brainard, *Six Came Back*, 25 (first quotation); Rice, Journal, October 1, 1882, Rice Papers, RSC (second quotation); Brainard, *The Outpost of the Lost*, 32 (third quotation).
17. "The Greely Party. Revelations of Sergeant Connell," *The San Francisco Chronicle*, July 25, 1886 (quotations).
18. Greely, Journal, August 27, 1881, Greely Papers, LOC (quotation).
19. Brainard, *The Outpost of the Lost*, 230-31. Brainard was the only one to record Pavy's outburst with Whistler.
20. Dick, *Muskox Land*, 410-13.

Chapter Twelve. The Farthest North (Pages 127-141)

1. Rice, Journal, October 30, 1881, Rice Papers, RSC.
2. Greely, *Three Years of Arctic Service*, 1:175-76 (quotation).
3. Ibid., 174 (quotation).

Chapter Notes

4. Ibid., 154 (quotation).
5. Adolphus Greely to Henrietta Greely, March 19, 1882 (quotation), Greely Papers, LOC; Pavy, Journal, January 22, 1882, LFBE Records, NA (the men "have no desire or interest to make discoveries and that if they could return next year, they would.").
6. Adolphus Greely to Henrietta Greely, March 19, 1882, Greely Papers, LOC (quotations).
7. Adolphus Greely to Henrietta Greely, May 12, 1882, Greely Papers, LOC (first and second quotations); Pavy, Journal, August 30, [1882], LFBE Records, NA.
8. Brainard, *Six Came Back,* 44 (quotation).
9. Ibid., 45 (quotation).
10. Greely, *Three Years of Arctic Service*, 1:229 (quotation).
11. Pavy to Commanding Officer, "Appendix No. 47-Dr. Pavy's Report on Journey" (quotation), in *Report of the Proceedings,* 1:169.
12. Ibid. (quotation).
13. Adolphus Greely to Henrietta Greely, May 12, 1882, Greely Papers, LOC (quotation).
14. Lanman, *Farthest North,* 150 (first quotation); Brainard, *Six Came Back*, 59 (second quotation).
15. Brainard, *Six Came Back* 62 (quotation).
16. Greely, *Three Years of Arctic Service,* 1:326, quoting Lockwood's field notebook.
17. Ibid., 1:335, quoting Brainard's field notebook (first quotation); Brainard, *Six Came Back*, 74 (second quotation).
18. Greely, *Three Years of Arctic Service*, 1:335 (quotation).
19. Ibid., 2:62 (first quotation); Brainard, *The Outpost of the Lost*, 33 (second quotation); Henry, Journal, May 1, 1882, LFBE Records, NA (third quotation).
20. Greely, Journal, June 22, 1882, Greely Papers, LOC (quotations).

Chapter Thirteen. Season of Despair (Pages 142-155)

1. Greely, Journal, October 2, 1882, Greely Papers, LOC (first quotation); Rice, Journal, October 1, 1882, Rice Papers, RSC (remaining quotations, including reference to "mutiny").
2. Brainard, *Six Came Back*, 104 (first quotation); Schneider, Journal, December 24, 1882, LFBE Records, NA (second quotation-"gloomy"); Rice, Journal, December 25, 1882, Rice Papers, RSC (third quotation).

Chapter Notes

3. Greely, Journal, January 12, 1883, Greely Papers, LOC (quotations).
4. Pavy to Commanding Officer, "Appendix No. 62-Dr. Pavy's letter of March 8, 1883" (quotation), in Greely, *Report of the Proceedings*, 1:242 (itals in original).
5. Greely, "Appendix No. 63-Lieutenant Greely's Answer to Dr. Pavy's letter of March 8, 1883" (quotation), in Greely, *Report of the Proceedings*, 1:243.
6. Greely, Journal, March 15, 1883, Greely Papers, LOC (quotations).
7. Ibid. (quotations).
8. Pavy, Journal, n.d. [p.188], LFBE Records, NA.
9. Hazen to Clay, February 22, 1883, quoted in Apple, "In Search of a Star," 25.
10. Brainard, *The Outpost of the Lost*, 54-55 (first quotation); Kislingbury, Journal, August 10, 1883, LFBE Records, NA (second quotation).
11. Elison, Journal, August 19, 1883, LFBE Records, NA (first quotation); Cross, Journal, August 10, 1883, LFBE Records, NA (second quotation).
12. Cross, Journal, August 13, 1883, LFBE Records, NA (quotation).
13. Brainard, Journal, August 15, 1883, LFBE Records, NA (quotations). See the Appendix for a more detailed account by Brainard of the event.
14. Pavy, Journal, n.d. [p.100], LFBE Records, NA (quotation).
15. Kislingbury, Journal, August 19 and 21, 1883, LFBE Records, NA (first and third quotations); Cross, Journal, August 21, 1883, LFBE Records, NA (second quotation).
16. Brainard, *Six Came Back*, 160 (first quotation); Greely, Journal, September 3, 1883, Greely Papers, LOC (second quotation); Kislingbury, Journal, September 3, 1883, LFBE Records, NA (third and fourth quotation).

Chapter Fourteen. "Here We Are Dying Like Men" (Pages 156-170)

1. Greely, Journal, October 7, 1883, LFBE Records, NA (quotations).
2. Brainard, *The Outpost of the Lost*, 110 (quotation);
3. Greely, Journal, October 9, 1883, LFBE Records, NA (quotation).
4. Kislingbury, Journal, February 22, 1884, LFBE Records, NA (first and second quotations); Greely, *Three Years of Arctic Service*, 2:252 (third quotation).
5. Kislingbury, Journal, April 24, 1884, LFBE Records, NA (quotation).
6. Weslawski and Legezynska, "Chances of Arctic Survival," 375.
7. Kislingbury, Journal, April 23, 1884, LFBE Records, NA (quotations).
8. Ibid., April 9, 1884 (quotation).
9. Biederbeck, Journal, April 9, 1884, LFBE Records, NA (quotation).

Chapter Notes

10. Greely, *Three Years of Arctic Service*, 2:289 (first quotation); Brainard, *Six Came Back*, 255 (second quotation).
11. Ralston, Journal, May 6, 1884, LFBE Records, NA (first quotation); Greely, *Three Years of Arctic Service*, 2:302 (second quotation); Kislingbury, Journal, April 30, 1884, LFBE Records, NA (third quotation).
12. Biederbeck, Journal, April 15, 1884, LFBE Records, NA (first quotation); Greely, *Report of the Proceedings*, 1:84 (second quotation); Greely, *Three Years of Arctic Service*, 2:291. Greely's extra rations were reduced the following Friday, April 18, but increased again on April 24 and 25.
13. Kislingbury, Journal, April 23, 1885, LFBE Records, NA (quotation).
14. Kislingbury, Journal, May 11, 1884, LFBE Records, NA (quotation).
15. Bender, Journal, May 11, 1884, LFBE Records, NA (quotation); Kislingbury, Journal, May 11, 1884, LFBE Records, NA (quotations).
16. Ibid., May 12, 1884 (first and second quotations); Henry, Journal, May 14, 1884 (third quotation), LFBE Records, NA.
17. Greely, *Report of the Proceedings*, 1:87 (quotation).
18. Connell to John Kislingbury, May 7, 1900, EC.
19. Henry, Journal, May 28, 1884, LFBE Records, NA (quotation). His original language being in German, this is the English translation.

Chapter Fifteen. Home Again (Pages 171-183)

1. "Return from the Arctic Regions," *Portsmouth Journal*, August 9, 1884 (quotation).
2. Ibid. (quotation).
3. "A Brave Man's Death. The Story of Lieutenant Kislingbury's Sufferings as Told by Greely," *Hamilton Daily Spectator* (Hamilton, Ontario), August 19, 1884 (quotation).
4. "Lieutenant Kislingbury's Boy," *New York Times*, July 26, 1884 (quotations).
5. "The Dead Arctic Heroes," *New York Sun*, August 9, 1884 (first quotation); "The Arctic's Dead," *New York Herald*, August 9, 1884 (second quotation); "Honor to the Greely Dead," *New York Tribune*, August 9, 1884 (third quotation).
6. Letters of Administration and Letters of Guardianship, Monroe County, City of Rochester, NY, July 22, 1884 (appointment of John Kislingbury administrator of Kislingbury's estate and guardian of Walter); Letters of Special Administration, County of Wayne, MI, August 2, 1884 (appointment

Chapter Notes

of Charles Clark administrator); and Letters of Guardianship, County of Wayne, MI, July 31, 1884 (appointment of Clark as guardian for Harry, Douglass and Wheeler), Clark Papers, UMI.

7. D. W. Selye to Clark, September 5, 1884 and William Kislingbury to Clark, July 26, 1884 (Kislingbury burial in Rochester), Clark Papers, UMI. The estate was valued at $10,773.07 with debts of $344.39. "State News," *Weekly Expositor* (Yale, MI), March 26, 1885.
8. "Honor the Arctic Hero," *Democrat and Chronicle* (Rochester), August 10, 1884.
9. "The Arctic Hero's Burial," *Democrat and Chronicle* (Rochester), August 11, 1884 (quotation).
10. Ibid. (quotation).
11. John Kislingbury to Clark, undated, 1884, Clark Papers, UMI (first quotation); "The Story Denied. No Cannibalism Practiced by Greely's Men in the North," *Harrisburg Patriot*, August 13, 1884 (second quotation); "Were They Cannibals?," *New York Herald*, August 14, 1884 (third quotation);
12. Bullock to Clark, August 21, 1884, Clark Papers, UMI (quotations).
13. Ibid. (quotation).
14. William Kislingbury to Clark, March 5, 1885 (first quotation) and William Kislingbury to Clark, March 12, 1885, Clark Papers, UMI (second quotation).
15. "The Second in Command. Lieut. Kislingbury's Mutilated Body Disinterred," *New York Times*, August 15, 1884 (quotations). Separately, in an extremely tactless and insensitive letter, William Kislingbury confided to young Harry Kislingbury that the real purpose behind the exhumation was to inspect the body of Harry's father for signs of cannibalism. William Kislingbury to Harry Kislingbury, August 22, 1884, Clark Papers, UMI. The Kislingbury exhumation led to the exhumation of Private William Whistler by Whistler's relatives a week later. The physicians performing the autopsy found the same state of affairs as Kislingbury, the flesh cut by a sharp instrument. "The Horrible Truth. Evidences of Cannibalism on Private Whistler's Body." *Cincinnati Commercial Gazette*, August 20, 1884. Years later, the administration of President Harry Truman had a commemorative marker placed on Whistler's grave.
16. "Proofs of Cannibalism. The Body of Lieutenant Kislingbury Exhumed in Rochester," *Sun* (New York), August 15, 1884 (quotation).
17. "Greely and his Dead Comrades," *New York Herald*, August 17, 1884 (quotations).

Chapter Notes

18. "Justifying the Survivors," *New York Times*, August 16, 1884 (quotation).
19. "Dying Amid Glaciers. Commodore Schley's Official Report," *New York Tribune*, October 23, 1884 (first quotation); Schley, *Report of Winfield S. Schley*, 50 (second quotation). In his 1885 popular narrative, *The Rescue of Greely*, Schley remarked that the six bodies had been cut and flesh removed, but made no conclusion as to the reason. Schley, *The Rescue of Greely*, 235. One rescuer, fireman Lewis C. Smith with the *Bear*, interviewed after the rescue in March 1885, stated that he located the body of Kislingbury under some two feet of snow and ice. According to Smith, the body was "badly mutilated. The skin on the front of the thigh had been cut straight up the leg and laid back, and the flesh cut out... I asked one of the survivors about it, and he said they had used the flesh for bait for shrimps... Of course we all knew the men had been eaten, and they knew that we knew it, but we had an understanding that we would not talk about it." "Glimpses of Lt. Greely," *Democrat and Chronicle* (Rochester), March 3, 1885.
20. Clark to Greely, October 7, 1884, Greely Papers, LOC (first two quotations); Clark to Greely, January 13, 1885, Greely Papers, LOC (third quotation); and Schley to Greely, June 16, 1885, Greely Papers, LOC; see also "Lieutenant Kislingbury's Children," *Detroit Free Press*, February 8, 1885 and "Lieut. Frederick F. Kislingbury," Report No. 2482, House of Representatives, 48th Congress, 2nd Session, February 4, 1885, for Greely's letter in support of the bill.

Chapter Sixteen. Aftermath (Pages 184–197)

1. "The Arctic Tragedy. Lieutenant Greely Replies to Lieutenant Kislingbury's Diary," *Democrat and Chronicle* (Rochester) February 12, 1885 (quotations); "The Greely Party's Quarrels. Lieut. Kislingbury's Diary Severe on Lieut. Greely," *New York Times*," February 11, 1885.
2. Connell to John Kislingbury April 24, 1886 (first quotation), KFP; Connell to Greely June 27, 1886 (second quotation), Greely Papers, LOC; Connell to Greely July 8, 1886 (third quotation), Greely Papers, LOC; Connell to John Kislingbury, July 28, 1886, KFP (last quotation).
3. "An Arctic Explorer. Complaints of Sergeant Connell," *San Francisco Chronicle*, July 18, 1886 (quotation). Though identified as "sergeant" in the headline, Connell was "ex-sergeant" in the text.
4. "The Greely Party. Revelations by Sergeant Connell," *San Francisco Chronicle*,

Chapter Notes

July 25, 1886 (quotations).

5. Brainard to Greely, August 18, 1886, Greely Papers, LOC (Brainard quotation); "Connell's Story. A Denial by one of the Expedition," *Los Angeles Herald*, July 27, 1886 ("obstructionist"); "Connell's Charges," St. Louis Post-Dispatch, July 26, 1886; "Let it Rest," *Evening News* (San Jose), July 25, 1886. Despite his show of support for Greely, Long subsequently caused his own trouble. In early 1898, Long told Brainard that he "had not received as much as the others and wishes to air his troubles through the newspapers." Long's complaint likely arose as a result of his discharge that year due to a staff reduction in the Signal Corps.
6. Connell to Clark, October 19, 1886, Clark Papers, UMI (quotation); Scott, *Yellowstone Denied*, 228.
7. Greely, *Three Years of Arctic Service*, 1:85 (quotation).
8. Brainard to Clark, June 9, 1886, Clark Papers, UMI (quotation).
9. Ibid (quotation).
10. Clark to Greely, July 2, 1886 (quotations), Greely Papers, LOC.
11. Brainard to Clark, January 15, 1887, Clark Papers, UMI (first and second quotations); Brainard to Henrietta Greely, November 5, 1885, Greely Papers, LOC (third and fourth quotations). Lilla Pavy had also reached out to Emma Gardiner, wife of Hampden Gardiner, to ascertain if Gardiner's journal reflected "in any unpleasant or bitter way upon Greely, or did it favor him." Pavy to Gardiner, March 23, [1886], Greely Papers, LOC. In a response fully supportive of Greely, Mrs. Gardiner advised Lilla that she was assured that Hampden "lived and died loyal to his commander." Emma Gardiner to Lilla Pavy, March 24, 1886, Greely Papers, LOC.
12. William Kislingbury to Clark, December 3, 1886, Clark Papers, UMI (quoting Mrs. Pavy). Evidently, the Kislingbury materials passed through the hands of George Meek, editor at the *San Francisco Chronicle,* to Mrs. Pavy. Meek had informed Clark that he had given Mrs. Pavy all the manuscripts and information in his possession to Mrs. Pavy for incorporation into her book. George Meek to Clark, January 13, 1887, Clark Papers, UMI.
13. Lilla Pavy to Clark, February 14, 1887, Clark Papers, UMI (quotation).
14. "Opposed to Capt. Greely," *St. Paul Daily Globe*, February 19, 1887; "Signal Officer Greely. Mrs. Pavy Objects to his Promotion, but the Senate will Confirm," *New York Herald,* February 23, 1887; Palmer to Clark, February 21, 1887, Clark Papers, UMI; Conger to Clark, February 21, 1887, Clark Papers, UMI. William Kislingbury leaned on Congressman Charles S. Baer (NY)

Chapter Notes

for opposition support. William Kislingbury to Clark, March 9, 1887, Clark Papers, UMI.

15. William Kislingbury to Clark, January 22, 1887, Clark Papers, UMI (first and third quotations); William Kislingbury to President Cleveland, January 21, 1887 (second quotation), AGO Letters Received by the Commission Branch, G702-CB1865, NA; "John Kislingbury's Mission," *Cincinnati Commercial Tribune*, August 28, 1887. John Kislingbury was pushing to understand how Private Henry could be stealing food on June 6, when the autopsy of Frederick Kislingbury, who died on June 1 showed that he had not eaten in six weeks.
16. William Kislingbury to Clark, March 8, 1887, Clark Papers, UMI. The Charles Clark Papers hold the litany of letters on the subject of guardianship.
17. Bullock to Clark, September 16, 1886, Clark Papers, UMI (quotation).
18. *Winslow Mail*, March 3, 1906; *The Coconino Sun* (Flagstaff, AZ), July 11, 1891; "Up from Arizona to pay a Visit," *Winslow Mail*, October 28, 1921; Urness, *Twenty-five Brave Men*, 59.
19. Urness, *Twenty-five Brave Men*, 59; "Tired of Life," *Arizona Champion* (Flagstaff, AZ), September 12, 1903; "Suicide Sequel," *The Town Talk* (Alexandria, LA), September 5, 1903.
20. Douglass Kislingbury to Donald Macmillan, undated typescript (ca 1932) (quotation), KFP; "Traveler Here may go to the Pole," *Wayne Herald* (Wayne, NE), April 28, 1928.
21. "Articles from Lost Polar Expedition of 1881 are seen here," *Elk City Daily News* (Elk City, OK), April 10, 1931; "Things Lost in Arctic are Given to Museum," *Sioux City Journal*, June 2, 1931; Urness, *Twenty-five Brave Men*, 59; "Son of Ill-Fated Arctic Explorer visits scenes of his Father's Last U.S. Home," *Morning Pioneer* (Mandan, ND), June 16, 1931.
22. Wheeler Kislingbury to Clark, May 7, 1913, Clark Papers, UMI (quotation).
23. Ibid. (quotation).

Appendix. The Transformation of David L. Brainard's LFBE Account (Pages 198-204)

1. Guttridge, *Ghosts of Cape Sabine*, 164; Levy, *Labyrinth of Ice*, 128; Todd, *Abandoned*, 89.
2. Brainard Journal, Vol. 2, flyleaf and August 15, 1883, Brainard Papers, NA. For details as to the various journals maintained by Brainard and their history,

Chapter Notes

as well as details of alterations, I have drawn upon Stein, "Appendix: The Evolution of Brainard's Lady Franklin Bay Expedition Writings."

3. Brainard Notebook No. 14, August 19 and 21, 1883 (quotations), Brainard Papers, NA.
4. Memorandum dated January 19, 1890 (included at August 15, 1883 entry in Brainard Journal, Vol. 2), Brainard Papers, NA.
5. Brainard, *The Outpost of the Lost*, 52–53; Brainard, *Six Came Back*, 153.
6. Brainard Notebook, April 10, 1884 (quotation), RSC.
7. Memorandum dated February 3, 1890 (included at April 10, 1884 entry in Brainard Journal, Vol. 2), Brainard Papers, NA
8. Brainard, *The Outpost of the Lost*, 230–31; see also Brainard, *Six Came Back*, 256.
9. Brainard Notebook, April 27, 1884 (quotation), RSC.

Bibliography

Manuscripts and Archival Collections

Abraham Lincoln Presidential Library and Museum, Springfield, IL
   Grierson, Benjamin H., Papers
Explorers Club, New York, NY
   Lady Franklin Bay Expedition, Papers
Fort Concho Library and Archives, San Angelo, TX
   Reports of Post Surgeons, 1873-76
Kislingbury, Linda, CA
   Kislingbury Family Papers
Library of Congress, Washington, D.C.
   Greely, Adolphus W., Papers
   Sheridan, Philip, Military Papers, 1853-1887
National Archives, Washington, D.C.
   Adjutant General's Office Letters Received (Main Series), 1871-1880, Microcopy 666
   Adjutant General's Office Letters Received (Main Series), 1881-1889, Microcopy 689
   Adjutant General's Office Letters Received by the Commission Branch, 1863-1917, Microcopy 1064
   Eleventh Infantry Regimental Returns, 1873-82, Microcopy 665
   Fort Concho Letters Received, Aug. 1867-June 1889
   Fort Concho Letters Sent, Dec. 1867-June 1889
   Fort Custer Letters, Endorsements and Telegrams Sent, 1877-1898, RG 393
   Fort Custer Letters and Telegrams Received, 1878-1889, RG 393
   Fort Yates Letters Sent, May 1870-Sept. 1903, RG 393
   Fort Yates Letters Received, Jan. 1876-May 1903, RG 393
   Fort Yates Endorsements Sent, June 1875-Sept. 1891, RG 393
   Fort Yates, Orders and Circulars, June 1875-Mar. 1881, RG 393
   Fort Yates, Special Orders, Jan. 1872-Oct. 1883, RG 393
   Kislingbury, Frederick, Appointment, Commission, Personal File, 3460 ACP 1973, RG 94
   Office of Indian Affairs, Letters Received, 1824-1881,

Bibliography

    Dakota Superintendency, 1861-1880, Microcopy 234
    Montana Superintendency, 1864-1880, Microcopy 234
    Standing Rock Agency, 1875-80, Microcopy 234
  Returns from U.S. Military Posts, 1800-1916, Microcopy 617
National Archives, College Park, MD
  Records of the Weather Bureau, Correspondence, Reports, Journals and Scientific Records of the Lady Franklin Bay Expedition, RG 27
  Brainard, David, Papers, RG 200/RG 27
Nebraska State Historical Society, Lincoln, NE
  North, Frank, Papers
  North, Luther, Papers
Rauner Special Collections Library, Dartmouth College, Hanover, NH
  Brainard, David, Papers
  Rice, George, Papers
State Historical Society of North Dakota Archives, Bismarck, ND
  Kislingbury, Frederick, Letters, Orin Grant Libby Collection
  Kislingbury, Frederick, Reports, U.S. Army Indian Scouts, Post Letters, 1876-1880
University of Michigan, William M. Clements Library, Ann Arbor, MI
  Clark, Charles, Papers (Frederick F. Kislingbury collection 1881-1919)
University of Mississippi, Starkville, MS
  Grant, U. S., Papers
Wamsley, Douglas
  Kislingbury, Frederick, Musselshell Account

Battle Reports

Carr, Eugene. "Report of Operations of the Republican River Expedition, Brevet Major General E. A. Carr Comm. from June 30th to July 20th, 1869," 816-31. Sheridan Papers, LOC.

Coale, J. H. "Report of Operations by Company C, Second Cavalry, March 26, 1880," 314-330. OIA Letters Received, 1824-1881, Montana Superintendency, 1878-80:1880.

Duncan, Thomas. "Operations of Republican River Expedition, Lieutenant Colonel Thos. Duncan, Fifth Cavalry Commanding from August 18th to October 7th, 1869," 868-76. Sheridan Papers, LOC.

Huggins, E. L. "Report of Operations Commencing March 25, 1880, in the District of the Yellowstone," 284-307, OIA Letters Received, 1824-1881, Montana Superintendency, 1878-80:1880.

Royall, W.B. "Report of the Operations of the Republican River Expedition, Report of Major and Brevt. Colonel W. B. Royall, Fifth Cavalry, Commanding from July 20th to August 14th, 1869," 861-67. Sheridan Papers, LOC.

Bibliography

Books and Articles

Annual Report of the Chief Signal-Officer to the Secretary of War for the Year 1876. Washington, D.C.: GPO, 1876.

Annual Report of the Chief Signal-Officer to the Secretary of War for the Year 1879. Washington, D.C.: GPO, 1880.

Anderson, Harry A. "A History of the Cheyenne River Indian Agency and its Military Post, Fort Bennett, 1868-1891." *South Dakota Historical Collections* 28 (1956), 390-551.

Apple, Lindsey. "In Search of a Star: A Kentucky Clay Goes to the Arctic." *The Filson Club History Quarterly*, 71, no. 1 (January 1997): 3-26.

"A Pythian Hero. Lieut. Frederick F. Kislingbury." *The Pythian Knight* 1, no. 6 (December 1886): 2-4, 20.

Barr, William. *The Expeditions of the First International Polar Year, 1882-83. Technical Paper 29.* Calgary: Arctic Institute of North America, 1985.

Booth, Ryan Wayne. "Crossed Arrows: The US Indian Scouts, 1866-1947." PhD diss., Washington State University, 2021.

Brainard, David L. *Six Came Back: The Arctic Adventure of David L. Brainard.* Edited by Bessie Rowland James. Indianapolis: Bobbs-Merrill, 1940.

Brainard, David L. *The Outpost of the Lost. An Arctic Adventure.* Edited by Bessie Rowland James. Indianapolis: Bobbs-Merrill, 1929.

Broome, Jeff. *Dog Soldier Justice: The Ordeal of Susanna Alderdice in the Kansas Indian War.* Lincoln: University of Nebraska Press, 2003.

Bruce, Robert. *The Fighting Norths and the Pawnee Scouts: Narratives and Reminiscences of Military Service on the Old Frontier.* Lincoln: Nebraska State Historical Society, 1932.

Butler, William Mill. "Lieutenant Frederick Kislingbury." In James R. Carnahan. *Pythian Knighthood, Its History and Literature: Being an Account of the Origin and Growth of the Order of Knights of Pythias.* Cincinnati: Pettibone Manufacturing Co., 1888.

Clark, George Washington and Charles Lamartine Clark. *The History and Genealogy of Our Branch of the Clark Family and its Connections.* Detroit: Morrison Printing Co., 1898.

Clow, Richmond L. "General Philip Sheridan's Legacy: The Sioux Pony Campaign of 1876." *Nebraska History* 57 (1976): 460-77.

Cody, William F. *Life and Adventures of "Buffalo Bill."* Chicago: Stanton and Van Vliet, 1917.

Cody, William F. *An Autobiography of Buffalo Bill.* New York: Farrar and Reinhart, 1920.

DeMallie, Raymond J. and Royal B. Hassrick. *Vestiges of a Proud Nation: The Ogden B. Read Northern Plains Collection.* Edited by Glenn E. Markoe. Burlington, VT: Robert Hull Fleming Museum, 1986.

Dick, Lyle. *Muskox Land: Ellesmere Island in the Age of Contact.* Calgary: University of Calgary Press, 2001.

Bibliography

Dutton, Allen & Co.'s Directory and Gazetteer of the Counties of Oxon, Berks and Bucks. Manchester: Dutton, Allen & Co., 1863.

Edwards, Wallace S. "Ranald Slidell Mackenzie: Indian Cavalryman." *Southwestern Historical Quarterly*, 56, no. 3 (January 1953): 378-96.

Fisher, John R. "The Royall and Duncan Pursuits: Aftermath of the Battle of Summit Springs, 1869." *Nebraska History* 50 (Fall 1969): 292-308.

Forrest, Daniel W. "Dismounting the Sioux." *North Dakota History, Journal of the Northern Plains* 41, no. 3 (Summer, 1974): 8-13.

Frank, James R. *Chief Gall and Chief John Grass: Cultural Mediators or Sellouts?* MA thesis, University of Montana, 2001.

Gaspar, Doris and Jennifer MacLeod. "A Case of Mistaken Identity: Bullock's Tavern and the Horsman Hotel." *Reflections, Newsletter of the Marsh Historical Collection* 7, no. 3 (Spring 2014): 1, 6.

Gray, Michael P. *The Business of Captivity. Elmira and its Civil War Prison*. Kent: Kent State University Press, 2001.

Greely, Adolphus W. *Reminiscences of Adventure and Service: A Record of Sixty-Five Years*. New York: Charles Scribner's Sons, 1927.

Greely, Adolphus W. *Report on the Proceedings of the United States Expedition to Lady Franklin Bay, Grinnell Land*. 2 vols. Washington, D.C.: GPO, 1888.

Greely, Adolphus W. *Three Years of Arctic Service: An Account of the Lady Franklin Bay Expedition of 1881-1884 and the Attainment of the Farthest North*. New York: Charles Scribner's Sons, 1886.

Gregory, J. N. *Fort Concho: Its Way and Wherefore*. San Angelo: Newsfoto Publishing Co., 1957.

Grierson, Alice Kirk, *The Colonel's Lady on the Western Frontier: The Correspondence of Alice Kirk Grierson*. Edited by Shirley Anne Leckie. Lincoln: University of Nebraska Press, 1989.

Grinnell, George Bird. *Two Great Scouts and their Pawnee Battalion*. Cleveland: Arthur H. Clark, 1928.

Guttridge, Leonard F. *Ghosts of Cape Sabine: The Harrowing True Story of the Greely Expedition*. New York: G. P. Putnam's Sons, 2000.

Hackett, Charles F. "Along the Upper Missouri in the '70s." In *South Dakota Historical Collections compiled by the State Department of History*, 27-55. Vol. 8. Pierre: State Publishing, 1916.

Haley, J. Evetts. *Fort Concho and the Texas Frontier*. San Angelo: San Angelo Standard-Times, 1952.

Haley, James L. *The Buffalo War: The History of the Red River Uprising of 1874*. Garden City: Doubleday & Company, 1976.

Hall, Charles Francis. *Narrative of the North Pole Expedition, U.S. Ship Polaris, Captain Charles Francis Hall Commanding*. Edited by G. M. Robeson and C. H. Davis. Washington, D.C.: GPO, 1876.

Hanson, Joseph Mills. *The Conquest of the Missouri: Being the Story of the Life and Exploits of Captain Grant Marsh*. Chicago: A. C. McClurg, 1909.

Hayes, Isaac I. *The Open Polar Sea: A Narrative of a Voyage of Discovery towards the

Bibliography

North Pole, in the Schooner "United States." New York: Hurd and Houghton, 1867.

Hedren, Paul L. *After Custer: Loss and Transformation in Sioux Country.* Norman: University of Oklahoma Press, 2011.

Hedren, Paul L. *Powder River: Disastrous Opening of the Great Sioux War.* Norman: University of Oklahoma Press, 2016.

Hedren, Paul L. *Rosebud June 17, 1876: Prelude to the Little Big Horn.* Norman: University of Oklahoma Press, 2019.

Heitman, Francis B. *Historical Register and Dictionary of the United States Army, from its Inception, September 29, 1789, to March 2 1903.* Washington, D.C.: GPO, 1903.

The History of the Dewitt Guard, Company A, 50th Regiment National Guard, New York. Ithaca: Andrus, McChain, 1866.

Holland, Clive. *Arctic Exploration and Development, c. 500 to 1915: An Encyclopedia.* New York: Garland, 1994.

Hooker, Forrestine C. *Child of the Fighting Tenth: On the Frontier with the Buffalo Soldiers.* Edited by Steve Wilson. Norman: University of Oklahoma Press, 2003.

Howgate, Henry W. *Polar Colonization: Memorial to Congress and Action of Scientific and Commercial Associations.* Washington, D.C.: Beresford, n.d. [1879].

Howgate, Henry W. *Polar Colonization and Exploration.* Washington, D.C.: Beresford, n.d. [1877].

Hyde, George E. *Life of George Bent Written from his Letters.* Edited by Savoie Lottinville. Norman: University of Oklahoma Press, 1968.

"Insolvent Debtors." *The Jurist* 12, no. 607 (August 26, 1848): 340.

Kane, Elisha Kent. *Arctic Explorations: The Second Grinnell Expedition in Search of Sir John Franklin, 1853, 54' 55'.* Philadelphia: Childs and Peterson, 1856.

King, James T. "The Republican River Expedition, June–July, 1869: I. On the March." *Nebraska History* 41 (1960): 165-199.

Lanman, Charles. *Farthest North; or The Life and Explorations Lieutenant James Booth Lockwood, of the Greely Arctic Expedition.* New York: D. Appleton and Company, 1885.

Leatherwood, Art. "*Llano Estacado*": *The Handbook of Tejano History.* Texas State Historical Assoc., 1952, updated June 18, 2020, https://www.tshaonline.org/handbook/entries/llano-estacado (accessed November 2, 2024).

Leckie, William H. and Shirley A. Leckie. *Unlikely Warriors: General Benjamin H. Grierson and his Family.* Norman: University of Oklahoma Press, 1998.

Levy, Buddy. *Labyrinth of Ice: The Triumphant and Tragic Greely Expedition.* New York: St. Martin's Press, 2019.

Lotz, Jim. *Canada's Forgotten Hero: George Rice and the Lady Franklin Bay Expedition, 1881-1884.* Breton Books: Sydney, NS, 2009.

Mackenzie, Ranald. *Ranald Mackenzie's Official Correspondence Relating to Texas, 1871-1873.* Edited by Ernest Wallace. Lubbock: West Texas Museum Association, 1967.

Bibliography

Matthews, James T. *Fort Concho: A History and a Guide.* Austin: Texas State Historical Association, 2005.

Maxfield, Derek. *Hellmira. The Union's Most Infamous Civil War Prison Camp.* Savas Beatie: El Dorado, CA, 2020.

Miles, Susan. "Fort Concho in 1877." *West Texas Historical Association Year Book* (1959): 29-49.

Mitchell, William. *General Greely: The Story of a Great American.* New York: G. P. Putnam's Sons, 1936.

Nelson, Mark J. *White Hat: The Military Career of Captain William Philo Clark.* Norman: University of Oklahoma Press, 2018.

North, Luther. *Man of the Plains: Recollections of Luther North, 1856-1882.* Edited by Donald F. Danker. Lincoln: University of Nebraska Press, 1961.

Notson, William M. *Fort Concho Medical History, January, 1869 to July, 1872.* San Angelo: Fort Concho Preservation and Museum, 1974.

Overfield II, Loyd J., comp. *The Little Big Horn: The Official Communications, Documents and Reports, with Rosters of the Officers and Troops of the Campaign.* Lincoln: University of Nebraska Press, 1971.

Peary, Robert. *The North Pole: Its Discovery in 1909 under the Auspices of the Peary Arctic Club.* New York: Frederick A. Stokes, 1910.

Plante, Trevor. "Lead the way: Researching U.S. Army Indian Scouts." *Prologue* 41, no. 2 (Summer 2009), 52-59.

Powell, William H. *A History of the Organization and Movements of the Fourth Regiment of Infantry, United States Army, From May 30, 1796 to December 31, 1870.* Washington, D.C.: M'Gill and Witherow, 1871.

Report of the Secretary of War for the Year 1876, vol. 1. Washington D.C.: GPO, 1877.

Report of the Secretary of War for the Year 1880, vol. 1. Washington, D.C.: GPO, 1880.

Riffenburgh, Beau. *The Myth of the Explorer.* London: Belhaven Press, 1993.

Rister, Carl Coke. *The Southwestern Frontier, 1865-1881.* Chicago: Arthur C. Clarke, 1928.

Roosevelt, Kermit. *The Happy Hunting-Grounds.* New York: Charles Scribner's Sons, 1912.

Saxton, Eric. "Lieutenant Frederick Kislingbury, 1846-1882." *Berkshire Family History Society* (March 1, 2022): 1-4, https://berksfhs.org/lieutenant-frederick-f-kislingbury-1846-1884/ (accessed September 7, 2024).

Saxton, Eric. "Sport and Leisure in East Ilsley." *East Ilsley Local History Society Newsletter* (Autumn 2017): 1-4.

Schledermann, Peter. *Voices in Stone: A Personal Journey into the Arctic Past.* Komatik Series, No. 5. Calgary: Arctic Institute of America, 1996.

Schley, Winfield S. *Report of Winfield S. Schley, Commander, U.S. Navy, Commanding the Greely Relief Expedition of 1884.* Washington, D.C.: GPO, 1887.

Schley, Winfield S. and J. R. Soley. *The Rescue of Greely.* New York: Charles Scribner's Sons, 1885.

Schmitt, Victoria Sandwick. "Rochester's Frederick Douglass-Part One."

Bibliography

Rochester History 67, no. 3 (Summer 2005): 1-28.

Scott, Kim Allen. *Yellowstone Denied. The Life of Gustavus Cheyney Doane.* Norman: University of Oklahoma Press, 2007.

"Scouting on the 'Staked Plains' (Llano Estacado) with Mackenzie, in 1874: One who was There." *The United Service* 13 (Oct, 1885): 400-12 and (Nov. 1885): 532-43.

Stein, Glenn. "Appendix: The Evolution of Brainard's Lady Franklin Bay Expedition Writings," https://www.library.dartmouth.edu/digital/digital-collections/david-brainard-diary/appendix (accessed March 24, 2025).

Stein, Glenn. "General David L. Brainard, U.S. Army: Last Survivor of the United States' Lady Franklin Bay Expedition." *The Polar Times*, July 2008/January 2009.

Thomas, Rodney G. *Bíilaachia-White Swan: Crow Warrior, Custer Scout, American Artist*. Jefferson, N.C.: McFarland, 2022.

Todd, Alden L. *Abandoned: The Story of the Greely Arctic Expedition 1881-1884.* New York: McGraw-Hill, 1961

Urness, James. *Twenty-Five Brave Men: Tales of an Arctic Journey*. Edited by Donald Kvamme. Tucson: Wheatmark, 2014.

Van De Logt, Mark. *War Party In Blue: Pawnee Scouts in the U.S. Army*. Norman: University of Oklahoma Press, 2010.

Wamsley, Douglas. "The Arctic Exploits of Dr. Octave Pavy." *Arctic* 68, no. 1 (February 2015): 1-15.

Warren, Louis S. *Buffalo Bill's America: William Cody and the Wild West Show*. New York: Alfred A. Knopf, 2005.

Watson, Robert Thomas. "A History of Fort Yates, 1875-1903." MA thesis, University of Nebraska, 1958.

Weslawski, Jan Marcin and Joanna Legezynska, "Chances of Arctic Survival: Greely's Expedition Revisited." *Arctic* 55, no. 4 (December 2002): 373-79.

Wolff, David. *Seth Bullock. Black Hills Lawman*. Pierre: South Dakota Historical Society Press, 2009.

Illustration Credits

Front cover:
  Portrait: Lieutenant Frederick F. Kislingbury. Private collection.
  Frontier images: Surprise Tactics demonstrated by the Indian Scouts, and Lieutenant Kislingbury and Indian Scouts on the Belle Fourche. Photographs by F. J. Haynes, Montana Historical Society Research Center.
  Arctic images: Departure of the steamship *Proteus*, and Return of "Farthest North" Party to Fort Conger, June 1, 1882. Library of Congress.
Rear cover: Rescue of Lieut. A. W. Greely and Party at Cape Sabine, June 22nd, 1884. The Explorers Club.
Page 3: Frederick F. Kislingbury near the time of his military enlistment. Private collection.
Page 5: Agnes ("Aggie") Bullock, first wife of Frederick Kislingbury. Private collection.
Page 11: Major Frank North, leader of the Pawnee Scouts, in 1867. RG2320 North Family, Nebraska State Historical Society.
Page 19: Frederick F. Kislingbury in 1872. Private collection.
Page 21: View of Fort Concho from above the Concho River. Fort Concho National Historic Landmark Archives and Library.
Page 25: Masquerade Party at Major Grierson's lodging, Aggie Kislingbury is fifth from left. Fort Concho National Historic Landmark Archives and Library.
Page 29: Lieutenant Adolphus W. Greely, U.S. Signal Corps. Author's collection.
Page 46: Eagle Man in 1872 taken by Alexander Gardner. National Archives.
Page 57: Lieutenant Kislingbury and Indian Scouts on the Belle Fourche. Photograph by F. J. Haynes. Montana Historical Society Research Center.
Page 58: Surprise Tactics demonstrated by the Indian Scouts. Photograph by F. J. Haynes. Montana Historical Society Research Center.
Page 62: Jessica ("Jessie") Lillian Bullock, second wife of Frederick Kislingbury. Private collection.
Page 65: Fort Custer in 1880. University of Montana, Maureen and Mike Mansfield Library.
Page 68: White Swan. Photograph by Frank Rinehart (No. 815). Boston Public

Illustration Credits

Library, Arts Department.

Page 71: White Swan (Apsáalooke, 1851 or 1852-1904), Pictographic War Record, ca. 1887, Muslin, watercolor, pencil, and ink. Raclin Murphy Museum of Art, University of Notre Dame. Gift of Rev. E. W. J. Lindesmith to the University of Notre Dame by transfer, 1963.009.005.

Page 80: Lieutenant Henry W. Howgate, U.S. Army Signal Corps. National Archives.

Page 89: Members of the Lady Franklin Bay Expedition. Author's collection.

Page 95: Charles Lamartine Clark between Walter and Harry Kislingbury. Frederick F. Kislingbury Collection, Williams L. Clements Library, University of Michigan.

Page 100: The Lady Franklin Bay Expedition visits Godhavn (Qeqertarsuaq). Library of Congress.

Page 109: Lieutenants Kislingbury and Lockwood on the Ice Pack. Latitude 81°35 North, August 5, 1884. Author's collection

Page 110: Fort Conger, headquarters of the Lady Franklin Bay Expedition. Library of Congress.

Page 119: Departure of the steamship *Proteus* from Lady Franklin Bay. Library of Congress.

Page 124: Octave Pavy and Jens Edwards skinning a seal. Library of Congress.

Page 129: December 15, 1881 issue of *The Arctic Moon*. Author's collection.

Page 139: "Farthest North," painting by Albert Operti (1852-1927), oil on canvas, signed "Albert Operti, N.Y./Copyrighted August 26, 1886." Gift of J. Watson Webb, Jr., 1916. Shelburne Museum, Shelburne, VT.

Page 140: Lieutenant Lockwood, Sergeant Brainard, and dog-driver Frederik Christiansen return to Fort Conger June 1, 1882. Library of Congress.

Page 150: Abandoning Launch *Lady Greely*, September 10, 1883. Watercolor by A. W. Greely. Private collection.

Page 169: The Greely tent at the time of rescue. Library of Congress.

Page 177: Funeral of Lieutenant Frederick Kislingbury, Rochester, New York. Rochester Local History Photo Images Database, Rochester Public Library, image number rpf 00548.

Page 194: Douglass Kislingbury at age thirty. Private collection.

Index

Note: Italicized numbers refer to illustrations

Alderdice, Susanna, 13
Aldrich, Pelham, 92
Alert (British ship), 92, 102, 168, 171
Alexander (British ship), 107
Alliance (U.S. ship), 97, 98, 171
Arctic Moon, 128, *129*
Arthur, Chester A., 168
Augur, Christopher C., 9

Baffin Bay, 80, 103, 106,
Batchelor (steamboat), 67, 72
Bear (U.S. ship), 168-69, 171-74, 221n19
Beaumont, Lewis A., 92, 133, 137
Beebe, William, 157
Belle Fourche River, 52-53, 56, *57*
Bender, Jacob (aka George Leyerzapf), 164-66; background, 90; death, 167; and Greely, 163
Biederbeck, Henry, 91; on food thefts, 164; extra Greely rations, 164; and Frederick Kislingbury, 162
Big Horn and Yellowstone Expedition, 34
Big Horn Mountains, 66
Big Horn River, 36
Black Hills, 6, 32-33, 52, 54, 56; purchase, 42-43, 46
Blanco Canyon, 27
Blue Cloud (chief), 53-54
Brainard, David L., xi, *140*, 144, 156-57, 159, 163, 169, 222n5; background, xiv, 91-92;
and Clark, 186, 188-90; receives extra rations, 164; on *Gulnare* expedition, 82, 92; serves in Indian wars, 92; criticism of Greely, 152, 198; the "Farthest North," 132-40; Henry execution, 167; and Frederick Kislingbury, 104-5, 119, 121, 126, 163, 165; and Lilla Pavy, 190; Pavy "mutiny," 152-53, 198-202; on the retreat, 149, 152-154; harvests "seafleas," 160; on silencing Connell, 186; sledge journeys, 124-25, 132-40; supports Greely, 121, 190; transformation of remarks, 198-204; Whistler confession, 203-4, 216n19
Brevoort Island, 168
Bristol, Edward, 176
British Arctic Expedition 1875-76, 92-93, 107, 109-110, 124, 133, 137, 138, 141, 147-48, 157
Buck, Charles Henry. *See* Henry, Charles B.
Budington, Sidney O., 107
Buffalo Soldiers, 22
Bullock, Agnes ("Aggie"). *See* Kislingbury, Agnes
Bullock, Jessica ("Jessie"). *See* Kislingbury, Jessie
Bullock, Martha (wife of Seth), 95
Bullock, George (father of Seth, Agnes, Alma and Jessica), 5, 206n9
Bullock, Seth (husband of Martha and brother of Agnes, Alma and Jessica),

Index

62; background, 5-6, 7; concern for Frederick Kislingbury's sons, 95, 178-79, 192-93; on Frederick's exhumation, 178-79
Burke, John, 38-39
Butler, William Mill, 178; and Frederick Kislingbury exhumation, 178, 180
Byrd, Richard E., 195

Cape Alexander, 107
Cape Britannia, 137, 138
Cape Cracroft, 142
Cape Isabella, 106, 107, 159
Cape Hawks, 109, 150, 154
Cape Joseph Henry, 132; and Pavy sledge journeys, 123-24, 134-35, 203
Cape Lieber, 109
Cape May, 137
Cape Sabine, xiii, 155-57, 178, 199; and Greely camp, 155, 168-69, 184, 199, 203; and *Neptune*, 142, 157; and *Proteus*, 148, 157; and Schley rescue, 168-69
Cape Sumner, 133
Cape Wrangel Bay, 126
Carey Islands, 105-6, 149
Carlin, William Passmore, 39, 54, 57, 60-61; appeals to keep Frederick Kislingbury, 58-59, 210n15; criticism of Burke, 39; on "civilizing" Indians, 50-51; commends Frederick Kislingbury, 45, 48, 55, 63; "Pony Campaign of 1876-77," 41-43, 47, 60
Carl Ritter Bay, 109
Carr, Eugene Asa, 10-13, 15, 30; commends Pawnees, 17
Cass School, 193
Catalpa (tug), 174
Chandler, William E., 168, 171
Chandler, Zachariah, 18
Cheyenne Agency, 41, 44, 54, 60, 68
Cheyenne River, 53, 55
Christiansen, Frederik Thorlip, 101, 165, 173; death, 161; and "Farthest North," 132, 135-40, *140*; sledge races, 128
Christman, Catherine (wife of Harry Kislingbury), 193
Clark, Charles Lamartine, *95,* 96, 98, 174, 180-81, 196, 206n9; background, 95; and Brainard, 188-89; and Seth Bullock, 178-79, 193; on cannibalism, 181; and Connell, 186-87; as executor and guardian, x, 95, 175, 182, 189, 192, 193, 195; and Greely, 173, 181, 182-83, 187-89, 191; and Frederick Kislingbury, 95-96, 181; and John Kislingbury, 98, 175, 177, 180-81, 183, 192; and William Kislingbury, 179, 183, 191; and Lilla Pavy, 190
Clark, William Philo, xv, 74,
Clay, Henry ("Harry"), 99, 103, 108, 124, 148, 157; death, 113; on *Gulnare* expedition, 84, 99; leaves LFBE, 112; Pavy dispute, 112-13
Coale, John H., 65-66
Coburn, Laura (wife of Walter Kislingbury), 193
Cocked Hat Island, 157
Cody, William "Buffalo Bill," 10, 12-13, 16
Cold Hand (U.S. scout), 46
Colwell, John C., 169
Conger, Omar D., 111, 191
Connell, Maurice, 104, 144, 154, 159, 173; critical of Greely, 121-22, 184, 186; demoted by Greely, 156; Pavy "mutiny" observer, 200-202; and Frederick Kislingbury, 121-22, 154, 166-67, 173, 186, 189, 200-202; threatens to publish his LFBE story, 184-87; re-enlists and promoted, 187
Crazy Horse (chief), 52
Crook, George, 33, 42, 52, 85, 90; Big Horn and Yellowstone Expedition, 34-36

Index

Cross, William, 150, 153, 154; alcoholism, 143; death, 159; Greely criticism of, 152
Crow scouts, xv, 36, 65, 68, 70, 73-75
Crozier Island, 150
Custer, George Armstrong, 34; and Little Big Horn, xvi, 36-37, 91
Cuthbertson, Joseph, 63

Daniel Webster (ship), 1
Davidson, John Wynn, 89
De Long, George Washington, 123
Detroit, MI, xv, 4-5, 7-8, 18, 20, 62, 77, 91, 95, 98, 175, 189, 192, 193, 207n1
Discovery (British ship), 92, 137
Discovery Harbour, 110
Disko Bay, 173
Disko Island, 84, 99-100
Doane, Gustavus C., 187; on *Gulnare* expedition, 81-84; and Julius Frederick, 187; rejected for LFBE, 93
"Dog Soldiers," 10-14
Douglass, Frederick, 2
Douglass, Henry, 24
Duncan, Thomas, 16-17
Dutch Island, 143, 144

Eagle Man (U.S. scout), 46; Black Hills negotiator, 46
Edwards, Jens, 101, *124,* 161; death, 164-65; sledge races, 128; sledge journeys, 124, 134, 156-57, 159, 203; wanders off, 130
Egelston, Miss, 98-99
Elison, Joseph, 164; background, 90-91; criticism of Greely, 150; death, 170; suffers frostbite, 159
Ellis, William A., 104, 128, 132, 144; background, 89-90; death, 165
Elmira prison, 3-4
Erie Canal, 2
Farthest North (Operti painting), 139
"Farthest North" (LFBE), 132, 135, 147; Pavy attempt, 124; achieved, 138, 141; Connell disputes, 186
Floeberg Beach, 92
Fort Assinniboine, 71-72, 88
Fort Concho, ix, 19-25, *21,* 32, 37; Red River War, 26-28; telegraph installation, 30-31
Fort Conger, *110,* 111, 119, 121, 124-25, 127, 130, 132, 134, 136, 140, 148, 158, 162-63, 166, 187-89, 191, 194-95, 199, 202-3; abandonment of, 145, 149-50, 198; proposal to return, 152, 154, 201
Fort Custer, ix, 63-68, *65,* 75-76, 78, 88-90, 99, 195
Fort Keogh, 63-64, 67, 69, 72-73, 75, 93
Fort Laramie Treaty of 1868, 32, 43
Fort McPherson, 11, 15
Fort Stockton, 31
Fort Yates (formerly, the Post at Standing Rock), 38, 43; and Frederick Kislingbury, 37, 47, 52, 61, 63, 56-60, 64; and scouts, 43
Franklin, Sir John, 92
Frederick, Julius R. ("Shorty"), 132, 152, 159; background, 82; Henry execution, 167; and Connell, 186; and Doane, 187

Gardiner, Emma (wife of Hampden), 222n11
Gardiner, Hampden, 128; background, 88; death, 167; and Lilla Pavy, 222n11; breaks leg, 131; scientific work, 127
Garfield, James A., 96
Garlington, Ernest A., 148-49
Gibbon, John, 34, 36
Gilbreath, Erasmus C., 28
Godhavn (Qeqertarsuaq), 84, 99, *100,* 173
Good-Toned Metal (U.S. scout), 49
Grand River, 37, 43-44, 49
Grand River Agency. *See* Standing Rock Agency

236

Index

Great Frozen Sea (book), 135
Great Sioux Reservation, 32, 33, 37
Great Sioux War, xi, 34, 36, 52
Greely, Adolphus W., ix-xv, 79, 84, 91, 96-101, 107, 125-29, 139, 142, 147, 155, 157, 168-72, 194-95, 203; abandons Fort Conger, 149; background and military service, 29-30; and British Arctic Expedition 1875-76, 93, 133; and Connell, 156, 184-86; and Clark, 173, 179-183, 187-91; and Cross, 152; denies knowledge of cannibalism, 177, 181; receives extra rations, 164; and "Farthest North," 92, 98, 122, 132, 135, 138; and Frederick Kislingbury, xiv, xv, 31, 64, 78, 81, 85-88, 92-93, 100, 103-6, 113-22, 126, 131-32, 141, 144-47, 154, 160-63, 165-66, 180-81, 188; and Frederick Kislingbury's children, 182-83, 195-96; lack of navigation skills, 150, 152-53; Linn demotion, 143; and Pavy, 112, 130-31, 134, 140, 145, 148, 158, 199-202; post-LFBE career, 196-97
Greely, Henrietta, 91, 120-22, 128, 135, 171, 190
Greely Expedition. *See* Lady Franklin Bay Expedition
Grant, Ulysses S., 18, 27, 33
Grierson, Alice, 22, 23
Grierson, Benjamin Henry, ix, 22-25
Grierson, John, 22
Grimm, Paul, 89
Gulnare (ship), 81, 108, 83
Gulnare expedition, 81-84, 92-93, 99, 123, 140

Hackett, Charles (owner *Parker New Era*), 57-58
Hall Basin, 106
Hall, Charles Francis, 107, 126, 133; death, 107
Hand, James J., 133, 137
Hancock, Winfield Scott, 174
Hawks, Annie (wife of Harry Kislingbury), 193
Hayes, Isaac Israel, 107, 124, 134-35
Hayes, Rutherford B., 43, 85
Haynes, Frank J., photographs Frederick Kislingbury and scouts, 56, 57, 58
Hazen, William B., 84, 87, 141, 148, 171; and Brainard, 188; and Clark, 189; and Connell, 185-87; and Greely, 85, 166, and Harry Kislingbury, 183
Henry, Charles B. (*aka* Charles Henry Buck), 166; background, 91; execution of, 167, 170, 180, 186; and Frederick Kislingbury, 141; food thefts by, 161, 164
Hickok, James Butler, "Wild Bill," 5
Howgate, Henry, W., *80*, 90; "colony" scheme, 80; *Gulnare* expedition, 81-82, 92; and Pavy, 82-83
Huggins, Eli L., 65-66

Ilges, Guido, 72-76; arrives Musselshell River, 73; praise of Frederick Kislingbury, 73-74; notes change in Frederick Kislingbury, 93
International Polar Year, xii-xiii, 79, 84, 98, 127
Israel, Edward, 156; background, 88; death, 165; scientific work, 127

Jeannette Expedition, 97, 123-24
Jewell, Winfield Scott, background, 88; death, 161; scientific work, 127; sledge journeys, 132-33, 135
Johnson, Andrew, 26
Johnson, Joseph, 66
Johnston, Robert E., 39
Kane, Elisha Kent, 107, 134, 148,
Kendrick, Frederick Monroe, 88
Kennedy Channel, xii-xiii, 109, 118, 142, 149, 153

Index

Kill Eagle, 42
Kislingbury, Agnes "Aggie" (*nee* Bullock, first wife of Frederick), 5, 7-8, 11, 16, 18, 59, 62, 81, 166, 173; marries Frederick Kislingbury, 5; at Fort Concho, 23-24, *25*; at Fort Yates, 59, 61; death, 61, 94
Kislingbury, Douglass Ebstian (son of Frederick), 62, 78, 93, 100-101, 108, *194*; birth, 24; death, 195; suffers from scarlet fever, 76; with Bullock family, 94-95, 178, 192; with John Kislingbury family, 192; given name "Bear Looking Back," 195; and Peary, 194-95; and Byrd and Macmillan expeditions, 195; post-LFBE, 194-95
Kislingbury, Frederick Foster
    personal
        birth and early years, 1-2; high character, 2, 28, 58; marries Aggie Bullock, 5; death of Aggie, 61; marries Jessie Bullock, 62; death of Jessie, 76; births of Harry, 7, Walter, 11, Douglass and Wheeler, 24; and Major Schofield, 94; and Clark, 95, 181-82; and Miss Egelston, 98-99; and John Kislingbury, 86, 166, 175-76, 180, 196, 223n15; and William Kislingbury, 174, 191, 213n8, 220n15
    military service (pre-LFBE)
        serves in NY 54th Infantry, 3-4; with U.S. Fourth Infantry, 4, 7-9; serves with Pawnee Scouts, 9, 14-17; commissioned second lieutenant, 19; assigned Fort Concho, 19; in Red River War, 26-28; works with Greely, 28-31; arrives Fort Yates, 33, 37; leads mounted detachments, 43-47, 49, 52-58; adopts Indian tactics, 14, 45-46; respected by Indian allies, 54, 74-75; Carlin commends, 58-59; Terry commends, 58, 63; praise from fellow soldiers, 66-67; drives herds, 47-48, 50; on "civilizing" Indians, 50-51; skilled in wilderness pursuit, 57; skirmish at O'Fallon Creek, 65-66; Musselshell engagement, 68-76; praise from Ilges, 73-74; expert in Indian sign language, 74
    LFBE
        recruited by Greely, 86; lack of scientific qualifications, 92; state of mind, 86-87, 93-94, 98-99, 101, 110, 122, 126, 129, 149, 161; and Ilges, 93; letters to his children, 99, 100-101, 103, 108, 110; letters to his "affianced," 98-99, 101, 110, 111; resignation and aborted withdrawal, 113-121; and Brainard, 104-5, 121; and Greely, 100, 104-06, 113-22, 131-32, 141, 144-46, 150, 152, 153, 155, 173, 187-99; and Pavy, 130-31, 140, 163; Pavy "mutiny," 153; respected by the men, 140-41; as hunter, 103, 124, 126, 154; sledge work, 154; scientific work, 147; suffers abdominal strain, 158; falls through ice, 160; ordered to duty, 161-62; order revoked, 163; Greely contrition, 165-66; in failing health, 164-66; death, 166; funeral, 175-76; exhumation, 177-80
Kislingbury, Howard "Harry" Grant (son of Frederick), 23, 62, *95*; birth, 7; and Clark, 95; death, 193; at Michigan Military Academy, 192; learns of Miss Egelston, 98-99; seeks U.S. Naval Academy, 182-83; post-LFBE 192-93
Kislingbury, Jessica ("Jessie") Lillian (*nee* Bullock, second wife of Frederick), *62,* 77, 86, 93, 99, 166,

238

Index

173; marries Frederick, 62; illness and death, 75-76

Kislingbury, John (brother of Frederick), 86, 176, 196; cannibalism claims, 180; and Clark, 192; and Connell, 166, 185; and Walter Kislingbury, 94, 192, 193; and Douglass Kislingbury, 192, 193, 194-95; files as executor and guardian, 175; and Greely, 191; and Miss Egelston, 98-99

Kislingbury, John (father of Frederick), 1-2

Kislingbury, Lillie Mae (wife of Douglass Kislingbury), 195

Kislingbury, Louis Polouze (sons of Frederick), 18

Kislingbury, Maria (*nee* Chenery) (mother of Frederick), 1

Kislingbury, Walter Frederick (son of Frederick), 23, 62, 78, *95*; birth, 11; death, 194; at Frederick Kislingbury's funeral, 174; and John Kislingbury, 94, 175; and Seth Bullock, 179; post-LFBE, 193-94

Kislingbury, Wheeler Schofield (son of Frederick), 62, 78, 94; birth, 24; death, 196; interviewed, 173-74; meets Greely, 196; publication of Frederick Kislingbury's journal, 195-96; suffers from scarlet fever, 76; and William Kislingbury, 192; post-LFBE, 195-96

Kislingbury, William (brother of Frederick); opinion of Greely, 179, 191; custody of Wheeler, 192; and Greely, 191, 213n8, 222-23n14; exhumation of Frederick Kislingbury, 220n15

Kittery, ME, 171

Lady Franklin Bay, 92, 106, 109, 110, *119,* 137, 142, 157

Lady Franklin Bay Expedition (or Greely Expedition), x-xiv, 79, 81-86, 96-99, 106, 110, 112-13, 115-22, 125-28, 141-42, 145-46, 156, 160, 171-73, 184-91, 196, 198-202; achieves "Farthest North," 138; members of, 82, 83, 85, 87-92, *89,* 101, 156; cannibalism on, xiii, 177-78. 180-82, 185

Lady Greely (steam launch), 101, 196, 142, 149-50, 214-15n11

Leyerzapf, George. *See* Bender, Jacob

Lincoln, Robert Todd, 84, 85, 94, 148, 174, 183

Lincoln Sea, 106

Linn, David, 134, 159; background, 89-90; death, 161; demoted by Greely, 143

Little Big Horn battle, 37, 39, 42, 49, 90; and White Swan, 68, 70

Little Big Horn River, 36

Littleton Island, 107, 142, 145, 146, 148-49, 157, 159, 160, 168; Greely plan to reach, 152-53, 199

Llano Estacado, 21, 27

Lockwood, James B., 96, 100-101, 106-7, *109,* 110, 117, 124, 125-26, 130-34, *140,* 146-47, 150, 153, 156, 200, 203, 214-15n11; background, 87-88; death, 161, 181; achieves "Farthest North," 135-40, 186; holds class and edits *The Arctic Moon*; breakfasts late, 113, 131, 143

Long, Francis, 90, 215n12; and Connell, 186

Low, William H., 82-83, 90

Luce, Stephen, B., 171

Macdona, Henry, 98

Mackenzie, Ranald Slidell, 27-28

MacMillan, Donald B., 110, 195

Mad Bear (Pawnee), 12

Mandeville, F. A., 180

Marcy, Randolph B., 21

Markham, Albert H., 92, 123, 135

Marsh. Grant, 67

239

Index

McClintock, Leopold, 103
McCrary, George W., 51
Meek, George, 186, 222n12
Melville Bay, 101, 105, 149
Michigan Military Academy, 193
Miles, Nelson A., 28, 52
Moldrup, K. M., 112
Morris, R. L., 88
Mount Hope Cemetery, 176, 177; cemetery chapel, 179
Mulgrew, Frank, 195-96
Myer, Albert J., 31, 79, 84

Nansen, Fridjtof (Farthest North), 141
Nares, George S., 92, 106, 109
Nares Strait, 107, 134
Neptune (U.S. ship), 142, 148, 157
New Castle, NH, 171
Newman Bay, 102
Niobrara Pursuit, 15-16

Open Polar Sea (book), 135
Open Polar Sea, 134-35, 138
Outpost of the Lost (book), 121, 202, 204

Palo Duro Canyon, 27
Pandora (British ship), 106, 107, 109
Paul, Charles W., 133, 137
Pawnee Scouts, ix, 9-17, 74, 208n11
Pavy, Lilla, 83, 187, 190-91, 222n11
Pavy, Octave Pierre, 106, 109, *124*, 128, 132, 138, 139, 143, 157, 190; background, 82, 88; and Brainard, 190, 198-203, 216n19; and Clay, 112-13; concern with second winter, 145; death, 167; food thefts by, 164, 186; on *Gulnare* expedition, 82-84, 99-100; and Greely, 112, 120-21, 130-31, 140-41, 145-48, 156, 158, 163, 178, 180, 215n2; and Frederick Kislingbury, 114, 115, 117, 130-31, 158, 163; medical skills, 127, 145, 158, 161; Pavy "mutiny," 152-53, 197-203; sledge journeys, 122-24,
126, 133-35; and Whistler, 124, 204, 216n19
Peary, Robert E., 110, 111, 125, 194, 195
Pike, Richard, xii, 103, 105, 114, 148
Pim Island, 148, 156, 157
Poland, John S., 38-39
Polaris (U.S. ship), 107-8, 150, 152
Polaris Boat Camp, 136
Portsmouth, NH, 97, 171, 172, 173, 180
Post at Standing Rock. *See* Fort Yates
Price, George Frederic, 91
Proteus (ship), xii, xiii, 96, 101, 103, 105-111, 112, 114, 117-19, *119*, 121, 142, 171, 187; sinks, 148, 157, 169, 181

Ralston, David C., 88, 127, 163; death, 165
Ray, Patrick Henry, 79
Red Cloud (chief), 33
Red Cloud Agency, 35, 42, 52
Red Cloud's War, 32
Reno, Marcus A., 42, 47, 68, 90
Republican River, 11, 16, 17
Republican River Expedition, 10, 16, 18, 30, 69, 208n11
Repulse Harbor, 147
Reynolds, Joseph, 34-35
Rice, George, 101, 110, 126, 130, 152; background, 88; death, 161, 165; and Greely, 121, 143-44; on *Gulnare* Expedition, 123; Pavy "mutiny," 153, 200-202; harvests "sea-fleas," 160; sledge journeys, 123, 134-35, 147, 156-57, 159
Rice Strait, 157
Robeson Channel, 106, 125, 136, 137
Rochester, NY, x, 1-3, 95, 167, 175-78, 182, 193, 214-15n11
Rochester Democrat and Chronicle, 189; Frederick Kislingbury funeral, 176; publishes Kislingbury journal extracts, 184

Index

Rochester Post-Express, 178-80
Rohe, Leonard, 83
Rohl, Paddy, 69, 71-72
Roosevelt, Theodore, 6
Ross, John, 103, 107
Royall, William B., 12, 15-16
Ryan, James, 82, 113

St. Paul, MN, 42, 47-48, 58, 59, 64
St. Paul Globe, 191
Salor, Nicholas, 82; death, 167
San Francisco, CA, 97, 185, 193, 195, 196
San Francisco Chronicle, 185-87, 189
Sandwich (now part of Windsor), Ontario, 175, 206n9; Aggie Kislingbury burial, 61; Jessie Kislingbury burial, 76-77
Schley, Winfield Scott, 171-72, 174, 183; on cannibalism, 177, 181-82, 221n19; leads Greely rescue, 168-69
Schofield, Alma "Allie" (*nee* Bullock), 24, 25, 86, 192; death 62, 94
Schofield, Frank, 25
Schofield, James Van Pelt, 94, 173-74, 192
Schofield, John McAllister, 25-26
Schofield, George Wheeler, 24, 25, 62, 94, 95; death, 25
Scott, Robert Falcon, 164
Sheridan, Philip H., xv, 37, 41-42, 55, 60, 63, 64, 85, 174
Sherman, William T., 63, 81; LFBE objections, 84-85, 87, 88
Signal Corps, 30-31, 80, 85, 79-80, 88, 184-85, 198, 222n5; Greely as chief signal officer, 190-91, 196
Sitting Bull, 35, 39, 41, 52, 63, 71, 73, 96-97
Six Came Back (book), 121, 163, 202
Smith, Sophus Theodor Krarup, 84, 99
Smith Sound, 103, 106-8, 142, 146, 149, 155, 168
Spotted Tail (chief), 33

Spotted Tail Agency, 42, 52, 54
Standing Rock Agency (formerly Grand River Agency), 37-39, 44-46, 50-52, 54-55, 60, 61-62; history, 37-38, 51-52; "Pony Campaign of 1876-77," 41-42, 60
Starr, Daniel, 82, 89, 105; leaves LFBE, 113
Stone, Jay, 94
Sturgis, Samuel D., 42
Summit Springs battle, 12, 14, 15, 17, 30, 208n11

Tall Bull (chief), 10, 13-14, 207n8
Tallapoosa (U.S. ship), 171
Tennessee (U.S. ship), 171
Terry, Alfred H., 34, 42, 47, 67, 85, 90; and Cold Hand, 46; and Frederick Kislingbury, xv, 45, 48, 50-51, 58, 63, 66
Thank God Harbor, 132-33, 147
Thetis (U.S. ship), 168, 171-72
Three Years of Arctic Service (book), 97, 146; and Clark, 188-89; and Frederick Kislingbury, 119-20, 162-63, 215n8; and Pavy, 140
Thunder Hawk (chief), 44

Upernavik, 84, 101, 214-15n11
U.S. Naval Academy, 87, 182, 183, 193

Wahl, Catherine (wife of Wheeler Kislingbury), 195
Weichell, Maria, 13
Wentworth (steam launch), 172
Weyprecht, Karl, 79-80, 98, 170
Whistler, William, 164; background, 90; death, 165; exhumation, 220n15; food thefts by, 164, 186; injured, 130; and Pavy, 124, 203
White Swan (U.S. scout), 68; background, 68; at Musselshell engagement, 70-71
Windsor Castle, 1

Index

Windsor, Ontario, x, 61, 206n9
Wood, William H., 41

Yanktonai, at Musselshell River, 73, 212n2; at Standing Rock, 37; as U.S. scouts, 43
Young, Allen, 106

ABOUT THE AUTHOR

Douglas W. Wamsley, an attorney by profession, is an independent researcher and scholar who has written extensively on the history of nineteenth-century Arctic exploration and its participants. He is the author of numerous publications that examine individual contributions to our knowledge and perceptions of the far northern regions, including *Big Wolf, the Adventurous Life of Lieutenant Frederick G. Schwatka*, published by American History Press, and *Polar Hayes, The Life and Contributions of Isaac Israel Hayes, M.D.* published by the American Philosophical Society.

www.ingramcontent.com/pod-product-compliance
Lightning Source LLC
Chambersburg PA
CBHW051538230426
43669CB00015B/2649